CHRISTIAN FAITH
IN THE BYZANTINE AND MEDIEVAL WORLDS

Faith in the Byzantine World

To Richard, Emily
and James

CHRISTIAN FAITH
IN THE BYZANTINE AND MEDIEVAL WORLDS

Mary Cunningham

Gillian R. Evans

Published by
Lion Hudson Limited
Wilkinson House, Jordan Hill Business Park
Banbury Road, Oxford OX2 8DR, England
www.lionhudson.com

ISBN 978 1 9125 5226 9

e-ISBN 978 1 9125 5229 0

'Faith in the Byzantine World': first paperback edition 2002
'Faith in the Medieval World': first paperback edition 2002

Acknowledgments

'Faith in the Byzantine World'

Scripture quotations taken from the *New Revised Standard Version Bible*, Anglicized edition, copyright © 1989, 1995 National Council of the Churches of Christ in the United States of America. Used by permission. All rights reserved worldwide.

'Faith in the Medieval World'

Unless otherwise stated, scriptures and additional materials quoted are from the *Good News Bible* © 1994 published by the Bible Societies/HarperCollins Publishers Ltd UK, Good News Bible © American Bible Society 1966, 1971, 1976, 1992. Used with permission.

Extracts from *Common Worship* (the Apostles' Creed and the Nicene Creed) copyright © The Archbishops' Council, 2000. Reproduced by permission. All rights reserved. copyright@churchofengland.org

Maps pp. 12–13, 14–15, 16–17, 237, 238–39 by Lion Hudson IP Limited

Cover image: © Raylipscombe / istockphoto.com

A catalogue record for this book is available from the British Library

CONTENTS

PART 1

FAITH
IN THE BYZANTINE WORLD

INTRODUCTION

From obscure roots in Palestine, Christianity slowly became the dominant religion in the territories of the later Roman empire and beyond. In this earliest period, the Christian Church was one entity, united by a network of bishops, as well as a shared faith and sacraments. It is out of this unified Church of the early centuries that the two main branches of Christian tradition, the Roman Catholic and the Eastern Orthodox Churches, developed. The former was based primarily in the region of Western Europe, whereas the latter developed in the empire which we now call 'Byzantine'; this had its centre in the capital city of Constantinople (now Istanbul, in modern Turkey). It is important to remember that the two halves of Christendom remained officially joined throughout the whole of the first Christian millennium.

The decisive split occurred in 1054, although a growing separation between Latin-speaking and Greek-speaking Christians had been visible long before this date. Nevertheless, we can speak of unity throughout the Christian world even after this time. Western and Eastern Christians shared essentially the same doctrine, methods of worship and objects of veneration – such as the cross and the Bible. Minor differences did exist, however, in musical traditions, disciplinary matters and the formulation of doctrine. The Orthodox use of holy icons, for example, remained foreign to Western Christians even though they also sponsored religious art in their cathedrals and homes. Perhaps the greatest source of friction lay in the issue of authority: Roman popes increasingly felt that they should represent the highest source of power in the Christian Church. Eastern bishops and patriarchs, on the other hand, believed in a pentarchy, that is, five ancient leading dioceses, or patriarchates, namely Rome, Constantinople, Alexandria, Antioch and Jerusalem. Although Eastern bishops acknowledged the pope as the first in importance among bishops, they were unwilling to grant him complete supremacy in the Church.

This account covers the history of the Byzantine Church between the dates 330 and 1453. To some extent these boundaries, especially that which is usually regarded as the beginning of the Eastern Roman empire, are open to debate. Nevertheless, Constantine's foundation of a new capital city at Constantinople in Asia Minor may legitimately be seen as the start of this new Christian empire. The fall of the city to the Ottoman Turks in 1453 effectively ended the long and varied history of Byzantine dominion. The title of this section, 'Faith in the Byzantine World', is also in some ways inaccurate. People of many different faiths lived in Byzantium at different times, including not only Christians, but also Jews, Samaritans, 'heretics' or those who deviated from the 'right' faith, and even pagans in the earlier period. Nevertheless, Orthodox Christianity had become the dominant faith in this empire by the end of the fourth century. Not only were the daily lives and attitudes of most citizens shaped by this faith, but the government and official Church were imbued with its teachings. Various aspects of this Christian civilization will be explored in the chapters which follow, including the close relationship between Church and State, doctrine and worldview.

The Byzantine empire has traditionally been viewed as a conservative and repressive society. Churchmen, scholars and politicians alike looked to a classical past and attempted to preserve its culture, laws and values – although, of course, within a Christian framework. Historians, beginning with Edward Gibbon in the eighteenth century, have stressed not only the traditionalism of this society, but also its corruption and lack of creativity. In fact, this view of Byzantium is inaccurate in many respects. If we study the texts and artefacts of the Byzantines carefully, it is clear that creative thought and religious views did flourish and develop in the course of 11 centuries. Most of these productions also reveal a deeply Christian view of the world, a sense of God's immanence and involvement in creation and human history. The expression of Orthodox Christian faith by means of the tools and ideas of classical civilization was consistently both innovative and successful.

Furthermore, the Eastern Roman empire contained in most periods a diverse, multi-ethnic population. The governing elite in Constantinople and a few other cities represented a tiny minority within the population as a whole. Perhaps as many as 90 per cent of the Byzantines were peasants living in rural areas, most of whom were probably illiterate. Not all of these people even spoke Greek; at the outer frontiers of the empire there were Armenian, Slavic and Syriac or Arabic-speaking communities, to name only a few. We are thus attempting to describe here a period and culture in Christian history which almost escapes precise definition. At the same time, however, it is clear on the basis of the surviving literary texts and artefacts that Byzantine Orthodoxy provided most of its adherents with a unified and comprehensive worldview. Belief in the triune God, whose definition was established by biblical revelation and in the course of the ecumenical councils, formed the basis of this worldview. Beyond this basic Christian doctrine, the cults of the Virgin Mary, the saints and holy symbols such as icons and relics, as well as religious practices such as attendance at church, keeping the fasts and celebrating the feast days, helped to define Byzantines' sense of cultural identity.

It is with some regret that I have decided not to cover in detail other faiths in the Byzantine world. The reasons for this are primarily those of space. Separate books on Byzantine Judaism, 'heretical' groups such as the Paulicians and Bogomils and, perhaps even more importantly, all the Churches now called the 'Oriental' Orthodox, which survive to this day in Syria, Lebanon, Israel, Egypt, Ethiopia, India and Armenia, are required for each of these topics. This account, alongside 'Faith in the Medieval World', is concerned primarily with the dominant religion in the region that it covers, in this case Orthodox Christianity. The first two chapters provide a broad chronological outline of the history of the Byzantine Church and State; after these, a more thematic approach is adopted. It is inevitable that some repetition will occur; nevertheless, it is hoped that each chapter may be read on its own as well as in conjunction with others. It would be impossible to cover every subject in detail in an account of this size. Further reading are therefore provided at the end, including both primary and secondary sources.

Finally, it is necessary to add a word about the technical terms and spellings that are used here. It seems impossible to avoid using certain terms which have very precise meanings when writing about the Byzantine Church. Many of these, such as 'patriarch', 'ecumenical' council or 'liturgy', in fact represent transliterations of Greek words. Most have been adopted for practical use in English both by scholars and writers of books for the general public. A short explanation of the meaning of each word is provided when it first occurs in the text. Whenever possible, however, simpler terms are substituted. Spellings follow the conventions of most books published on Byzantine topics. That is, names of people or places which have a well-known English equivalent, such as 'Rome', 'Antony' or 'Michael', appear in that form. Those which have not previously been translated, such as 'Herakleios' or 'Kosmas Indikopleustes', are spelled according to Greek, rather than Latin, conventions.

I would like to acknowledge here the generous help of Augustine Casiday and Zaga Gavrilović, who both read through earlier drafts of the text and suggested a number of changes. I would also like to thank Claire Sauer for her meticulous work in improving the narrative.

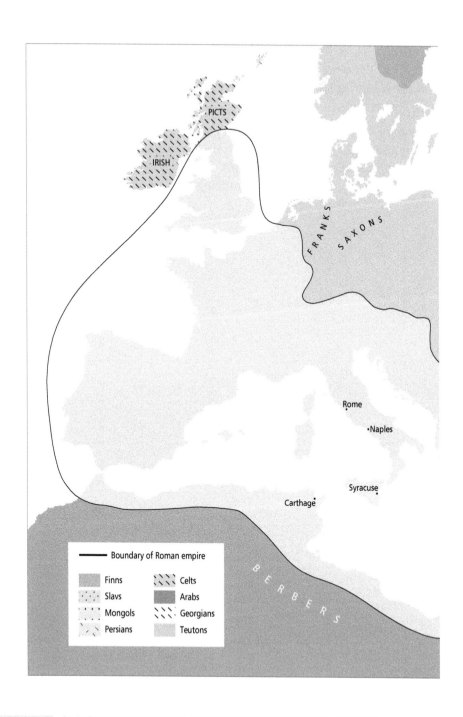

PICTS

IRISH

FRANKS

SAXONS

Rome

•Naples

Syracuse•

Carthage•

BERBERS

—— Boundary of Roman empire

Finns	Celts
Slavs	Arabs
Mongols	Georgians
Persians	Teutons

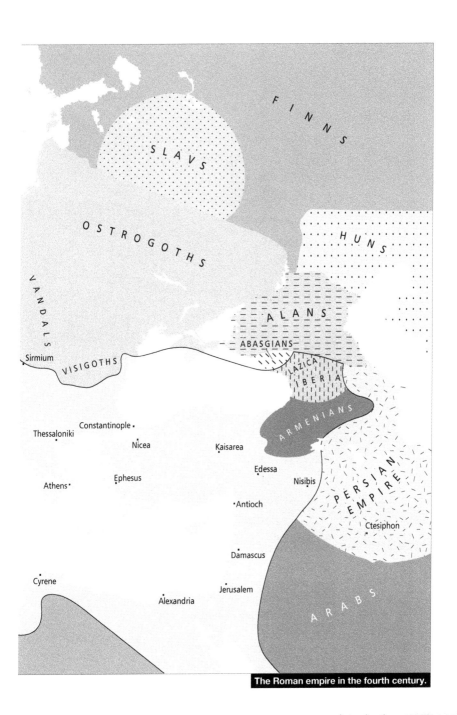

The Roman empire in the fourth century.

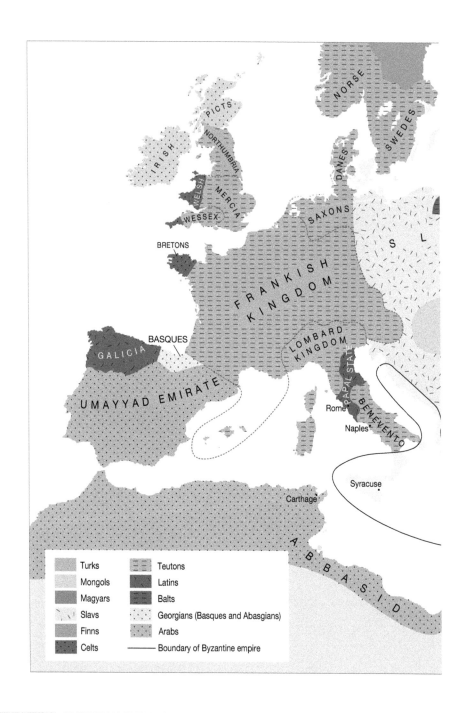

Turks
Mongols
Magyars
Slavs
Finns
Celts
Teutons
Latins
Balts
Georgians (Basques and Abasgians)
Arabs
Boundary of Byzantine empire

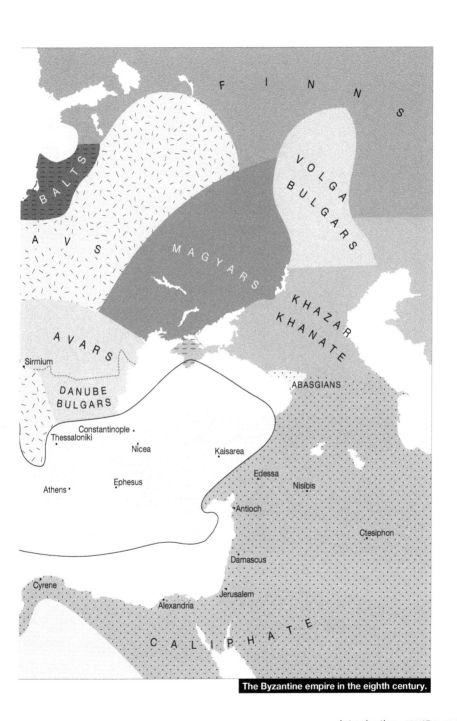

The following place names and peoples are labelled on the map:

FINNS

BALTS

VOLGA BULGARS

AVS

MAGYARS

KHAZAR KHANATE

AVARS

Sirmium

DANUBE BULGARS

ABASGIANS

Thessaloniki

Constantinople

Nicea

Kaisarea

Edessa

Nisibis

Athens

Ephesus

Antioch

Ctesiphon

Damascus

Cyrene

Jerusalem

Alexandria

CALIPHATE

The Byzantine empire in the eighth century.

CHRISTIAN FAITH IN THE BYZANTINE AND MEDIEVAL WORLDS

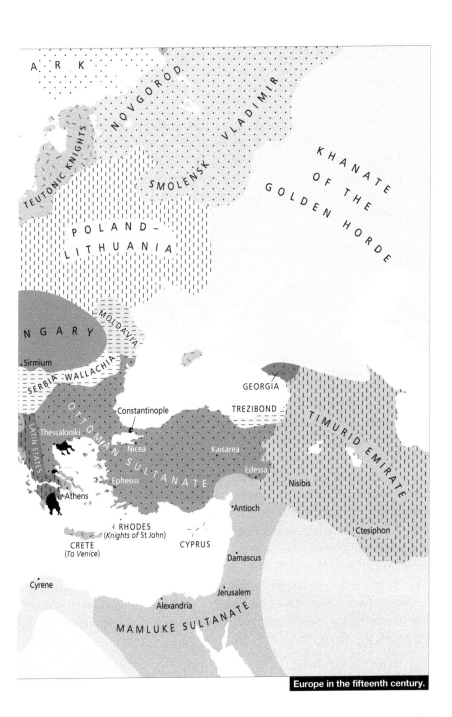

A· R K

NOVGOROD

TEUTONIC KNIGHTS

VLADIMIR

SMOLENSK

POLAND-
LITHUANIA

KHANATE
OF THE
GOLDEN HORDE

MOLDAVIA

N G A R Y

Sirmium

SERBIA WALLACHIA

GEORGIA

Constantinople

TREZIBOND

O
T
T
O
M
A
N

TIMURID EMIRATE

LATIN STATES

Thessaloniki

Nicea

Kaisarea

S
U
L
T
A
N
A
T
E

Ephesus

Edessa

Nisibis

Athens

•Antioch

RHODES
(Knights of St John)

CRETE
(To Venice)

CYPRUS

Ctesiphon

Cyrene

Damascus

Jerusalem

Alexandria

MAMLUKE SULTANATE

Europe in the fifteenth century.

CHAPTER 1

A CHRISTIAN ROMAN EMPIRE
(330–843)

When did the Byzantine Church, or for that matter the Byzantine empire, begin? The time when it ended, at the sack of Constantinople by the Ottoman Turks in 1453, is indisputable, but the point of transition between the later Roman and the Byzantine empires is less obvious. Some historians indeed would argue that there is no beginning: Byzantium represented (and its own citizens in fact adhered to this idea) the continuation of the Roman empire in the East. Many, however, would signal the reign of Constantine the Great, who finally gained sole authority as Roman emperor when he defeated Licinius in 324, and whose dramatic conversion to Christianity ended the period of persecution by pagan emperors, as the starting point for both empire and Church.

Constantinople, the 'New Rome'

Constantine's decision to found an administrative capital, or 'New Rome', at the site of the ancient city of Byzantion shifted the centre of gravity eastwards in the empire. Several ideas seem to have motivated Constantine in this decision. First, the site was strategically well placed. At a vantage point which divided not only Asia Minor from the rest of Europe, but also the Black Sea from the Mediterranean, Constantinople represented a link between all the territories of the Roman world. Second, it is likely that Constantine saw political advantages in distancing himself from the power structures and traditions of the old Rome. In Constantinople, he was able to establish a new order, with a newly appointed senate and administration. Henceforth, Constantinople would represent the centre of the largely Greek-speaking, Eastern Roman empire which slowly and inexorably became separated, both culturally and politically, from the Latin West.

Constantine's conversion

Although it may be purely legendary, the story of Constantine's dramatic conversion at the Milvian Bridge outside Rome and the successful defeat of his first main rival, the usurper Maxentius, in 312 was regarded even by contemporary historians as the starting point for a new, Christian Roman empire. The true sequence of events before this famous battle remains obscure and was embroidered in subsequent years. An account written by the Christian historian Lactantius sometime before 324 relates that Constantine, following instructions he had received in a dream the night before, instructed his troops to inscribe the chi-rho sign, ☧, representing the first two letters in the name of Christ in Greek, on their shields. Nearly 30 years later, Eusebius elaborated this story in his biography of Constantine, saying that the emperor had a vision of a luminous cross in the sky, accompanied by the inscription 'Conquer by this'. After this battle, Constantine went on to defeat his other rivals and by 324 had become sole ruler of the entire Roman empire. He also decided to introduce Christianity as the state religion, providing the Church for the first time with money and imperial backing. The extent of Constantine's own conversion remains open to debate. It is likely that while viewing the Christian God as the most powerful force in the universe, he continued to express allegiance to the ancient gods of pagan Rome. Constantine was finally baptized on his deathbed in 337, and was buried with much pomp in a mausoleum which he had built in Constantinople

The Christianization of the empire

Perhaps the most important effect of Constantine's conversion was on the Christian Church itself. As a result of Constantine's active patronage and legal reforms from the 320s onwards, the Church began to develop as an institution with wealth and property at its disposal. For the first time, churches on a monumental scale could be endowed and built. Basilicas intended for large urban congregations, shrines in honour of martyrs or saints, and churches built on holy sites of pilgrimage began to proliferate in Eastern and Western Christendom. The internal organization of the Church also changed in response to imperial patronage and protection. Although bishops had led the

Constantinople

Constantine founded his new capital city on the site of Byzantion, an ancient Greek city-state, or *polis*, located on the Bosphorus between Golden Horn, an inlet which leads to the Black Sea, and the Sea of Marmara. Byzantion was insignificant before Constantine chose it for the 'New Rome', but he added or enlarged all the necessary ingredients of a late-Roman city: wide avenues bordered by colonnades, squares or forums, public baths, a racecourse or hippodrome, a palace and several new Christian churches, including the two central basilicas, Hagia Sophia (Holy Wisdom) and St Irene. Constantine also moved the city walls outwards to allow for expansion; a further set of defensive walls, about 1.5 kilometres beyond Constantine's, was added by the emperor Theodosius II at the beginning of the fifth century. These outer walls proved virtually impregnable on various later occasions, when enemies laid siege to the 'Queen City'.

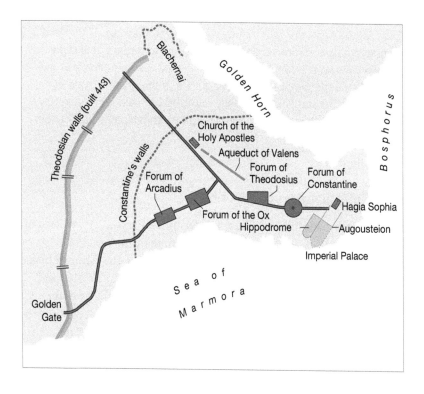

Christian community in its decisions since as early as the second century, their organization into various ranks and dioceses seems to date from the period of Constantine. It is interesting to note that Christian dioceses followed closely the secular organization of the state and its division into local provinces by Diocletian and his successors. Each province had its principal bishop, who was responsible for organizing meetings and ordaining all the clerics under his jurisdiction. A hierarchical power structure for the Church came into being at the same time that it began to exert significant influence and authority within the secular state.

The Christianization of the Roman empire continued after the death of Constantine I. Laws which date back to Constantine's successors, such as his son Constantius, reveal increasing restrictions on pagans and more favourable conditions for Christians. The conversion of the masses to Christianity did not happen immediately, however, and the emperor Julian (361–63) initiated a brief return to paganism as the official state religion. By the end of the fourth century, and with the return of Christian rulers, legislation in favour of Christianity became increasingly pronounced. The *Codex Theodosianus*, published between 429 and 438, but incorporating laws promulgated during the reigns of Constantine I and his successors, reveals an ever-increasing intent on the part of emperors to promote Christianity and eradicate paganism. Sundays and important Christian feast days were declared holidays, with the prohibition of secular lawsuits and business transactions. By the end of the fourth century, laws forbidding pagan sacrifices and ordering the closure of temples were being enforced. Pagans were forbidden to hold jobs in the imperial court or in military or civil service. Increasingly, all non-orthodox citizens, including pagans, Jews and heretical Christians, became second-class citizens throughout the empire.

'It is our will that all the peoples who are ruled by the administration of our clemency shall practise that religion which the divine Peter the Apostle transmitted to the Romans . . . according to the apostolic discipline and the evangelic doctrine, we shall believe in the single Deity of the Father, the Son, and the Holy Spirit, under the concept of equal majesty and of the Holy Trinity.'

An edict on the profession of the Catholic faith, 380

The beginnings of political and religious disunity

After Constantine's brief rule as sole Christian Roman emperor, the empire was divided into Eastern and Western territories under his sons. The shape of late-Roman Christendom began to change irrevocably in the fifth century, owing to military and political upheavals in the West. As Goths, Vandals and Huns invaded the Balkans and Western Europe, Christians in these regions increasingly looked to Rome or Constantinople for protection and spiritual direction. There can be no doubt that the political instability of this period contributed to a need for religious authority, based now primarily in the main episcopal dioceses

Jews in the later Roman empire

Jewish communities survived and even flourished in the later Roman empire after the destruction of the Temple (AD 70) and their expulsion from Jerusalem in 135. New communities were established in Palestine and Jews were allowed to govern themselves. Jewish communities in many Eastern cities such as Antioch thus remained strong and vibrant for several centuries, even attracting converts from among the Christian population. After the beginning of the fifth century, however, life in the Roman empire became increasingly difficult for Jews as imperial legislation began to restrict their rights. Privileges such as holding slaves, teaching in public institutions, building new synagogues or serving in the army were henceforth barred. Outside Palestine, a Jewish *diaspora* existed in most of the major cities of the Roman empire. Here the Jews tended to live in small enclaves; in Constantinople they were located in the commercial quarters and worked as dyers, weavers, furriers, glass-makers and even merchants and physicians. Prejudice against the Jews was strong in all periods of Byzantine history, however, and was frequently expressed both in devotional literature and in legislation. Byzantine Christians regarded themselves as the New Israel and believed that the Jews deliberately refused to acknowledge Christ as Messiah. The emperors Herakleios, Leo III and others all ordered the compulsory baptism of Jews at various periods of military stress or economic hardship. There is evidence, however, that some bishops in the Byzantine Church consistently opposed such measures and upheld the right of Jews to practise their ancestral religion.

of the Roman empire. It is also important to recognize, however, that the barbarian invasions in the West did not topple Roman civilization or the Church. In most cases, the invaders were keen to adopt the culture and institutions of the Roman world; many of them had been converted to Christianity earlier (although, in the case of the Visigoths and Ostrogoths, this was the heretical Arian form of the faith).

Disunity and eventually schism were introduced into the Christian Church as controversy over theological doctrines developed. In the fourth century, the main issue of contention had been the formulation of ideas concerning the Trinity. In the fifth century, discussion moved on to Jesus Christ himself and to the manner in which two natures, the divine and the human, came together in his person. The unfortunate result of the controversy is that after the ecumenical councils of 431 and 451, bishops who felt that their views had not been represented began to split away from the mainstream Church. The Assyrian, or 'Nestorian', Church of the East, which still exists in parts of Iran, Iraq and Northern Syria, remains out of communion to this day with mainstream Orthodox Christianity because of the irregularities which its members perceived in the organization of the third ecumenical council of Ephesus (431). Similarly, the so-called 'Monophysite' churches began to be formed after the Council of Chalcedon (451) as bishops mainly from Egypt, Palestine and Syria found that they could not accept the formulations of that council. The effect of these early schisms on the Christian Church as a whole, but especially on the Chalcedonian Byzantine Church, was significant. Emperors of the fifth, sixth and seventh centuries expended much energy on attempts to heal the schisms, only abandoning the effort after most of the Near East fell to the Arabs in the middle of the seventh century.

Reunification under Justinian

The reign of the emperor Justinian I (527–65) represented the last attempt at political reunification of the Eastern and Western halves of the Roman empire. By his reconquest of North Africa, Italy, and even a small part of Spain, Justinian aimed to regain the territories which had been under Roman jurisdiction. At the same time, he hoped to rebuild a unified Church in the course of his reign. This would be accomplished by various means, including the building of many more churches and monasteries throughout the empire, attempts to resolve the disputes which still divided bishops within the Church, and finally, by suppressing religious minorities within the empire, especially such 'outsiders' as pagans, Jews and Samaritans.

Justinian's contributions to the development of the Byzantine Church were significant and far-reaching. Due to the increase of commerce and industry during his reign, imperial patronage of art and architecture was carried out on an unprecedented scale. The Great Church of Hagia Sophia, completed in 537, represents a stupendous feat of engineering for the period. Justinian is said to have exclaimed after the completion of the church, 'Solomon, I have surpassed you!' Contemporaries marvelled at the building, with its massive, centralized interior and huge dome, which appears to be balanced on nothing. As Constantinople's main cathedral, Hagia Sophia came to represent for Byzantines of all periods the archetypal church building, a veritable 'heaven on earth'.

Justinian's other achievements include the codification of Roman law, a process which drew on the writings of classical Roman jurists, but which also created an orderly and up-to-date system out of their sometimes contradictory rulings, the further elaboration of the liturgy and the creation of an even closer relationship between Church and State than had existed previously. Building on the ideal image of the Christian emperor established by Eusebius in the fourth century, Justinian was fully conscious of his role as a divinely sanctioned ruler. He summoned Church councils, wrote theological treatises and composed hymns.

The Byzantine 'Dark Age'

Soon after the death of Justinian, the territories which he had worked so hard to reconquer began to crumble. The empire's resources had been exhausted by the years of military campaigns, making it impossible for Justinian's successors to maintain his achievements. The first area to be lost was Italy, when the Lombards invaded from the north in 568. The Visigoths in Spain began a counter-offensive and by the end of the sixth century had recaptured all of the territories they had lost to the

Byzantines. Even greater threats soon appeared in the north and the east, when Turkic peoples such as the Avars, who had originated on the steppes of Asia, began to invade the Crimea and the Balkans, and when Justin II (565–78) broke a peace treaty with Persia. The late sixth and early seventh centuries thus represented a period of great stress for the East Roman, or Byzantine, empire. Increasingly, people looked to God as their only source of protection and consolation.

A catastrophic event for the Byzantines in symbolic terms was the loss of the relic of the true cross when the Persians captured Jerusalem in 614. The newly enthroned Herakleios, one of the few emperors of this period who was able to reverse the tide of military defeats for the Byzantines, did not rest until he had conquered the Persians and restored the relic to Jerusalem. Ironically, however, Herakleios' achievements in the East were swiftly reversed when a new and much more formidable invader overthrew first the Persian empire and then the remaining Byzantine territories in Syria, Palestine, Egypt and even North Africa. The rise of Islam after 632 represents one of the most remarkable and dramatic events in the history of the world. The success and rapid spread of this new and highly unified religious movement completely changed the aspect of the Mediterranean basin and what remained of the later Roman empire.

Iconoclasm

At the beginning of the eighth century, a combination of usurpations, invasions by the Muslims and natural disasters helped to create even more chaos and uncertainty in the Byzantine world. Historians have long debated the possible reasons why Leo III (717–41) decided to introduce Iconoclasm (literally, the breaking of icons or images), the policy of destroying the holy icons within the Church and forbidding their veneration. Whatever the emperor's personal motivations may have been, it is clear that he was backed by a powerful lobby within the Church, which opposed the growing devotion to holy images, seeing this as a return to the idolatrous practices of pre-Christian times. It is also likely that contact in this period with Muslims, Jews and a heretical sect called the Paulicians contributed to the belief that representational art contravened God's second commandment in Exodus 20:4–5.

The rise of Islam

The religion of Islam originated in northern Arabia, a desert region which had been ruled for centuries by competing Arab tribes with pagan beliefs. Owing both to Arabia's importance on the trade routes to the Far East and to the presence of Christian and Jewish communities, its inhabitants had come into contact with monotheistic religions before. In the middle of the seventh century, the prophet Muhammad began to teach the existence of one, transcendent God. Born in the holy city of Mecca and orphaned at the age of six, Muhammad had been trained as a merchant by his grandfather and uncle. At the age of 24 he entered the service of a rich widow named Khadija and eventually married her. Although he continued his job as a merchant, Muhammad became increasingly drawn to religious contemplation and prayer. Some time after 600 (the traditional date is 610), he began to receive revelations from Allah, the supreme God. These teachings, which were collected into the 114 chapters of the Qur'an, commanded the destruction of pagan idols and the worship of one God. In 622, when this new religious group lost support in Mecca, Muhammad was invited to move to the city of Yathrib. This migration, called the Hijra, represents the beginning of the Muslim era. The name of the new city was changed at this time to Medina, 'the city of the prophet'. By 629 Muhammad and his followers took control of Mecca. After his death in 632, the Muslims fought internally for a brief period, but went on to spread into Persian and Roman territories. Partly due to their exhaustion after years of warfare, both powers collapsed in the Middle East in a remarkably short space of time. In 636 the Persian capital Ctesiphon fell to the Muslims; ten years later the Arabs had conquered most of Syria, Palestine, Mesopotamia and Egypt. The Muslim *caliphate* became Byzantium's most formidable enemy on the Eastern frontier for several centuries after this date.

Although the extent and severity of Leo III's iconoclastic policy is open to question, his son, Constantine V (741–75), undertook to enforce the edict against images actively and at times aggressively. This emperor considered himself a theologian and wrote several treatises arguing the case against the use of icons in the Church. Constantine V adopted extreme measures in order to eradicate icons and their cult from the empire. According to the chroniclers Theophanes and Nikephoros, both of whom were writing at the beginning of the following century, the emperor persecuted iconophiles in the civil services, the army and the Church. He seems especially to have targeted monks and monasteries, although it is not clear whether this was specifically because of their defensive stance towards the holy icons. For whatever reason he undertook this anti-monastic policy, there is evidence that he systematically razed monasteries or turned them into secular public buildings. Monks and abbots were publicly humiliated and forced to take up professions in secular life. During Constantine V's reign a number of monks and other iconophiles fled to Rome where they received protection from the pope, who publicly supported the cause of the holy images.

> 'You shall not make for yourself an idol, whether in the form of anything that is in heaven above, or that is on the earth beneath, or that is in the water under the earth. You shall not bow down to them or worship them.'
>
> **Exodus 20:4–5**

The campaign against icons was already losing impetus when Irene, widow of Constantine V's successor, Leo IV, called the seventh ecumenical council at Nicea in 787 to overturn the official iconoclastic policy. At this council the defenders of icons amassed numerous arguments against the charges which had been brought against them, basing these on scripture, tradition and the writings of the Fathers.

Unfortunately, political and military setbacks under Irene's successors in the early ninth century, including the major defeat and death of the emperor Nikephoros I at the hands of the Bulgars, paved the way for a return to iconoclastic policies in 815. Leo V, perhaps associating strong imperial rule and military victory with the iconoclast emperors of the eighth century, summoned a council at Hagia Sophia which reversed the decisions of the Council of Nicea. Leo and his successors appear to have acted more moderately than Constantine V in their suppression of religious images, however. Enforcement of the ban on images seems to have been confined to Constantinople and its immediate environs during this period, even during the reign of Theophilos (829–42), who enforced these policies the most rigorously.

> 'In every village and town one could witness the weeping and lamentation of the pious, whereas, on the part of the impious, one saw sacred things trodden upon, liturgical vessels turned to other use, churches scraped down and smeared with ashes because they contained holy images.'
>
> **Life of St Stephen the Younger, early ninth century**

The formal restoration of holy images in the Byzantine empire occurred in March 843; this is still remembered and celebrated in the Orthodox Church as the 'Triumph of Orthodoxy' on the first Sunday in Lent. The arguments in defence of icons were this time expressed in a document called the *Synodikon*, which proclaimed not only the validity, but even the *necessity* of images in Christian worship. To deny the legitimacy of images of Christ is to undermine the significance of his incarnation, when God willingly put on human flesh and involved himself in the created world. The Orthodox belief in the potential for material creation to be divinely transfigured is also reaffirmed in the *Synodikon*. From this time onwards, the Byzantine Church formally accepted the importance of material symbols such as icons in Christian worship, along with their veneration through physical acts such as kneeling before them or kissing them.

The first five centuries of the Byzantine empire, lasting from approximately 330 to 843, represented a period of enormous transition and change. Beginning as the continuation of the Roman empire in the East, the state underwent internal changes as it embraced Christianity as its official religion, and began to resolve theological controversies within the Church. Externally, the Eastern empire first extended its dominion under the sixth-century emperor Justinian, and then shrank to only a remnant of its former territories due to invasions by Slavs, Persians, Arabs and other enemies. The seventh and eighth centuries are usually seen as a period of transition from the Roman empire to a vulnerable, medieval state centred on its capital city, Constantinople. The self-questioning that accompanied this change manifested itself in the official policy of banning religious images in the Church, or Iconoclasm. After the restoration of icons to the Byzantine Church, or the Triumph of Orthodoxy, in 843, a new period of confidence and expansion began.

CHAPTER 2

THE PARTING OF THE WAYS
(843–1453)

In the later period of Byzantine history, we see the flowering of this remarkable and unique civilization, as well as its continuing interaction with the other two dominant cultures in the Mediterranean region: Western Christendom and Islam. The Byzantine Church experienced successes and failures in this period: perhaps the most difficult crisis was the period (1204–61) when the Latins occupied Constantinople and surrounding Byzantine territories after the disastrous climax of the Fourth Crusade. The Byzantines survived this setback, however, and their Church, officially in schism with the Roman papacy since 1054, flourished once more after the Latins were finally thrown out of the occupied territories. The period between 1261 and 1453, sometimes described as the 'twilight' years of Byzantium, was one of extraordinary religious and cultural revival, in spite of the inexorable advance of the Ottoman Turks into Asia Minor, the Balkans and eventually Constantinople itself.

> 'By the ninth century the process of separation was complete. Out of the ruins of the Roman world had emerged three quite distinct civilizations . . . Islam, Byzantium and the West.'
>
> **Michael Angold, *Byzantium: The Bridge from Antiquity to the Middle Ages*, 2001**

The restoration of Orthodoxy

After the official end of Iconoclasm in 843, a number of significant changes took place both in Byzantine society and the Church. First, and perhaps most important for the population as a whole, the empire began to experience a period of prosperity and military success which lasted nearly two centuries. This allowed commerce, culture and religious life to flourish, thus initiating a period of revival which has been called after the dynasty which ruled at the time, the 'Macedonian' Renaissance. Second, it is after the period of Iconoclasm and partly due to the role which monks played in that controversy as the defenders of icons, that monasticism flourished as never before. This led to the formation of a powerful monastic lobby which exerted influence in both the Church and the secular government. Finally, it is in this period that the long-standing cultural and political separation between the Byzantine patriarchate and the Roman papacy began to be felt. This process took place slowly and not, as might appear at first glance, in response to a few isolated events.

To begin with the first of these developments, the cultural renaissance of the mid-ninth century manifested itself in a number of areas. After a decline of higher education and learning in the so-called 'Dark Age' of Byzantine history, the seventh and eighth centuries, a revival began to get underway in the early ninth century. It is possible that this was fuelled to some extent by monasteries, which in turn were influenced by monastic emigration from the Holy Land in the face of civil war among the Arabs who now ruled this territory. Theodore, abbot of the monastery of Studios in Constantinople, undertook to reform his monastery, introducing Palestinian liturgical practices and a return to the coenobitic ideals of Basil of Caesarea, with an emphasis on manual labour and productivity. One area of manual labour in which skilled monks could work was the copying of manuscripts in the monastic scriptorium. It can scarcely be accidental that the new cursive script, which rendered the copying of manuscripts so much faster and more economical, was introduced in just this period, sometime between the middle of the eighth and early ninth centuries. Theodore also set his monks to compose hymns and prayers to fill the hours of the entire liturgical year.

After 843 a revival of secular education in the Byzantine empire also took place. A school in a part of the palace called the Magnaura had been established under the emperor Theophilos (829–42), which taught the secular disciplines of rhetoric and philosophy, as well as mathematics, astronomy and grammar. Patriarchs in ninth-century Constantinople such as Tarasios, Methodios, Ignatios and Photios tended to be well educated in Greek rhetoric, to the extent that their surviving treatises and sermons are difficult for all but the classically educated reader to understand. Religious art experienced a similar revival after its vindication by the Triumph of Orthodoxy. After the middle of the ninth century, a proliferation of church decoration – such as the splendid mosaic of the Virgin and Child in the apse of Hagia Sophia – manuscript illumination and other examples of artistic production took place.

Monasticism also entered a period of growth and prosperity in Byzantine society from the mid-ninth century onwards. Several factors probably contributed to this development. As we saw above, monks were believed to have played a major role in resisting the iconoclast emperors and in bringing about the restoration of holy icons in the Church. After the end of Iconoclasm many of these figures were rewarded with high positions in the Church as the incumbent iconoclast bishops were deposed and disciplined. Soon patronage of monasteries also increased and many became extremely wealthy institutions. As more and more houses were founded and endowed with both land and movable property, monasteries and their leaders formed an important and powerful pressure group within society. By the mid-tenth century, a series of emperors were so worried by this phenomenon that they enacted laws aimed at limiting the growth of monastic properties. That this legislation ultimately failed reflects the enormous respect and support for monastic life that existed by this time throughout the Byzantine world.

Growing separation between East and West

Tension had been growing between the patriarchate in Constantinople and the Roman papacy for several centuries before flaring up again in the late ninth century. Culturally, the Eastern and Western halves of the former Roman empire had been drifting apart from as early as the fifth century. The political and military disintegration of much of Western Europe provided an important backdrop for this increasing sense of isolation. In addition, however, the main languages of communication, Greek and Latin, had become mutually unintelligible for most members of the population.

Doctrinal disagreements, such as the controversy over holy icons in the eighth and ninth centuries, provoked further misunderstanding and distrust. During the period of Iconoclasm, a succession of popes refused to accept the Byzantine Church's rulings and provided a safe haven for iconophile monks and bishops fleeing persecution. On this occasion, the papacy was vindicated in its stance when these policies were eventually declared unorthodox.

The filioque

In the late ninth century, another issue which might at first glance appear insignificant began to cause controversy between Roman popes and Byzantine patriarchates. This was the issue of the *filioque*, a short clause meaning 'and the Son', which some Western Churches had been adding since as early as the sixth century to the section of the Creed which describes the procession of the Holy Spirit. The addition of this clause probably originated in Spain in the sixth century; by the eighth and ninth most Frankish churches were also reciting the Creed in this way. Although popes had consistently opposed the official addition of the *filioque* to the Creed, they did not take active steps to stamp out its inclusion in Western Churches. Byzantine patriarchs, beginning with Photios (858–67 and 878–86), attacked the doctrine of 'the double procession', eventually even excommunicating the pope at a local Constantinopolitan synod.

'I believe in one God, Father Almighty, Maker of heaven and earth and of all things visible and invisible . . . and in the Holy Spirit, the Lord, the Giver of life, who proceeds from the Father, who together with the Father and the Son is worshipped and glorified.'

The Creed in its original form and as it is still recited in the Orthodox Church

Papal supremacy

The issue of authority also played a major part in the disagreement between popes and patriarchs in this period. One of the reasons that Photios entered into a debate with Rome over the issue of the *filioque* was probably that the pope had opposed his appointment as uncanonical. Pope Nicholas I, an able and energetic leader of the Western Church, felt that he should have the final say over the choice of patriarchs in Constantinople. Photios, like many Eastern patriarchs both before and after, upheld the principle of five leaders of the universal Church, with the pope as the first *among equals*. In other words, the pope, as successor to the apostle Peter, should be recognized as first bishop in the Church, but to the Eastern bishops this did not imply supreme authority.

Mission

Another cause for increasing tension between East and West from the ninth century onwards was Christian mission. Since as early as the fifth century the Roman empire had been threatened by invasion as waves of Gothic, Slavic and Turkic peoples moved westwards and southwards into the civilized world. By the ninth century, both secular and ecclesiastical leaders had begun to explore methods of civilizing these people as an alternative to remaining in a permanent state of war. In the case of the Byzantines, diplomacy had long been used to pacify one enemy so that the army could concentrate its energy on combating another. In the 860s, during the patriarchate of Photios, the most serious effort yet to convert neighbouring peoples such as the Slavs and the Bulgars to Christianity got underway. Unfortunately, the drive to convert these groups also led to rivalry with Latin missionaries who were working at this time in many of the same areas.

Missions to the Slavs

In 863 two Greek brothers named Cyril and Methodios set out, at the invitation of Rastislav, its ruler, to the kingdom of Moravia, a Slavic state which was located roughly in the area of modern Czechoslovakia. Rastislav requested that the Christian missionaries from Byzantium bring scriptures and service books translated into Slavonic so that his people could understand what they were being taught. Cyril and Methodios immediately embarked on this task. Having been raised in Thessaloniki, a city which had been surrounded by Slavic immigrants from the sixth century onwards, the brothers were fluent in the language of this neighbouring culture. The dialect that they used for their translations of Christian texts was that of the Macedonian Slavs: this remains the liturgical language of all the Slavic churches to this day and is now called Old Church Slavonic. Unfortunately, the Greek mission to Moravia soon came into conflict with German evangelists who were working in the same area. Cyril and Methodios appealed to the pope in Rome for help, which was granted, but the Germans ignored the papal decision and continued to obstruct the brothers' mission. Eventually, after Cyril and Methodios had died in 869 and 885 respectively, the

Basil II 'the Bulgar-Slayer' (976–1025)

In spite of their conversion to Christianity, the Bulgars continued to represent a military threat to Byzantium through the beginning of the eleventh century. The tsar Samuel, who established a massive Bulgarian and Macedonian empire extending from the Adriatic to the Black Sea, exerted continuous pressure on the frontiers of Byzantium. However, in July 1014, after a carefully planned series of military campaigns against the Bulgars, Basil II succeeded in defeating Samuel's army by subtle tactics of pursuit and ambush. According to legend (historians now believe this story may have been embroidered by later chroniclers), the entire Bulgarian army, allegedly numbering 15,000, was blinded and sent back to their leader in groups of 100 men. Each group was led by a one-eyed man. When Samuel saw this gruesome procession approaching, he fell into a coma and died two days later (6 October 1014).

Germans expelled their disciples from Moravia and eradicated all signs of their mission there.

Although the Orthodox mission to Moravia thus failed, the decision to translate Christian texts into Old Church Slavonic was immensely significant. Soon the Byzantines began to send evangelists to other neighbouring peoples, including the Bulgars, the Serbs and eventually the Rus'. The translations begun by Cyril and Methodios continued to be used in these areas and also to be expanded. Thus the Christian message was presented to these peoples in a way which they could understand and assimilate. The Bulgars, after vacillating for some time between the Latins and the Greeks, eventually placed themselves under the protection of the patriarchate in Constantinople. Boris, the khan of Bulgaria, was baptized in 864 or 865.

The Rus'

The earliest Greek reference to a northern people called the Rus' (ancestors of the Russian people) occurs in a sermon preached by the patriarch Photios, describing their attack on Constantinople in 860. The earliest Rus' were Scandinavians who migrated south and settled initially in the region around Novgorod. During the ninth and tenth centuries the Viking Rus' settled along the river routes of modern Russia and gradually merged with the native Slav population, eventually establishing a capital city in Kiev. With their periodic raids into Byzantine territory, the Rus' represented an increasing threat to the empire and it was not long before the tactics of diplomacy and mission were tried. A first attempt at evangelization in 864 failed, but steady Christian infiltration both from Byzantium and from the neighbouring Bulgarian state eventually had an effect. The Kievan princess Olga, who travelled to Constantinople and witnessed for herself the splendours of the imperial liturgy in Hagia Sophia, was baptized probably in 954 or 955. Although her son Svyatoslav refused to follow her example, her grandson Vladimir embraced Christianity in 988. This is accepted in the Russian Orthodox Church today as the date of its foundation: after being baptized himself, Vladimir set out to Christianize the whole of his realm.

In addition to adopting the Byzantine Orthodox liturgy and encouraging the growth of monasticism within his realm, Vladimir and his followers seem to have taken the social implications of Christ's teachings seriously. Tenth-century Kiev represented a model of a true Christian state, with organized social services and distributions of food to the poor. When Vladimir introduced Byzantine law codes into Rus' society, he made sure that the most severe punishments and abuses were eliminated from them. Thus there was no death penalty in Kievan Rus' and only rarely did rulers resort to corporal punishment or torture. The

The conversion of the Rus'

The earliest written record of the Russian nation, called the *Primary Chronicle*, was probably composed in the twelfth century, but drew on earlier sources. It describes how the ruler Vladimir sent embassies to observe many different religions before deciding which one to adopt. When the envoys returned, they described their experience in Constantinople as follows: 'Then we went on to Greece, and the Greeks led us to the edifices where they worship their God, and we knew not whether we were in heaven or on earth. For on earth there is no such splendour or such beauty, and we are at a loss how to describe it. We know only that God dwells there among men, and their service is fairer than the ceremonies of other nations.'

story of Vladimir's two sons, Boris and Gleb, also exemplifies the new Christian ethos of this period. On Vladimir's death in 1015, the realm was divided between these two sons and their brother, Svyatopolk. When Svyatopolk illegally seized their principalities, Boris and Gleb offered no resistance, choosing instead to die at his hands.

Schism between Constantinople and Rome

Tension between the Roman papacy and the Eastern patriarchates continued to grow in the course of the 10th and 11th centuries. Rival missions to the Slavs did not help matters, especially as the differences between the two religious traditions, minor though they were, seemed significant in the context of the daily life of the Church. For example, the Greek Church had always allowed priests to marry, whereas the Latins enforced celibacy. The Orthodox Churches used leavened bread in the eucharist, as opposed to the Latins' unleavened wafers, and the rules of fasting also differed in the two halves of Christendom. An even more fundamental problem, as we saw above, was the issue of papal primacy; while the Eastern Orthodox patriarchs could accept that the pope wielded sole power in the whole of the Western Church, they could not admit his authority over their own affairs.

An official schism between East and West eventually occurred in 1054. The dispute which led up to this rupture seems trivial, even petty. Nevertheless, these events should be seen against a background of political insecurity, especially on the Byzantine side, which helps to explain the hasty reactions that led to long-term separation. In the course of the eleventh century, the Normans had occupied much of what had been Byzantine territory in Southern Italy and proceeded to force the Greeks still living in these areas to adopt Latin ecclesiastical customs. The patriarch Kerularios of Constantinople, a strong-willed and combative individual, refused to let this pass and retaliated by imposing similar measures against all the Latin churches in the imperial city and closing them when they refused to comply. The pope sent three legates to Constantinople, one of whom was the rigorous Cardinal Humbert, a reformer within the Western Church in this period. When communications broke down between Kerularios and the Latin delegation, Humbert and his colleagues left a Bull of Excommunication on the altar of the Great Church of Hagia Sophia, in which they accused the Greeks of many breaches of discipline, including the exclusion of the *filioque* from the Creed.

Mutual excommunications by Roman popes and Constantinopolitan patriarchs had occurred several times before; it is perhaps a historical accident that the Schism of 1054 was not healed soon afterwards. As we have seen, however, this event should be viewed against a background of a mutual distrust which had been developing for several centuries and which inhibited each side's desire for reconciliation. The final seal of separation in any case was provided by another major event in Christian history, namely the four crusades which took place between 1095 and 1204.

The Crusades

A Byzantine emperor, Alexios I, was responsible for initiating the Crusades. After a series of military reverses, beginning with the disastrous battle of Manzikert in 1071, the Byzantine empire stood in grave peril from the relentless advance of the Seljuk Turks. Alexios, in desperation, turned to the West for help. In March 1095, his envoys met Pope Urban II at Piacenza and asked for military aid to save Eastern Christendom from the threat of destruction and to free the Holy Land, especially Jerusalem, from the infidels. The First Crusade began with great success: Antioch was captured from the Turks in 1098 and Jerusalem in 1099. The Western crusaders immediately carved out principalities for themselves and installed Latin patriarchs in both of these cities. Although this did not perhaps constitute part of the original bargain, the Greek and Latin populations in these areas appear to have coexisted fairly harmoniously under the new arrangements. The next three crusades, however, were by no means so successful. Tension and distrust between Greek and Latin leaders increased as the crusaders began to experience military reverses at the hands of the Turks and Arabs. Finally, the Fourth Crusade resulted in catastrophe for the Greeks when, on the pretext of reinstating a dispossessed Byzantine emperor, the Latins sacked Constantinople for three days in April 1204. The Greeks viewed the destruction and pillaging of Constantinople on this occasion as an act of treachery on the part of the Latins. It is fair to say that this event represents the real moment when the schism between East and West became final.

The period of Latin domination

After their capture of the capital city, the Latins ruled the various territories of the Byzantine empire, with the exception of a few small principalities that remained under Byzantine rule, for nearly 60 years. In general, this period of Latin occupation (1204–61) was peaceful as far as the two Churches were concerned. Greek Orthodox priests were allowed to continue their ministry in accordance with their Eastern

> 'The crusaders brought not peace but a sword; and the sword was to sever Christendom.'
>
> **Sir Steven Runciman, *The Eastern Schism*, 1955**

traditions. However, there can be no doubt that the Roman papacy had as its long-term aim the restoration of unity between East and West. To achieve this goal the Latins hoped gradually to replace the Greek ecclesiastical hierarchy by Latin clergy and gradually to enforce the use of Western customs in the Church. None of these measures helped to overcome the Greeks' distrust and resentment towards their Latin overlords; when Michael VIII Palaiologos succeeded in recapturing Constantinople and ousting the Western leaders from most of the Byzantine territories, Orthodox Christians were jubilant.

The final centuries

The restored Byzantine empire after 1261 covered only a fraction of the territory that it had once controlled. Confined to the Western half of Asia Minor, Constantinople and parts of what is now mainland Greece, the empire faced a hostile Seljuk Sultanate in the East and various European kingdoms in the West. One of the surprising aspects of this period of Byzantine history is that Orthodox faith and culture flourished as never before. This is the period when some of the greatest mosaic and frescoed wall paintings were created, when philosophical and mystical writings proliferated, and monasticism flourished again. It is possible that a sense of isolation and defensiveness promotes a stronger sense of cultural identity. More and more, Constantinople represented for Byzantine Christians the symbolic centre of their civilization. This city alone stood firm once again against the incursions of a hostile and aggressive world outside.

As Byzantine imperial power declined between 1261 and 1453, the Church, rather surprisingly, gained prestige and authority. This may be partly due to the fact that patriarchs played an important political role in this period, promoting culture, negotiating with the West and lending legitimacy to the newly formed state. Although imperial finances were reduced, owing to the loss of taxable territories, private patrons funded many new monasteries in Constantinople and also in the Balkans and the Peloponnese.

The sense of isolation and frailty in the face of an ever-advancing Turkish enemy in these centuries led the Byzantines once again to seek reconciliation with their fellow Christians in the West. Even though the humiliation of 1204 and the years of Latin domination must have been fresh in his mind, the emperor Michael VIII Palaiologos sent delegates to the Council of Lyons in 1274. Although the official reunion with the West which was achieved at this council bore with it the promise of greater security, both against the Turks in the East and aggressive Western leaders such as Charles of Anjou, the Orthodox people at home and their bishops vigorously rejected it.

By the early fifteenth century the situation in Byzantium was desperate. A new clan of Turks, called the Ottomans, had succeeded the Seljuks and conquered the whole of Asia Minor and much of mainland Greece. By attending the Council of Ferrara/Florence in 1438–39, the emperor John VIII Palaiologos hoped to gain Western military aid in fighting the Turks. In addition to the emperor, two important Greek theologians attended the council: the unionist Bessarion and the anti-unionist Mark, metropolitans of Nicea and Ephesus, respectively. A number of issues were discussed at this council, including the procession of the Holy Spirit, the use of leavened or unleavened bread in the eucharist, the existence of purgatory and the primacy of the pope. The Orthodox delegation ended up capitulating on almost every one, although Mark of Ephesus refused to add his signature to the Decree of Union. Once again, the Greek delegation met with opposition from the majority of Orthodox Christians when they returned to Constantinople. When the imperial city finally fell to the Turks in 1453, the quest for unity, along with the agreements of this council, was abandoned for ever. As the Byzantine Orthodox Church began to find its feet under Ottoman domination, the prospect of reunion with Latin Christendom no longer seemed relevant.

When studying the later history of Eastern Christendom, it is worth asking who the Byzantines were and how they viewed themselves. There can be no doubt that, just as in the West, the Church represented the most important unifying aspect of this culture. In spite of the catastrophic loss of their imperial territories to the Turks and other hostile invaders, Orthodox Christians in the late Byzantine period also could view themselves as part of a larger commonwealth. The neighbouring Slavic nations, including the Bulgars, the Serbs and the Rus', shared with the Byzantines their Orthodox beliefs and traditions. Thus, even after the fall of Constantinople to the Ottomans in 1453, the Eastern Orthodox Church maintained a sense of its own independence and identity within a wider Christian world.

CHAPTER 3

CHURCH AND STATE

The conversion of Constantine I in 312 and the gradual Christianization of the empire throughout the fourth century brought about a number of significant changes in political ideology. For the first time the Christian Church found itself in a powerful position. The emperor, whose job was to defend the state and overcome his political rivals by force, must at the same time live a Christian life according to the example set by Jesus Christ. The need to explain and justify Constantine's new role as Christian emperor appears in the writings of Eusebius of Caesarea, bishop and advisor to the emperor. Eusebius wrote not only a lengthy *History of the Christian Church*, one of the earliest examples of this genre, but also a biography and several orations in praise of Constantine. It is in the latter works, in particular the *Oration on the Tricennalia*, or *Thirty Years' Rule*, of Constantine, that we see the full development of a new and creative ideology justifying the whole concept of a Christian empire.

Byzantine political ideology

Eusebius based his ideas on a tradition of divine kingship which originated in the Hellenistic period and became influential in the later Roman empire. He was able successfully to unite the pagan concept of kingship with a new, specifically Christian, philosophy. Monotheism, according to Eusebius, requires an autocracy: just as one all-powerful God in heaven rules over his subjects, so should one supreme emperor administer justice on earth. The earthly emperor is invested with power by his divine prototype. He is the image, or representative, of the divine Ruler in heaven. The Christian emperor thus embodies not only God's power, but also his benevolence and protection towards humankind. His job is

'The only begotten Word of God reigns, from ages which had no beginning, to infinite and endless ages, the partner of his Father's kingdom. And our emperor ever beloved by him, who derives the source of imperial authority from above, and is strong in the power of his sacred title, has controlled the empire of the world for a long period of years.'

Eusebius of Caesarea, in an oration celebrating 30 years of Constantine's rule, probably written in 336

to protect the empire from barbarians and unbelievers and to promote peace within both Church and empire.

The importance of Eusebius' political ideology for the future development of the Eastern Roman empire was incalculable. In their role as God's representatives on earth, Byzantine rulers henceforth wielded absolute power over their subjects. It is important to note that usurpers were not ruled out from assuming this privileged position. If a powerful general or other suitably qualified candidate succeeded in overthrowing a weak emperor and assuming power himself, this could be justified on the grounds that he had gained God's favour. All in all, Eusebius' vision of the ideal political system being based on one, autocratic ruler proved both flexible and lasting, even in the highly unstable political and economic circumstances which prevailed in later centuries.

The link between Church and State was thus much stronger in the Byzantine empire than is the case in most modern nations. A distinction between the two entities would have seemed meaningless to most Byzantines: they viewed the polity, which was made up of both secular and religious powers, as one organic whole. The emperor and his government could not operate without the sanction of the Church, nor could the bishops and patriarch serve their flocks without imperial support. As we shall see later in this chapter, however, this ideal picture of the harmonious relationship between the secular and religious spheres of life did not always prevail in later Byzantine history. On a number of occasions, emperors came into conflict with their highest bishops. It is at times such as these that churchmen expressed the view that emperors should not interfere in matters of the Church. In general, however, it remained the duty of the secular government to enforce and implement ecclesiastical policy. Indeed, Byzantines believed that the security of the empire depended on the successful enactment of God's kingdom here on earth.

The idea of the Christian Roman empire envisioned by Eusebius and adhered to throughout the Byzantine period was thus a strictly hierarchical structure. At the top stood the emperor, God's representative on earth, who was responsible for maintaining harmony in his name both in Church and State. Michael II, writing to the Frankish ruler Louis the Pious in the early ninth century, speaks of having his power from God. Basil I, who like many Byzantine emperors crowned his own son as his successor, wrote, 'The crown which you receive at my

Coronation

The formal acceptance of a Byzantine emperor was a complex event, made up of a number of different elements. The ceremonies also appear to have changed somewhat in the course of Byzantine history. The practice of raising the emperor on a shield and acclaiming him was borrowed from Germanic tradition and was first used for the emperor Julian in the fourth century. By the middle of the fifth century, parts of the ceremony were taking place in church, where the patriarch blessed and participated in the investiture of the imperial candidate. At this period, however, the patriarch's role was not yet seen as lending legitimacy to the emperor's rule. The coronation of Constans II in Hagia Sophia (641) represented the beginning of full-scale ceremonies in the Great Church, which became the practice thereafter. The patriarch would crown the emperor on the ambo, a raised platform in the centre of the church, while the congregation acclaimed him. The coronation ceremony would be followed by a *eucharistic liturgy*, thus fully integrating the secular and the religious spheres. A tenth-century text called the *Book of Ceremonies*, attributed to the emperor Constantine VII Porphyrogennetos, provides detailed accounts of the coronation procedures in this period. According to this source, empresses were crowned not in Hagia Sophia, but in a square called the Augusteion, or in a smaller church.

hands comes from God.' Although in theory the legitimacy of emperors' reigns was validated by the people's (in other words, the senate's) and the army's acclaim, in accordance with the customs of the later Roman empire, in practice many later Byzantine emperors were crowned dynastically by their fathers. It was only by the mid-fifth century that the full ecclesiastical ceremony surrounding the coronation of an emperor developed; from the seventh century onwards it became customary for the ceremony to be performed in the Great Church, Hagia Sophia.

The role of the emperor

When Eusebius writes that the emperor is God's representative on earth, or that he is a living icon of Christ, he of course does not mean that the emperor himself is divine. Eusebius' picture of the emperor and state is in fact based on a Platonic view of the world. The emperor represents an image or reflection of divine majesty, but he himself remains firmly in the realm of the created world. It is also important to note that Byzantine emperors did not represent priest-kings such as one would find in a true religious state. The emperor was technically a layman in the Church. It is true that he played an important role in looking after the welfare of the Church, calling church councils and implementing their decisions. He also took part on a daily basis in elaborate religious ceremonies which took place both in the palace and in the main churches of the capital city. Byzantine emperors never, however, fulfilled a priestly role in these liturgies. Although they were allowed to enter the inner sanctuary of the Great Church and to receive communion with the clergy, emperors could not themselves administer the sacraments.

Byzantine emperors also played an important role in helping to resolve the doctrinal controversies which broke out in the Church from the fourth century onwards. Thus we see Constantine I summoning the first universal, or 'ecumenical', council in 325. The fact that he presided over the council and regarded himself responsible for enforcing its decisions represents a highly significant precedent for the religious administration of the Byzantine Church in subsequent centuries. Ecumenical councils, of which the Byzantines recognized seven, beginning and ending in the small town of Nicea (325 and 787) near Constantinople, became the accepted method for discussing and defining religious doctrine in response to opposing, or 'heretical', views.

> 'The constitution consists, like the human person, of parts and members . . . and of these the greatest and most necessary are the emperor and the patriarch. Thus the peace and felicity of subjects, in body and soul, depends on the agreement and concord of the kingship and the priesthood in all things.'
>
> The *Epanagoge Aucta*, a legal handbook probably compiled in Constantinople soon after 912

The ecumenical patriarch

After the emperor, the main leader of the Church in the Byzantine empire was the ecumenical patriarch. The term 'ecumenical' comes from the Greek word *oikoumene*, meaning the inhabited world. The title thus conveys the importance of the Patriarch of Constantinople within the empire as a whole. By the end of the sixth century, five major sees within the Roman world had been officially designated 'patriarchates' and given an order of precedence. These were the dioceses of Rome, Constantinople, Alexandria, Antioch and Jerusalem. Constantinople in fact had the least claim to apostolic foundation, but Theodosius I made sure at the Council of Constantinople in 381 that it should nevertheless be placed after Rome in power and dignity.

Soon political and military developments began to influence the shape and organization of Christendom as a whole. After the Near East and North Africa fell to Islam in the mid-seventh century, the patriarchates of Alexandria, Antioch and Jerusalem ceased to wield any significant influence in the affairs of the Byzantine and Western Churches. The ecumenical patriarch in Constantinople increasingly came to represent the leader of the Eastern Christian Church. As the emperor's right-hand man in all matters of ecclesiastical jurisdiction, the Patriarch of Constantinople ideally operated in a close, symbiotic relationship with the secular head of the empire. It certainly made life easier for both men if they could agree on important issues of doctrine and church practice. Occasionally in the course of Byzantine history, however, we see the relationship between an emperor and his ecumenical patriarch becoming strained or even breaking down. In order to set the theoretical model of the Byzantine Church, which has so far been set out into perspective, it might be useful to look at a few examples of emperors and patriarchs in conflict.

Tension between emperors and ecumenical patriarchs

As the subsequent events of Byzantine history showed, tension between emperors and their ecumenical patriarchs could develop, thus dividing the body politic and causing great strain within both Church and State. The period of Iconoclasm, which lasted from the early eighth to the mid-ninth century, provides the background for one such rift. When the emperor Leo III decided to introduce Iconoclasm as an imperial policy, Patriarch Germanos I was strongly opposed to the idea. Christian imagery, he argued, was strongly established in the Church since apostolic times; the charge of idolatry could only be levelled at ancient Jews, pagans or barbarians who had not accepted the truth of Christian revelation. It is still not known how seriously Leo III imposed Iconoclasm as an imperial policy. It is likely that severe persecution of the defenders of holy icons only began under his son, Constantine V. Nevertheless, Germanos felt morally incapable of remaining in the office of ecumenical patriarch. In 730 he resigned and went to live on his private estate near Constantinople, where he died three years later.

After a brief period between 787 and 815 when icons were formally reinstated in the Church, the first iconoclast emperor's namesake, Leo V, decided to reintroduce the ban against images. On this occasion, the emperor tried to justify his policies by establishing a small committee of clerics to compile arguments against the use of icons in the Church, backed up with passages supporting this position taken from scripture and the writings of the Church Fathers. The incumbent ecumenical patriarch, Nikephoros, however, refused to have anything to do with this commission. Gathering together a group of supporters just before Christmas in 815, he persuaded them formally to reject the emperor's iconoclast compilation. Leo then summoned him to the palace where Nikephoros continued to defend his position, although strong measures of intimidation were employed. Eventually, after several months in which the patriarch remained virtually under house arrest, he resigned from his office and was exiled on the Asian side of the Bosphorus. Although Nikephoros was by this time an old and sick man, he spent his remaining years writing voluminous treatises in which he refuted Iconoclasm and developed further the theological defence of Christian imagery.

It is clear from contemporary writings that some of the defenders of icons were aware of the political dimensions of the controversy. John of Damascus, for example, in one of the three treatises which he wrote in defence of icons, states: 'What right have emperors to style themselves lawgivers in the Church?' Iconoclasm represented one of a few instances in the Byzantine Church when a series of emperors enacted religious policies which, although supported by many bishops at the time, were later declared heretical. Thus, while their interference in Church affairs was generally tolerated and even expected by Christians, Orthodox rulers remained laymen

'Your responsibility, Emperor, is with affairs of the state and military matters. Give your mind to these and leave the Church to its pastors and teachers.'

Theodore of Studios, ninth-century monk and defender of icons

and could frequently make catastrophic mistakes. The conceptual difference between Church and State expressed in a few outspoken texts contrasts strikingly with the more usual contemporary depictions of a deeply symbiotic relationship between the two bodies.

Church discipline as a source of tension

Matters of discipline rather than doctrine could also frequently cause tension between emperors and patriarchs. In 795 the emperor Constantine VI divorced his wife and remarried. Byzantine canon law does not completely ban these actions if there are mitigating circumstances, but Tarasios, the current patriarch, was widely condemned by his colleagues for allowing Constantine VI's remarriage. A highly vocal monastic party, led by Abbot Plato of Saccudion and his nephew Theodore of Studios, called for the excommunication of the priest, Joseph, who had presided over it. The resulting controversy, called the 'moechian' (adultery) affair, rumbled on for a decade or so, with subsequent patriarchs being obliged to take one side or the other. Nikephoros followed the example of Tarasios in overlooking the emperor's transgression; furthermore, he reinstated Joseph in 809, thereby infuriating the Studite monks. It is clear that this early-ninth-century patriarch was diplomatic in his response to imperial policy. He was prepared to give way on a matter of discipline, exercising the principle of compromise, while standing firm on the issue of icons which he regarded as fundamental to Orthodox doctrine. Many subsequent examples of tension between Byzantine emperors and their patriarchs also illustrate the fact that this relationship was not uniformly harmonious. It is noticeable that after the period of Iconoclasm, it was not usually doctrinal issues which divided the secular from the ecclesiastical realms.

Church politics after 1204

One of the most important and lasting rifts between Church and State took place after the period of Latin occupation which followed the Fourth Crusade and the sack of Constantinople in 1204. Under the pretext of driving the Latins out of Byzantine territories, Michael

Condemnation of Leo VI for divorce and remarriage

In the early tenth century, the issue of the emperor Leo VI's *fourth* marriage caused controversy. Leo, who ruled between 886 and 912, became worried that he had no male heir. When his first wife, Theophano, died in 897, the emperor took a second wife, who also died without issue in 899. According to canon law, two imperial marriages could be tolerated, but any further unions were strictly prohibited. Leo was undeterred by this ruling. He married again, and when this wife died in 901, in connection with childbirth, he took a mistress who finally provided him with a son, the future Constantine VII. The current patriarch, Nicholas I Mystikos, although accepting the illegitimate heir of this union, refused to forgive the emperor for his immoral behaviour. He prohibited Leo VI from entering the Great Church, actually turning him back from its doors at Christmas and Epiphany 906–07. The emperor resorted to deposing the patriarch and seeking pardon from the Roman pope. He also secretly married his consort, probably around the time of Easter 906. After his death in 912, however, the patriarch Nicholas was reinstated and thus vindicated for his firm stance in opposition to the emperor.

VIII usurped the throne which belonged rightfully to Theodore II, a member of the Lascarid dynasty, and was crowned in Hagia Sophia on 15 August 1261. The patriarch Arsenios, who remained loyal to the Lascarids, excommunicated Michael both because of his usurpation and because five months later he blinded the rightful heir and designated his own son Andronikos as his successor. After several years of tension, Arsenios was deposed from his patriarchal seat in 1264 and exiled to the island of Proconnesus. On this occasion the deposition of the patriarch caused a schism within the Church which lasted for most of the rest of Michael VIII's reign. The followers of Arsenios refused to recognize the patriarchs who replaced him; that many of them were monks, described as 'zealots' and 'extremists' by those who opposed them, reinforces the impression that it was frequently the monastic elements in the Church who took the lead in moral disputes of this kind.

Church and State thus did not represent one entity in the Eastern Roman empire. They supported each other, depending on an active, symbiotic relationship, but it is fair to say that their values and goals were not always closely matched. Bishops, along with the metropolitans and patriarchs who led them, usually backed the political aims of emperors, but when matters of church discipline or doctrine were breached, they could oppose their secular rulers. The emperor in turn regarded it as his duty to uphold the decisions of ecclesiastical councils and to maintain stability and harmony within society. If he failed to carry out these functions responsibly he risked incurring the disapproval not only of priests and bishops, but also of an increasingly powerful monastic lobby.

In the whole course of Byzantine history, it is possible to find many instances in which the secular and ecclesiastical realms became divided. On the other hand, the checks and balances of this system ensured that in most cases stability could be restored, sometimes at the expense of a patriarch's career. In spite of the questions concerning the right of an emperor to interfere in the affairs of the Church posed by John of Damascus and Theodore of Studios at the beginning of the ninth century, the Eusebian vision of the emperor as 'God's friend, acting as interpreter to the Word of God' prevailed until 1453, when there was no longer an Orthodox emperor to reign over the Eastern Christian empire.

CHAPTER 4
SERVICE TO THE COMMUNITY

The medieval Church, in both East and West, was hierarchical in its organization. The clergy was organized into three major orders: bishops, priests or presbyters, and deacons. Beneath this threefold structure were the minor orders, including subdeacons, readers and all the officials who looked after church buildings or ministered to the public. Each office had its own ceremony of ordination, a sacred ritual which conferred both the blessing of the Holy Spirit and the approval of the Church as a whole. Bishops, at the top of the hierarchy, in theory represented the highest source of authority within the Christian Church. They were led in their decisions, however, by five bishops who presided over the most influential sees in the Roman world. In the sixth century, these five bishops came to be called patriarchs or, in the cases of Rome and Alexandria, popes. The five apostolic sees, or patriarchates, were, in order of their importance: Rome, Constantinople, Alexandria, Antioch and Jerusalem.

> 'For as in one body we have many members, and not all the members have the same function, so we, who are many, are one body in Christ, and individually we are members one of another.'
>
> **Romans 12:4–5**

The threefold structure

Such a strictly hierarchical structure had not, of course, existed in the earliest Christian Church. During the first and second centuries, texts of the New Testament and the Apostolic Fathers testify to the leadership of self-appointed 'prophets', teachers and even distinguished women in the ministry of the early Church. Charismatic leadership had a place in the Church in this period, as Paul testifies in 1 Corinthians 12:28: 'And God has appointed in the church first apostles, second prophets, third teachers; then deeds of power, then gifts of healing, forms of assistance, forms of leadership, various kinds of tongues.' It is clear even in this passage, however, that Paul envisaged an order of precedence with regard to these various offices. The apostles came first; it was their direct successors, or the men whom they approved and blessed, who in the course of the second century became the leaders, or bishops, of the Church.

Problems and challenges of many kinds assailed the Church in the first few centuries: schism within individual communities, issues of authority and differences over doctrine or discipline represent only a few of the internal problems facing early Christian communities. Persecution by various Roman emperors probably strengthened rather than divided the Church, but it also eliminated some of its most talented leaders. In the course of the second century, various groups collectively called the Gnostics emerged and challenged both the teachings and leadership of the mainstream Church. In response to this threat, Irenaeus of Lyons, a bishop who was active in the 170s, wrote treatises in which he addressed the issue of authority. Irenaeus supported the principle of 'apostolic succession', the idea that Christian bishops follow a direct line of succession from the first apostles. Two main principles emerge from this analysis: first, bishops of the orthodox or right-believing Church possess the authority conferred on them by their apostolic succession; and second, they are unified and consistent in their teaching of the Christian faith.

> 'This unity firmly should we hold and maintain, especially we bishops presiding within the Church, in order that we may approve the episcopate itself to be one and undivided.'
>
> Cyprian, a third-century bishop of Carthage, who argued for unity among bishops as they sought to resolve conflicts within the Church.

After the adoption of Christianity as the state religion throughout the Roman empire by Constantine and his successors, bishops continued to be ordained and to function in accordance with this tradition. The organization of episcopal sees followed closely the patterns of secular government. Every major city would have its bishop and, following the administrative division of the empire, provincial capitals would be home to a superior bishop, or metropolitan. Most important doctrinal or disciplinary decisions had to be discussed in councils, at which all bishops had an equal vote. When an issue was judged to be of overwhelming importance within the Church, an ecumenical or 'universal' council would be called. In theory, representatives (these could be any bishops) of all five patriarchates were expected to attend the ecumenical councils in order to render their decisions valid. In practice, owing to the increasingly precarious military position of the Byzantine empire in the fifth to the eighth centuries, bishops from Rome and from the three Near-Eastern patriarchates were frequently absent at the later ecumenical councils.

The five patriarchs each held supreme authority within their areas of jurisdiction. The Bishop of Rome, or pope, as he came to be called, increasingly was sole leader of the whole of the Western Church. In the Eastern Roman empire, it was the Patriarch of Constantinople, called the 'ecumenical' patriarch, who came to dominate church politics, especially after the Eastern territories including Palestine, Syria, Egypt and North Africa were conquered by the Muslims in the course of the seventh century. In addition to crowning the emperor and carrying out with him the numerous liturgical ceremonies which formed an important part of the duties of each, the ecumenical patriarch helped to enforce ecclesiastical policies throughout the empire. Patriarchs were elected by all the metropolitans who met for this purpose in a synod at Constantinople. They would present the names of three candidates to the emperor. He could choose one of these, but if none was acceptable, the emperor had the right to appoint a patriarch of his own choice, subject to the metropolitans' approval.

Under the patriarchs came the bishops, led in each province by their metropolitans. Bishops and metropolitans were concerned with all aspects of religious life and worship. They looked after not only churches and monasteries but all other ecclesiastical properties, including charitable foundations and hospitals. In their administrative roles, bishops were responsible for the smooth running of affairs within their dioceses, as well as for preserving harmony within the universal Church. As ordained priests of God, they also administered the sacraments and acted as teachers of the faith. Many sermons delivered by Byzantine bishops of all periods survive. Although some of these are written in a highly rhetorical and poetic style and have obviously been carefully edited after their first delivery, others, mostly dating from the fourth to the sixth centuries, provide instructive explanations of scriptural readings. We know much less about Byzantine bishops' pastoral work among their flocks: sometimes details are recorded in their biographies, letters or in ecclesiastical histories, but it is often difficult to learn much about their relations with parishioners on the basis of their own preaching. A prerequisite for ordination to the episcopate was monastic status: thus, all bishops were unmarried and ideally celibate. This tradition reflects the idea that bishops were chosen originally from the ranks of holy men or ascetics who had renounced the world and chosen a solitary way of life.

The second order of priests or presbyters (the terms eventually became interchangeable) had, in the early Church, served to assist the bishop in his administrative and teaching roles. By the fourth century, resident priests were being put in charge of parishes and were performing the sacramental rites. Priests were also allowed to preach, although their sermons always followed that of the bishop, if he happened to be present. Unlike bishops, priests in the Byzantine Church were allowed to marry. This later became a point of contention with the West, where celibacy had become the rule for priests as well as bishops. The image of the humble village priest, often employed in another profession, such as farming or teaching, and supporting a family, held true in the Byzantine provinces as it does in some outlying districts of Greece and other Orthodox countries today. The advantage of matrimony among the lower clergy was that it kept priests closely involved in their communities and aware of the joys and difficulties of married and family life.

The duties of the deacon and the deaconess were mostly pastoral. As the title suggests in Greek, deacons were expected primarily to assist priests and bishops in their duties. They helped with baptisms, served at the celebration and administration of the eucharist in the Divine Liturgy, performed administrative tasks and sometimes acted as bishops' secretaries. In spite of the fact that they occupied one of the lower ranks of the Church hierarchy, deacons represented an essential order within the clergy, carrying out many important functions. Female deacons, or deaconesses, were ordained in the Church from a very early period. The initial reason for ordaining women to this office seems to have been their assistance at the baptisms of women. Since baptism took place by full immersion in this period and many of the converts to Christianity were adult women, it was deemed improper and distracting for male clergy to preside at their initiation into the Church. The office of deaconess survived until as late as the eleventh century in the Byzantine Church, even though the number of adult baptisms soon declined; in the West, the female diaconate seems to have died out much earlier.

Although the Byzantine Orthodox Church was hierarchical, it remained true to its apostolic origins in considering the laity as the foundation of the Church: 'a royal priesthood, a holy nation' (1 Peter 2:9). Unfortunately we hear little from ordinary laypeople of the Byzantine period, since they did not usually write theological discourses, sermons or religious texts. Indeed, it has been estimated that only a tiny percentage of the Byzantine population was literate, even to the extent of reading simple Bible passages. On the other hand, the wealth of surviving biographies of saints and collections of miracle stories provide some information about the beliefs and conduct of ordinary Orthodox Christians. Some of these narratives suggest that lay Byzantine Christians attended church especially when they sought divine protection or help. A familiar theme, for example, is that of the barren mother who seeks God's help in conceiving a child. The mother of a ninth-century Palestinian saint called Michael the Synkellos spent much time in church praying for a child before she became pregnant with Michael. Brief references such as these, even though they may represent conventional set pieces in the

'If we take seriously the bond between God and his Church, then we must inevitably think of the Church as one, even as God is one: there is only one Christ, and so there can be only one body of Christ. Nor is this unity merely ideal and invisible; Orthodox theology refuses to separate the "invisible" and the "visible Church", and therefore it refuses to say that the Church is invisibly one but visibly divided.'

Timothy Ware, The Orthodox Church, 1993

Church rules

A collection of rules for the Church called the *Apostolic Constitutions*, probably dating from the late fourth century and of Syrian provenance, contains valuable information about the three orders of clergy and their functions in the Church in this period. For example, the appropriate qualities of a bishop are listed as follows: 'Let him therefore be sober, prudent, decent, firm, stable, not given to wine; no striker, but gentle; not a brawler, not covetous.' The passage goes on to state that the bishop may be married, but that he should have had no more than one wife. It later became the custom for bishops to be chosen from the monastic profession and thus to be celibate. The *Apostolic Constitutions* also provide rules for the correct conduct of laymen and laywomen, giving advice on clothing, married life, social conduct and many other topics.

biographies of saints, provide precious information about the customs and piety of ordinary Byzantine people.

Although the Church hierarchy was loosely ordered in the early Christian period, it had become extremely well defined by the middle and later periods of Byzantine history. A strong sense of order, called *taxis*, prevailed. Lists of precedence, called the *Notitiae Episcopatum*, were drawn up and revised in successive centuries: these set out official lists of bishoprics and determined the order in which signatures would appear in the acts of Church councils. As we have seen, the ecumenical patriarch wielded ultimate authority in the Byzantine Church, especially as the Eastern, or 'Oriental', patriarchates of Alexandria, Antioch and Jerusalem came under Muslim rule. Beneath him, the bishops, led by their metropolitans, reached important decisions concerning church doctrine or discipline in councils. In spite of this hierarchy, however, it is important to realize that Orthodox Byzantines continued to think of their Church as one, unified body. This communion consisted not only of all ordained clergy and the laity here on earth, but also of God and his heavenly kingdom.

Canon law

Besides making decisions about Christian doctrine, ecumenical councils drew up rules, or canons, dealing with organizational and disciplinary matters. Canons could also be established in smaller, local synods and added to the growing list of ecclesiastical laws. The canons of the Church are thus contained in the Acts or Definitions of the various councils. In the later period of Byzantine history, they were arranged into collections and provided with commentaries. The vast number of canons, established as they were over a number of centuries and in response to very different circumstances, inevitably repeat and even at times contradict each other. These canons do not possess the same authority as the formal definitions of doctrine which emerged from the ecumenical councils. They deal with earthly life, whereas doctrine is concerned with eternal truths. Nevertheless, the canons did provide guidelines for the daily administration of the Byzantine Church and for its response to controversy over issues such as morality, ethics and discipline.

Emperors also frequently enacted laws on ecclesiastical matters; here again it is clear that no sharp distinction between Church and State existed for the Byzantines. Secular rulers were closely involved with the Church in dealing with matters of heresy and could attend the synod in Constantinople where trials of this kind took place. Many emperors also legislated on matters of church discipline: a good example of this can be found in the 'new decrees', or Novels, of the sixth-century emperor Justinian. The late-ninth and tenth-century emperors, Leo VI and Nikephoros II, issued laws concerning the foundation and maintenance of monastic properties or regulating Christian marriage. Sometimes bishops opposed emperors' ecclesiastical legislation, but more often it was accepted as a legitimate part of the imperial prerogative.

Bishops were responsible for dealing with breaches of canon law and church discipline within their own dioceses. In effect, they acted as judges within their own courts. The bishop might also receive appeals from the laity in matters of discipline or morality. In Constantinople, the synod of bishops, led by the patriarch, would handle serious cases of heresy or discipline in the ranks of the higher clergy, as we saw above. Punishment for breaches of ecclesiastical law usually could consist in temporary exclusion from the Church or even excommunication. If members of the clergy were accused of misconduct they might be defrocked, relegated to a monastery or excommunicated. In the most serious cases of all, when penalties of exile or death were recommended, the convicts were handed over to the secular authority for punishment.

It is thus clear that the laws and courts of the Byzantine Church played a significant role in the jurisdiction of the empire. At the same time, however, the application of canon law in Byzantium possessed in all periods a certain willingness to take into account individual circumstances. This feature of Orthodox jurisdiction is technically known as 'economy', or *oikonomia*, which may be roughly translated as 'the working out of God's Law on earth'. Thus, divorce and remarriage, although officially condemned, were frequently permitted for ordinary civilians as well as for emperors. This willingness to consider the special background of each petitioner when judging his or her case preserved the Byzantine Church from the more rigid approach to ecclesiastical law which sometimes prevailed in the West.

Education and higher learning

Education in the Byzantine empire was effectively divided into two streams from the earliest period onwards. Christian learning was understood as knowledge of scripture, either through reading or memorization of the sacred texts of the Old and New Testaments. On the other hand, from as early as the second century, Christian writers had employed the language and conceptual frameworks of the pagan, classical tradition. This was justified by the idea that Christian teaching must be expressed eloquently and persuasively for its mission to become truly universal. In most periods of Byzantine history, only a small elite, mostly consisting of professional people, civil servants and churchmen, received an advanced education in pagan rhetoric and philosophy. Nevertheless, these individuals wielded power in society; their ability to understand and express themselves in the archaic, classicizing language would have represented a badge of membership to the upper classes.

Illiteracy was less widespread in the Byzantine empire than in the medieval West, but even so it is likely that a high proportion of citizens were unable to read or write. Records suggest that even some monastic superiors were unable to sign their names to documents; one of Justinian's laws in the sixth century prohibits an illiterate person being elected bishop. It is important to realize, however, that the term 'illiteracy' is in some ways inappropriate for a civilization that used oral communication to a much greater degree than do most modern societies. Many Christians who could not read or write could nevertheless understand the scriptural readings in church, or even absorb the meaning of a highly rhetorical sermon. Byzantine sources also stress the importance of images in this largely illiterate culture. During the period of Iconoclasm, in the eighth and ninth centuries, pictorial representations of scenes from the life of Christ were defended on the grounds that they served an educational purpose in the Church.

Most monasteries would have run a small school, but unlike those in the West, these taught mostly at a primary level. It was sufficient for a monk to be able to read the Bible or to recite the Psalms from memory. Higher education, on the other hand, underwent many vicissitudes in the course of Byzantine history. Justinian closed down the Academy of Athens in 529 on the grounds that it taught only pagan, classical culture, and the secular university in Constantinople seems to have closed by about the seventh century. Pagan, secular education was provided after this by private teachers, some of whom travelled about from city to city. In the course of the ninth century, a revival of higher education began to take place. A school was established in a part of the palace called the Magnaura, where grammar, philosophy, mathematics and astronomy were taught. In the early twelfth century, a patriarchal school was established, which concentrated on scriptural studies. Later in the same century the field of rhetoric was added to this curriculum. Judging by the writings of bishops and patriarchs throughout the Byzantine period, classical and scriptural literary training represented necessary prerequisites for ordination to important sees.

Philanthropy and social activities

The virtue of love for humankind, or philanthropy, is not an invention of the Christian Church. In classical Greece and pagan Rome, philanthropy was regarded as an essential attribute of civilized human beings. On an individual level it implied a willingness to help one's fellow humans in any way possible, whereas collectively it meant the provisions made by society for its weaker members, especially the sick, the aged, widows and orphans. In a book on Byzantine philanthropy, the historian Demetrios J. Constantelos suggests a fundamental distinction between pagan and Christian views of philanthropy. Whereas pagans were motivated to do good because of shared social values, concern for their fellow citizens, or in some cases, in order to gain honour and approbation from the rest of society, Christians, while sharing many of these impulses, possessed a further reason for practising benevolence. This was the idea that the philanthropist is serving God by assisting other human beings. Christians who do good works are also imitating Christ since 'the Son of man came not to be served but to serve, and to give his life a ransom for many' (Matthew 20:28; Mark 10:45).

Ever since the coming of Christ, his followers had attempted to carry out his injunction to serve others, especially the weakest and poorest members of society. Early Christians organized common meals and raised money for the care of the poor, the widows and the orphans. They also extended their mission to prisoners and travellers, providing

Christian charity

Some Byzantine saints were remembered and praised for their example of active social service. A seventh-century patriarch called John the Almsgiver established a number of charitable institutions in the Egyptian city of Alexandria and its environs. His biographer records his activities in the following passage:

Once when a severe famine was oppressing the city and the holy man's stewards were, as usual, ceaselessly distributing money or some small gift to the needy, some destitute women overcome with hunger and but lately risen from child-bed were obliged to hasten to receive help from the distributors while they were still in the grip of abdominal pains, deadly pale, and suffering grievously; when the wondrous man was told of this, he built seven lying-in hospitals in different parts of the city, ordered 40 beds to be kept ready in each and arranged that every woman should rest quietly in these for seven full days after her confinement and then receive the third of a nomisma and go home.

Leontios of Neapolis, *Life of St John the Almsgiver*

food, accommodation and other material assistance to anyone in need. When Constantine and his successors adopted Christianity as the official religion of the Roman empire, such philanthropic work could be carried out on a larger and more organized scale. Canon 70 of the Council of Nicea (325) decrees that hospitals should be erected in every city of the empire. The Council of Chalcedon (451) provides evidence of other Christian foundations in its injunction that hostels for travellers, poorhouses and orphanages should be well administered. It is clear from these and other texts that the Church did not forget its traditional commitment to service after gaining imperial backing in the early fourth century.

It is also clear that philanthropy and social service remained important values in Byzantine society throughout its later history. The motivation to imitate Christ and to serve God through service to the community provided the basis not only for individual donations, but also for the work undertaken by both Church and State. It is important to reiterate here, as in other areas covered in this account, that a strong distinction between individual Christians, the Church and the State did not exist in this society. The Byzantine Church was an all-embracing organism; thus all of these categories were involved in funding charitable institutions throughout Byzantine history. The Church probably represented the most important source for endowments; as a result, many hostels and poorhouses were located next to churches or monasteries and were administered by their officers.

Charitable institutions

A number of different forms of institution were founded throughout the Byzantine period to serve the weak or poorer members of society. Perhaps one of the most loosely organized of these, which must have developed directly out of early Christian fellowships of service, was the confraternity or *diakonia* (not to be confused with the ordained diaconate). The confraternity was a voluntary organization made up of both lay and clerical members of the Church. Many dioceses, local churches and monasteries supported such organizations. The members of the confraternity were in charge of distributing charity to the community in the form of money or food, ministering to the sick and the poor, and helping any travellers who might visit the parish or diocese.

Other charitable institutions founded throughout the major cities of the empire included hospices, hospitals, orphanages, old peoples' homes and hostels for travellers and pilgrims. Occasionally the sources tell us of imperial foundations, which reflect the obligation felt by Byzantine rulers to display the qualities of benevolence and philanthropy. We hear, for example, of the fourth-century empress Flacilla, who was especially compassionate towards lepers. In the sixth century, the historian Procopius writes that the empress Theodora established a monastery and attached hostel intended for the rescue and rehabilitation of prostitutes. Basil I, the founder of the Macedonian dynasty in the late ninth century, erected more than 100 foundations for the poor, including hospitals, hostels and other institutions, both in Constantinople and in the provinces. The individual dioceses of the Church also funded philanthropic institutions throughout the empire. The money to pay for these foundations came from imperial grants, revenues from land and property, and voluntary donations from individuals. A mandatory system of tithes was instituted only fairly late in Byzantine history.

In the later centuries, that is, from the tenth century onwards, monasteries increasingly took on the responsibility of establishing and maintaining hospitals and other philanthropic institutions. Hospitals were usually built next to the church, or *katholikon*, of the monastery, while hospices for the aged and hostels for travellers were usually located outside the monastery walls. Although professional doctors might be appointed to provide specialized care, the monks would care for the sick and the needy as part of their monastic duties. The monastery of the Pantokrator, which was founded in 1136 by the emperor John II Komnenos and his wife Irene and which still stands as a broken shell in the middle of modern Istanbul, housed a large and complex hospital. Fortunately, we know a great deal about the layout and administration of this hospital because the founding charter, or *Typikon*, still survives. According to this document, the Pantokrator hospital possessed five clinics, each of which had about 10 or 12 beds. These wards were assigned to different groups, including patients suffering from illnesses of the eyes and the intestines, women (the *Typikon* does not specify whether these were gynaecological or maternity cases), emergency and general cases. In this hospital of 61 beds there were 35 doctors, some of whom may even have been female.

Byzantine Christians, from the emperor downwards, thus believed collectively in the importance of philanthropy and social service. The institutional Church and monasteries came increasingly to administer the larger charitable foundations, but it should not be forgotten that the funding for these institutions came ultimately from individual donors, whether imperial or otherwise. The importance of the role played by emperors and empresses in the support of charitable organizations cannot be overemphasized. The image of the Christian Roman emperor, which was expressed so eloquently by Eusebius in the fourth century, included the idea that as the representative of God on earth the Byzantine ruler embodies the virtues of benevolence and mercy. Byzantines thus expected their emperors to practise philanthropy. Individual Christians could also imitate their ruler's example and donate money for the service of the poor. Imitation of Christ and a genuine desire to act ethically probably represented one aspect of their motivation; the hope of divine reward and eternal salvation may have been the other.

The Byzantine system of social welfare inevitably looks haphazard to the modern eye. The extent and availability of social services would have varied according to the district in which one lived, nor did the weaker members of society possess any 'right' to claim help or treatment. Furthermore, it could be argued that by offering charity to the poor, Byzantines did nothing to improve their situation or enable them to help themselves. Nevertheless, it is undeniable that charitable institutions of all kinds provided relief to many underprivileged members of society in the larger cities of Byzantium. The fact that philanthropy remained such a prized ideal among all wealthy citizens, including the emperor, meant that the system continued to work effectively through the final years of Byzantine sovereignty. Even just after the fall of Constantinople to the Turks in 1453, an eye witness lamented that the city would no longer be able to maintain its many philanthropic institutions.

CHAPTER 5
THE SOLITARY IDEAL

One of the greatest legacies of the Byzantine Orthodox Church to Christianity is its spiritual tradition. This tradition has at its core the lives and teachings of the 'Desert Fathers and Mothers' – the early Christian men and women who left the temptations and distractions of everyday life for a life of solitude. These individuals literally entered the deserted places surrounding the urban centres of the later Roman empire. Although monasticism was originally thought to have begun in Egypt, we now know that it developed independently in various regions around the Mediterranean basin, attracting both men and women who felt the call to retire from the world. The object of this life was primarily to seek closeness to God without distraction from material or personal attachments. It is clear from the texts written both by and about monks in every period that they were also conscious of imitating Christ, who demonstrated in his own life complete self-sacrifice and devotion to God the Father.

Monasticism in subsequent centuries took many forms, but the solitary and mystical ideal remained at its heart. Thus we find monks in communal, or coenobitic, monasteries all over the Byzantine empire, reading the *Lives* and *Sayings* of the early Desert Fathers for inspiration and spiritual advancement. Although the completely solitary life was later not permitted for most monks and nuns, abbots might allow those few individuals who demonstrated outstanding commitment to retreat to a hermitage nearby or to a cell within the confines of the monastic walls. In the later centuries of the Byzantine period, monasticism had become important not only as a way of life for committed Christians, but also as an institution endowed with much wealth and property. Such economic prosperity naturally implied power, and there can be no doubt that monastic interests played an important part in later Byzantine history. Nevertheless, the power of the monasteries was based on Byzantines' continuing belief in the importance of the spiritual life and Christian ideals that they represented.

The origins of monasticism

How did Christian monasticism come into being and how did it differ from similar movements in other religions? It seems likely that the earliest Christian ascetics emerged in the context of pagan persecution in the third century. In Egypt men such as Chaeremon, bishop of Neapolis, and a certain Paul of Thebes fled into the desert rather than face persecution at the hands of the pagan authorities. Perhaps having tasted the sweetness of solitude and freedom from the burdens of worldly life, such individuals decided to pursue this solitary way even after the period of oppression had ended.

Asceticism as a way of life did not, of course, originate with third-century Christians. Antecedents exist in the Greek and Roman pagan traditions, with examples such as the philosopher Pythagorus, who flourished in the sixth century BC, and a more recent follower of his

Asceticism

The term 'asceticism' comes from the Greek *askesis*, which means 'exercise' or 'training'. Early Christians who embraced a life of poverty, fasting, celibacy and solitary prayer believed that these activities served to discipline their bodies and selfish instincts. The concept is summed up in Christ's call to his disciples: 'If any want to become my followers, let them deny themselves and take up their cross and follow me' (Mark 8:34). The degrees of asceticism undertaken by holy people in different periods and places varied widely: in spite of the extreme example provided by St Antony and a few other important figures in Egypt, moderation seems to have been a dominant theme in this area. An emphasis on interior self-denial and on the cultivation of virtues is noticeable in the sayings and writings of the Desert Fathers. In parts of Syria and Asia Minor, on the other hand, a few individuals such as St Symeon, who lived in the early fifth century near Antioch, practised extreme forms of asceticism. After subjecting himself to various other difficult feats, Symeon had a pillar raised slowly to a height of about 16 metres. The holy man stood on the top of this column for a number of years, praying, preaching and helping a stream of pilgrims who came to seek spiritual advice and miraculous intercession.

named Apollonius of Tyana, who lived a wandering holy life in the first century AD. Judaism was not a stranger to such spiritual endeavours either, with figures such as John the Baptist and the sect of the Essenes representing the best-known examples. Ascetic and mystical movements have also featured in other main world religions, such as Hinduism and Buddhism; these may well have influenced late-Roman asceticism, including both its pagan and Judeo-Christian manifestations.

St Antony

The most famous of all the early Egyptian ascetics, remembered in the Christian Church as the first Christian monk, is a holy man called Antony. It is worth looking at his story in detail for two reasons: first, because St Antony's way of life became the model for all ascetics, both male and female, who followed in his footsteps; and second, because his life exemplifies many distinctive aspects of Christian monasticism. One of the main reasons for Antony's subsequent fame is that a biography in his honour was written by the important Alexandrian bishop and theologian, Athanasius (c. 297–373). The author relates how Antony, a wealthy young landowner, heard the 19th chapter of the Gospel of Matthew read out one Sunday in church: 'If you wish to be perfect, go, sell your possessions, and give the money to the poor, and you will have treasure in heaven; then come, follow me.' After reflecting on the meaning of these words, Antony decided to sell all his property, entrust his sister to the care of a community of virgins and devote himself to a life of prayer in the desert.

St Antony trained first with an older ascetic, but then decided to retreat into greater solitude. First, he shut himself up in a tomb near his village where, according to his biographer Athanasius, he spent most of his time praying and combating the evil beings who inhabited this place. The late-antique belief in demons, who could take many forms and devoted themselves to obstructing spiritual endeavour, remained as strong among Christians as it did among pagans. The force of their assaults caused physical harm to the saint but he refused to give up his solitary vigil. Eventually Antony retreated even further into the desert, shutting himself up in an abandoned fort on the other side of the Nile. After 20 years of solitude, during which he survived on a diet of a tiny amount of bread, the holy man emerged in a purified but apparently completely healthy physical state.

As the biography of St Antony shows, early Christian ascetics drew much of their inspiration from the Bible, and in particular the Gospels. Aspects of their lives, such as temptation by demons and the ability to work miracles, resemble events in the life of Christ. As we see in the *Life of St Antony*, fasting, avoiding sleep and remaining celibate were never viewed as goals in themselves; instead, the early saints regarded these as exercises in physical discipline. Biographers such as Athanasius emphasize that the saints' bodies and souls are involved in the process of transformation from an ordinary existence into holiness. This idea excludes the dualist belief that the material world, which includes the human body, is inherently evil and may never be redeemed.

> 'Antony appeared to [his followers] with an aura of holiness as if he had emerged from some divine sanctuary. They were all stunned at the beauty of his countenance and the dignified bearing of his body which had not grown flabby through lack of exercise; neither had his face grown pale as a result of fasting and fighting with demons.'
>
> **Athanasius (c. 297–373) writing of St Antony's emergence from his solitary vigil**

Pachomios and the rise of communal monasticism

A second, but very different, figure to emerge in the Egyptian desert in the early fourth century was Pachomios, the legendary founder of coenobitic (or communal) monasticism. Pachomios was born into a pagan family and was conscripted into the Roman army during the war of 312/13 between the two emperors Licinius and Maximinus Daia. According to his biographies, which exist in various versions, Pachomios was impressed by the charity of local Christians while billeted in Thebes. The young soldier then prayed to God, promising that he would serve humanity in the same way. After his release from the army he was instructed in the Christian faith and baptized. On the eve of his baptism, Pachomios had a vision 'in which he saw dew falling on him from heaven, spilling into his hand in the form of honey, and flowing from there over the surface of the earth. A voice informed him that this was an augury for his future' (Philip Rousseau, *Pachomios*, 1985).

Pachomios carried out his mission to serve the rest of humanity as well as God by establishing monasteries. In about 320, Pachomios founded a community at Tabennesis in Upper Egypt. This consisted of separate buildings in which 30 to 40 monks lived together, each subject to a head, or *hegumenos*, who was responsible for the spiritual direction and discipline of the monks. It is possible that Pachomios' military background influenced his vision of monastic life. The emphasis within the monastic houses, which in some ways resembled military barracks, lay on discipline and obedience rather than the pursuit of more individualistic spiritual aims.

In fourth-century Egypt, we thus see the development of two very different strands in Christian monasticism. The first, which was probably the earliest, consisted of individuals living in cells that they had constructed in the desert, sometimes loosely grouped together and sometimes entirely alone, following a life of asceticism, prayer, celibacy and some manual labour. St Antony represents a good example of this style of monasticism and was imitated by many other early hermits. The lives and sayings of many such men and women are witnessed in collections of stories which were first transmitted orally and later written down. Many emerge as distinct individuals who achieved reputations of great holiness and wisdom. The cells and caves of Nitria and Scetis in Lower Egypt must indeed have resembled 'cities' at some points in their history, as when the Western pilgrim Rufinus visited the area in 375, with individual monks continually visiting one another in search of wise 'words' from their elders.

> 'And so there were on the mountain monastic cells like tents, filled with divine choirs of people singing psalms, reading and praying . . . They appeared to inhabit an infinitely large area, a town removed from worldly matters, full of piety and justice.'
>
> **Athanasius,** *Life of Saint Antony*, **fourth century**

The second tradition, which developed not only in the Pachomian foundations of Upper Egypt, but also independently in various coenobitic monasteries in the Delta region, embraced a much more regulated and disciplined form of religious life. In foundations such as these, the emphasis was on obedience and conformity, rather than on feats of asceticism or solitary prayer. Both of these strands survived in the later Byzantine monastic tradition and continued to be regarded as equally valid forms of Christian life.

St Basil of Caesarea and the development of monasticism in Asia Minor

Another important figure in the history of Christian monasticism is undoubtedly the bishop and theologian Basil of Caesarea, who, along with his brother, Gregory of Nyssa, and friend, Gregory Nazianzen, became an important contributor to the development of trinitarian doctrine in the Christian Church. Basil was born in about 329 into a large, land-owning Christian family in north-eastern and central Asia Minor (now modern Turkey). He spent most of his life in his native Pontus and Cappadocia, but received an excellent education in classical letters and philosophy at the Academy of Athens.

It is clear from the activities of Basil of Caesarea and others, including his family and friend Gregory, that monasticism was 'in the air' at this stage in Byzantine history. The perfect Christian life, as described and lived out by Jesus Christ himself, represented a way of poverty, charity and, ideally, celibacy. At the same time, Basil recognized that more formal arrangements needed to be made for Christians who wished to live together according to a rule. Sometime between 355 and 358, Basil undertook an extended trip through Egypt, Palestine and Syria. In Egypt, Basil came across the Pachomian monasteries and was deeply impressed by the well-ordered and systematic structure of these houses. It was this form of monasticism, with its emphasis on discipline and obedience, that Basil brought back to Asia Minor and which he oversaw in the numerous monasteries that he founded.

St Basil left a number of writings, which played a significant role in both Eastern and Western monasticism in subsequent centuries. These include the 'moral rules', or *Moralia*, which were composed early in his career, and the longer *Asketikon*, a collection of questions and answers concerning the monastic life, which may have been written in the 360s. The latter text went through various rewritings even during Basil's lifetime; later it helped to inspire the Rule of St Benedict of Nursia in the West and, as we shall see, the monastic reforms of Theodore of Studios in ninth-century Constantinople. Basil's vision of organized monasticism, in which the hours of prayer, manual labour, eating and sleeping are clearly defined, and obedience to one's abbot is regarded as the highest virtue, set the tone for the development of coenobitic monasticism hereafter. This is not to suggest, however, that the more individualistic and extreme examples of Christian asceticism did not continue to flourish throughout the territories of the Eastern empire.

Women and asceticism in the early Byzantine world

Women played an important role in the development of asceticism in the early Christian and Byzantine worlds. There can be no doubt that some women solitaries in the Egyptian desert, including Syncletica, Sarah and a few others, achieved an equal status with their male colleagues. The 'desert mothers', as they are called, attracted disciples of their own and their teachings survive in the collections of 'Sayings' which developed out of this milieu.

Somewhat later, however, many women did struggle with the difficulty of breaking into roles that were defined primarily as masculine in this strongly patriarchal society. A group of nuns emerged between the fifth and ninth centuries who achieved sanctity by pretending to be men and entering male monasteries. The biographies written in their honour stress the fact that women such as St Mary/Marinos succeeded in *overcoming* their femininity, becoming like men in their strength of purpose and ascetic prowess. The unspoken assumption behind statements such as these is that women start from a position of greater weakness and vulnerability; both as temptresses and as objects of temptation, they are implicated with Eve more heavily than men in the fall of humankind from grace.

Another feature which is evident in the literary accounts of holy women is the tendency to classify them according to certain stereotypes. Holy virgins such as St Macrina, the redoubtable sister of Basil of Caesarea, and the women who surrounded St Jerome form one class, while another may be identified in the women who renounced prostitution to embrace a life of asceticism, such as Pelagia and Mary of Egypt. From the depths of depravity to the heights of holiness, the latter seem to sum up in their persons the contemporary view of females as 'harlots, witches or saints'. On the other hand, many of the biographies written in honour of these figures are moving accounts of real individuals, struggling to overcome the prejudices of their age and to enter into the spiritual arena on an equal footing with men.

It is interesting that after about the ninth century, asceticism and the undertaking of monastic vows seems to have opened up for women of many different backgrounds, including those who were married or widowed. The pursuit of a solitary, self-directed ascetic life also declined after this time, as women increasingly entered organized, coenobitic monasteries in their pursuit of spiritual aims.

The reforms of Theodore of Studios in the ninth century

After Basil of Caesarea's strong endorsement of coenobitic (communal) monasticism in Asia Minor, houses for both men and women continued to be founded throughout the Byzantine empire and especially in its capital city, Constantinople. The first recorded monastery in Constantinople was established in the late fourth century; by the mid-sixth century about 70 monasteries existed in the capital city alone. Institutional monasticism appears to have gone into something of a decline during the turbulent period of the early iconoclast emperors, Leo III and Constantine V. Accurately or not, later chroniclers and hagiographers linked monks with the defence of the holy icons. For this reason, when icons were reinstated after the Triumph of Orthodoxy in 843, the monastic movement received an enormous boost: in public perception at least, monks belonged to the winning side and deserved extra honour and veneration for their brave opposition to the iconoclast emperors.

> 'Two old men, great anchorites, came to the district of Pelusia to visit [Sarah] . . . Amma Sarah said to them, "According to nature I am a woman, but not according to my thoughts" . . . She also said to the brothers, "It is I who am a man, you who are women."'
>
> **The Sayings of the Desert Fathers**, translated by Benedicta Ward SLG, 1977

Monastic regulation

Institutional monasticism received another important stimulus in the early ninth century from the example and writings of Theodore, abbot of the monastery of Studios in Constantinople. Theodore, who was born in 759, entered with vigour into the task of renovating and reforming the urban monastery of which he became abbot towards the end of the eighth century. Theodore used as his model the surviving rules of his fourth-century predecessor, Basil of Caesarea. Like Basil, Theodore stressed absolute obedience in his monastery, urging moderation in ascetic practice and the importance of manual labour. The monastery became a self-contained economic unit, with workshops in which various necessities such as clothing and shoes were manufactured; it also contained a scriptorium in which manuscripts were copied, and gardens that supplied most of the food for the monastery. Most of Theodore's teachings concerning the coenobitic way of life are contained in a series of short sermons which he delivered daily to his monks after the early morning service. These teachings, called the *Great* and *Little Catecheses*, soon came to represent, along with the writings of St Basil, the most influential rules for monasticism throughout the Byzantine empire.

Monasticism after the ninth century

It is impossible to overemphasize the growing importance of monasticism in every aspect of Byzantine social and religious life after the ninth century. In this period, monastic foundations began to proliferate throughout the empire. Everyone from wealthy landowners and emperors to prosperous peasant-farmers wished to bequeath property to existing monasteries, or even to found new ones on their land. In return for the gifts of property and money, monks and nuns could be asked to pray for the souls of the donor and his family, as well as for their descendants. Endowing property to monasteries also represented a way of securing the survival of an estate or piece of land if a family possessed no obvious heir to manage it. It is clear from the historical sources that people saw monasticism as a calling which could be embraced at any stage in their lives. Deposed emperors, empresses left as widows or divorcées, landowners who had fallen on hard times – all of these groups could, at any age, choose to retreat to the peace and regularity of the monastic way of life.

Monasticism as a landed and wealthy institution finally began to represent a threat to imperial finances by the early tenth century. Monasteries were often exempted from paying the taxes which peasant-

Monastic Rules

Unlike the monastic houses in Western Europe, Byzantine foundations were not formally grouped into specific orders following standard rules. In Eastern Christendom the monastic world remained much less regulated, with individual monasteries following their own regulations, depending on the directives of their patrons or abbots. The Rule or *Typikon* provided at the time of foundation reflected the unique concerns and needs of each house, but also usually depended on earlier models and especially on the writings of such influential figures as Saints Basil and Theodore. It is also striking that within individual monasteries various styles of spiritual life might be undertaken. Whereas most novices and less spiritually advanced members of the community would follow a communal way of life, the monastery might also contain one or more individuals who were allowed (at the abbot's discretion) to live and pray in solitude. Another striking difference between Eastern and Western monasticism was the lack of stability among monks: in spite of canonical directives which enjoined them to stay in one monastery, many moved frequently from one monastery to another or from monasteries to solitary hermitages.

farmers had previously supplied. Eventually emperors were forced to introduce legislation aimed at prohibiting the foundation of monastic estates and restricting the growth of new ones. In 964 Nikephoros II Phokas banned all new foundations of monasteries and philanthropic institutions. The reason given to justify this restriction was that existing foundations were being neglected and were consequently falling into disrepair. At the same time, however, the emperor identified and deplored avarice as a motive for the foundation of new monasteries, stressing the importance of poverty in the true Christian life. All such legislation came to nothing in the end, however, which perhaps reflects the irreversible importance of monasticism in both popular and imperial opinion. In 988 Basil II repealed the laws of his predecessor and by the middle of the eleventh century, the vested interests of both monastic and lay property owners had prevailed. Many historians view the failure of such legislation against large landowners, including monasteries, as contributing to the long-term financial and military decline of the Byzantine empire.

The close relationship between Byzantine monasteries and the local communities in which they were founded is best described as symbiotic. Far from being completely isolated, both male and female monasteries performed many important services in society which had an impact on most members of the population. Perhaps most importantly, monasteries frequently provided charitable institutions which were served by the monks and nuns themselves. From a spiritual point of view, Byzantine monasteries provided ordinary Christians with guidance, as we know from the records of many laypeople who sought spiritual direction from the abbots of neighbouring monasteries. The importance attached by lay Orthodox to the prayers and commemorations of monastics in return for their patronage has already been mentioned; this represents another example of the close interaction between the secular and religious spheres in the Byzantine world.

Male and female monasteries

Monasteries for both men and women flourished throughout the Byzantine era. It is interesting to note, however, that far fewer convents than male monasteries existed at any given time. It has been estimated, on the basis of a tally of all the known monasteries of Constantinople during all 11 centuries of its history, that there were only 77 nunneries in comparison with 270 monasteries. It is also striking that most of the known female monasteries in the Byzantine world were located within cities, rather than in most of the rural areas inhabited by monks. The reasons for this discrepancy are not difficult to find. According to contemporary sources, the founders of convents were worried about the security of nuns in outlying districts; throughout the turbulent Byzantine centuries women in these areas would have been vulnerable to attacks by invaders, pirates and other marauders. In the eyes of pious Byzantines, there could be no worse crime than the dishonouring of a woman who had been dedicated to God. It is also significant that many of the founders of convents, most of whom were imperial or aristocratic laywomen, themselves lived in the capital city. Female monasticism thus remained for the most part an urban phenomenon, closely associated with its benevolent founders and their families.

'Holy mountains'

One specifically Byzantine phenomenon which seems to have developed at an early date, but also to have flourished with all other forms of monasticism after the ninth century, was the 'holy mountain'. The reason for clusters of monasteries appearing in one area is clear: foundations might break away from their parent houses or a particularly eminent spiritual figure might attract more disciples than could fit into one monastery. In certain areas of Asia Minor and mainland Greece, such clusters were formed on hills or mountains, which henceforth became designated as 'holy mountains'. The choice of mountainous places was certainly symbolic: in both classical and Judeo-Christian traditions these represent both wildernesses and places that are closer to God. Most of the 'holy mountains' which existed in Asia Minor, for example on Mount Olympus in Bithynia, Mount Latros on the south-western coast, Mount St Auxentios, above Chalcedon, and Mount Kyminas, on the border of Paphlagonia and Bithynia, survive only as accounts in literary sources or as ruins. The greatest of all the holy mountains, however, called Mount Athos, was established by a monk called Athanasius in the ninth century on a hilly peninsula in northern Greece. This important monastic centre survives to this day and is still inhabited by Orthodox monks.

In the early and later periods of Byzantine history, there are instances of 'double' monasteries, that is, foundations in which men and women lived in separate communities within one main enclosure. These monasteries tended to be under the supervision of one superior and were supported by the same sources of revenue. On the other hand, every aspect of daily life within these foundations would be carried out separately so as to avoid mutual distraction. The monks and nuns in double monasteries tended to be assigned jobs in accordance with traditional views of gender: whereas the monks might tend the garden and work in the fields, the nuns were responsible for the preparation of food and manufacture of cloth. During the middle period of Byzantine history (approximately from the sixth to the thirteenth centuries), many double houses were closed down in response to imperial legislation against them. There was a resurgence of such houses, however, in the Palaiologan period (13th–15th centuries), sometimes in response to the needs of their founders, who wished to stay together as a family even after entering into the monastic way of life.

It is clear that the position of nuns reflected underlying Byzantine attitudes towards gender. Even in monastic life women could play only a subordinate role, remaining dependent on men for practical needs and for their priestly offices in the running of the convent or double monastery. On the other hand, the responsibility and authority of the female superior and the active participation of ordinary nuns in the life of the convent must have provided these women with some degree of autonomy and self-direction. The important role played by wealthy female patronesses, both in founding monasteries and in overseeing them, reinforces the impression that monasticism provided a significant outlet for female energy in the Byzantine world.

Spirituality in the Byzantine world

At the beginning of this chapter we saw the importance of asceticism and prayer in early Christian spirituality. These ideals remained central to the monastic movement throughout the later centuries in Byzantium, even after the communal, or coenobitic, way of life became the accepted norm. The highest goal for all monks and nuns remained the practice of *hesychia*, which is variously translated as 'solitude', 'stillness' or 'solitary prayer'. Several outstanding figures taught and exemplified this tradition in the course of Byzantine history. These spiritual teachers drew on a large body of writings which began to be collected and disseminated within monasteries as early as the fourth century. The tradition continued to develop, however, as new insights and personal revelations were added over the centuries.

One figure who stands out in the late tenth century is the mystic St Symeon the New Theologian, abbot of the monastery of St Mamas in Constantinople. In his numerous writings, which include short sermons, treatises and hymns, Symeon discusses the steps that lead the mystic to a complete apprehension of God. He describes his own mystical experience, which he attained on more than one occasion, as a vision of divine light. Symeon believed that any human being may, if sufficiently purified and dedicated to prayer, be capable of such a revelation.

Symeon, like many monastic teachers before him, believed in the concept of deification (*theôsis*). According to this doctrine, human beings, created in God's image and restored after the fall by the incarnation of Christ, are capable of regaining their likeness to God to the extent that they may become by grace what God is by nature. The process is of course a long and slow one: asceticism and prayer form only one part of a journey which is dependent also on the grace of the Holy Spirit.

Another important figure in the history of Byzantine spirituality is the monk Gregory Palamas, who began his career on Mount Athos and then became Archbishop of Thessaloniki in the mid-fourteenth century. Palamas believed that Christians, and especially monks, may achieve complete revelation of God's glory through contemplation. While preserving a completely Orthodox belief in God's complete unknowability and transcendence, Palamas argued that human beings may nevertheless perceive what he called God's 'uncreated energies'. The concept is best exemplified by the vision of uncreated light that shone about Christ at his transfiguration on Mount Tabor (Luke 9:28–36). In most icons of the transfiguration, the three disciples are shown experiencing a divine revelation. They fall down at Christ's feet, covering their faces with their hands. The practical technique for achieving such a mystical experience, which came to be known by the technical term 'Hesychasm', involved deep breathing and quiet repetition of the Jesus Prayer ('Lord Jesus Christ, have mercy on me a sinner'). Like St Symeon the New Theologian, Gregory Palamas based his teachings on the idea that humanity, created in the image of God, is capable and worthy of participation in divine existence.

> 'The third method of attention and prayer is the following: the mind should be in the heart . . . Keep your attention within yourself (not in your head but heart). Wrestling thus the mind will find the place of the heart . . . From that moment, whenever a thought appears, the mind at once dispels it, before it has time to enter and become a thought or image, destroying it by repeating Jesus' name [prayer], "Lord Jesus Christ, have mercy upon me."'
>
> **Gregory Palamas, mid-fourteenth century**

Controversy over Gregory Palamas' teachings arose when a Calabrian monk named Barlaam entered into an exchange of letters with him. Barlaam objected to the idea that human beings through their own efforts could achieve a revelation of God. Barlaam felt that the Athonite monk's teachings threatened God's transcendence and unknowability, besides stressing too much the role of human endeavour in the process of spiritual enlightenment. A council was called at Constantinople in 1341 to resolve the dispute and decided in Palamas' favour. After his opponents succeeded in the following few years to secure his conviction for heresy and excommunication, however, it took another two councils to reaffirm the orthodoxy of the Palamite teachings. Gregory Palamas was eventually canonized by the Byzantine Church in 1368.

The approval of the teachings of Gregory Palamas in the mid-fourteenth century was a deeply significant event in the history of Byzantine monasticism. Building on centuries of personal endeavour and spiritual knowledge, Palamas summed up in his writings the Orthodox belief in the unknowable transcendence of God, but also the ability of human beings to ascend through prayer to a mystical understanding of his uncreated energies. This positive view of human potential is based on the doctrine that humanity is capable of deification or transfiguration in the presence of God. The mystical writings of Gregory Palamas, Symeon the New Theologian and earlier spiritual teachers continued to provide inspiration for both monastic and lay Orthodox Christians through the difficult centuries which followed the Turks' domination of most Byzantine territories after 1453. These writings, which emerged out of the heart of Orthodox monasticism, represent one of the Byzantium's abiding contributions to the history of Christian spirituality.

CHAPTER 6
HOLY PLACES, HOLY PEOPLE

For the Byzantines, the heavenly and earthly worlds were closely entwined. God's power and mercy could be experienced at any time by the humblest believer in various ways, whether through acts of nature or healing miracles, or in the sacramental rites of the Church. It is clear that from a very early date some places, objects or people were seen as channels to divine power. In this chapter we will explore the various cults which received special veneration in the Byzantine world. These included the holy sites in Palestine and Jerusalem, the relics of martyrs and saints, the Virgin Mary or *Theotokos* ('God-bearer') as she was more commonly called, and icons.

Holy places

The evidence of Christian visits to the Holy Land begins very early, with accounts written by important figures such as Melito of Sardis and Origen in the second and third centuries respectively. In the fourth century, according to legend, the mother of Constantine I, the aged Helena, visited Jerusalem as a pilgrim and funded archaeological investigations both inside and outside the city. She was delighted with the discoveries that resulted: the sites of Christ's crucifixion and tomb represented by far the most important of these. Constantine immediately set about building churches to commemorate these sites. A huge complex incorporating the Anastasis, a circular area surrounding the tomb itself, Golgotha, a rocky outcrop believed to be the site of the crucifixion, and a magnificent basilica was collectively known as the Holy Sepulchre. The relic of the true cross formed a centrepiece in this holy site. Constantine and

'Here then, impelled by Christ our God and assisted by the prayers of the holy men who accompanied us, we made the great effort of the climb. It was quite impossible to ride up, but though I had to go on foot I was not conscious of the effort – in fact I hardly noticed it because, by God's will, I was seeing my hopes coming true. So at 10 o'clock we arrived on the summit of Sinai, the Mount of God where the Law was given, and the place where God's glory came down on the day when the mountain was smoking.'

J. Wilkinson, *Egeria's Travels*, 1999

Helena also discovered places outside Jerusalem which they believed to be the actual sites of important events in Jesus' life. The cave in which the Christ child was born was honoured by another basilica in the town of Bethlehem. Various places on the Mount of Olives and in Galilee also became centres of pilgrimage and commemoration.

We are fortunate in possessing several early accounts written by pilgrims who visited the Holy Land in the fourth century or later. In 333 an anonymous pilgrim from the west coast of France, probably near Bordeaux, travelled overland to Palestine and, once there, described the sites that he saw. He mentions in his account approximately 21 sites associated with the New Testament and 32 recalling pre-Christian biblical history. Even more fascinating, however, is the account by a Western woman, possibly a nun from Galicia in Spain, called Egeria, who probably travelled eastwards between 381 and 384. She writes in great detail of her leisurely pilgrimage through Palestine, Jerusalem and even the Sinai desert, describing both the sites and the liturgical celebrations that she witnessed in all of these places.

Martyrs and relics

The bodies of martyrs were honoured from a very early period in the Christian Church. People who died in the pagan persecutions represented the ultimate example of Christian sacrifice as they followed the example of the Saviour himself. Inspired by the martyrs' own belief in paradise and the afterlife, Christians believed that these individuals continued to intercede on their behalf in the heavenly kingdom. It is clear from the many texts that were written about martyrs and their cults that their material remains were also imbued with special powers. Shrines were established to honour these holy relics. Many Christians journeyed long distances to venerate the martyrs' graves and to seek healing or other miracles at these sites.

The veneration of relics at the shrines and churches erected in honour of the early martyrs continued throughout the Byzantine period. No city would have been without some share of these precious remains, which were believed to protect the citizens from enemy attack, besides providing miraculous help on an individual basis. Cities which lacked any saintly relics sometimes managed to acquire them as gifts, purchases or even stolen goods. Thus Constantinople, a city that did not feature as the site of any famous martyrdoms at the time of its foundation, nevertheless possessed a huge number of holy relics by the end of the eleventh century. A letter which purports to be written by the emperor Alexios Komnenos to a count of Flanders enumerates all of these relics, listing such precious objects as the pillar to which Christ was bound when he was flogged, the lash, the crown of thorns, the head of John the Baptist, and many others.

The veneration of saints

After the end of persecution and the establishment of Christianity as the state religion in the Roman empire, ascetic saints joined martyrs as objects of veneration. The literary accounts of these holy people suggest that most of them achieved special powers even during their lives. Whereas the ascetics in the Egyptian desert practised a more moderate form of asceticism, fasting and praying but also supporting themselves by manual labour, more extreme styles of monastic life emerged in other parts of the empire, especially in Syria. Symeon, the fifth-century Stylite saint has already been introduced in a previous chapter; before erecting the column on which he stood exposed to the elements for a number of years, St Symeon subjected himself to many other physical trials. These included enclosure in a dry cistern and the chaining of his right leg to a stone. Several saints in Asia Minor later imitated Symeon. A slightly younger contemporary, named Daniel the Stylite, had a pillar erected on the outskirts of Constantinople in 460 from which he preached, performed miracles and even advised the emperor.

The historian Peter Brown has studied the phenomenon of holy men and argued that they came to represent the archetypal 'outsiders' in Syrian and, later, Byzantine society. They acquired closeness to God by means of fasting and other ascetic feats, but even more important than this was their self-imposed exile from the rest of society. This enabled these individuals to act as channels between the created and the divine worlds, having direct access to God in a way that even the ordained clergy was denied. Holy men such as Symeon and Daniel were revered after their deaths, since their bodies retained the miraculous powers which they

Holy fools

One of the most remarkable forms of sanctity to emerge in Eastern Christendom was that exemplified by 'holy fools'. Such figures include the Syrian saint, Symeon of Emesa, and later the Greek saint, Andrew the Fool, as well as many others. This group of ascetics turned all the rules of Christian life, so to speak, upside down. Saint Symeon pretended to be half-witted, acting in outrageous and unpredictable ways. According to his seventh-century biographer, Leontios of Neapolis, Symeon entered a church one Sunday and began throwing nuts at the candles. When the congregation tried to chase him out, he went up into the pulpit and began pelting the women with nuts. As Symeon finally left the church, he overturned the tables of the pastry chefs (presumably selling cakes at the front of the church). Many other incidents in the life of this holy fool seem to mock the customs of the church, but also to recall events in the life of Christ. For example, the saint is said to have first entered the city of Emesa in Syria, where he stayed for the remainder of his life, dragging a dead dog behind him. As he advanced, local children shouted, 'Hey, a crazy abba!' There can be no doubt that Symeon mimics in this scene the entrance of Christ into Jerusalem, reversing the story, however, by making himself an object of ridicule rather than celebration. The holy fool, basing his way of life on the passage 'We are fools for Christ's sake' (1 Corinthians 4:10) experienced humility more completely than even the most impoverished and hungry ascetic could ever do. The tradition of 'holy fools' survived through the later centuries of the Byzantine era and was adopted in Orthodox Russia. St Basil's Cathedral in Red Square, Moscow, is named for a holy fool (Basil of Mangazeia, who died in 1552); in Russian literature the concept is treated most famously in Dostoevsky's *The Idiot*.

had acquired through their ascetic labours. Many miracle stories survive, commemorating the cults of both male and female ascetic saints.

Mary the 'God-bearer', or Theotokos

Evidence of Christian veneration of the Virgin Mary before the early fifth century is patchy, but incontrovertible. Although references to the Virgin Mary are infrequent in the New Testament, Christians honoured her from an early date for her role in the incarnation of Christ. By the end of the second century some apocryphal writings, especially a text called the *Protoevangelion* of James, which recounts the story of her conception, birth and childhood, were circulating among the faithful. The bishop Irenaeus of Lyons stressed Mary's importance in the birth of Christ as the antithesis of Eve: 'for it was necessary . . . that a virgin, become an advocate for a virgin, might undo and destroy the virginal disobedience by virginal obedience'. The Old Testament books that had prophesied the virgin birth along with every other aspect of the new dispensation provided further backing for the growing cult in honour of Mary.

It is interesting to note that some of the fourth-century texts which honour the Virgin Mary stress her role as a saintly human being. A letter which is preserved only in Coptic, but which was probably written by the patriarch Athanasius, describes Mary as the ideal model for Christian virgins. She was calm and pure, modest, loved good works and prayed constantly to God. She wanted to make progress every day and worked tirelessly to improve her spiritual state. The Virgin is presented in this text as a model of good behaviour, but the author nevertheless stresses her humanity, stating that her good works are not perfect and that 'bad thoughts' occasionally enter her mind. Such a description would be unthinkable several centuries later, when the Virgin Mary had become an object of devotion in the Church second only to Christ himself.

The early fifth century was the period in which the budding cult of the Virgin suddenly acquired official sanction and theological justification in the Byzantine empire. The controversy initiated by Nestorios and Cyril, patriarchs of Constantinople and Alexandria respectively, focused on the title 'God-bearer', or *Theotokos*, for Mary. This was sparked off by their conflicting views concerning the manner in which humanity and divinity were combined in the person of Christ. There can be no doubt that the party led by the Alexandrians, which backed the idea that the Virgin gave birth to God, were motivated in part by their reverence for Mary herself. Nestorios, on the other hand, felt that her exaltation was out of proportion to the role that she actually played in Christ's incarnation. It is likely too that he felt that her true humanity, as well as that of her Son, was compromised by such exalted praise.

After the triumph of the Alexandrians at the Council of Ephesus (431), the cult of the *Theotokos* was allowed to develop unchecked. From this period onwards, liturgical praise of the Virgin, which appeared both in poetic sermons and in hymns, proliferated. As feast days in her honour were introduced into the Church calendar in the course of the sixth century, texts extolling her nativity, presentation as a child in the Temple, annunciation and death were composed. More historical sources begin to record the Virgin's miraculous interventions in human history from the late sixth century onwards. It is probably in this period that the city of Constantinople adopted the *Theotokos* as its special patroness.

'To you, Mother of God, champion and leader, I, your city [Constantinople], delivered from sufferings, ascribe the prize of victory and my thanks. And may you, in your invincible power, free me from all kinds of dangers, that I may cry to you: "Hail, wedded maiden and virgin."'

Prologue of the *Akathistos Hymn*, probably written after the siege of Constantinople by Avars and Persians in 626

The most famous story concerning the Virgin's role as defender of the imperial city is that of the siege by the Avars and Persians in 626. With these two enemies mounting a combined and highly organized assault on Constantinople, both from the land and the sea, the situation seemed desperate. The emperor Herakleios was away on campaign in Asia Minor, but Patriarch Sergios, in whose care he had left Constantinople, rallied the citizens by calling on the *Theotokos* for help. The patriarch organized processions around the walls of the city, in which the clergy and people carried icons of Christ and the Virgin and chanted hymns and prayers. This unprecedented involvement of all the citizens in the defence of the city may indeed have played a part in undermining the confidence of the enemies. The Avars and Persians suffered a humiliating defeat and eventually retreated. The Byzantines themselves attributed their salvation to divine protection. According to a contemporary source, the Virgin Mary herself was seen fighting from the walls beside the soldiers. The siege of 626 soon became part of the city's folklore and a popular hymn in her honour, called the Akathistos, acquired a new prologue commemorating these events.

Icons

Scholars are still debating when Byzantine Christians began to use and venerate icons, which mostly took the form of images of holy figures painted on wooden panels. Some argue that this cult developed in the late sixth century, a time when the population as a whole began to sense the breakdown of the civilized, Roman world and to turn to God for reassurance. Others have suggested that the veneration of icons began somewhat later and that holy relics were still viewed in the late sixth and early seventh centuries as the main channels of divine power. Relics included not only the precious remains of the bodies of martyrs and saints, but also their clothing or possessions, or the substances, such as oil, that flowed from their tombs. No bodily remains, of course, survived from Christ and his mother Mary, since both were believed to have been raised to heaven soon after their deaths. However, from as early as the fifth century, relics such as the Virgin's robe and belt had been discovered and brought with great ceremony to Constantinople.

A group of icons which appeared early, but which may still be classed with relics rather than with man-made images, are those known as icons 'made without hands', or *acheiropoietai*. Perhaps the most famous of these was the icon of Christ found in the city of Edessa, in eastern Syria. According to a legend which is first related in the late sixth century, the king of the city who was contemporary with Christ, named Abgar, fell ill and sent a message to the Saviour, begging him to come and cure him. Instead, Christ gave the king's messenger a towel, or *mandylion*, that he had pressed to his face and which retained the impression of his features. The king was cured by the miraculous image, which was then preserved in the city and used as an object of divine protection, or 'palladium', in times of danger.

Icons 'made without hands' were used to justify the cult of more ordinary icons which was developing in the course of the seventh century. Literary texts of the period suggest that the growing veneration of icons attracted criticism, mainly from members of other religions which were stricter about the use of figural imagery, especially Muslims and Jews. The miraculous icons of Christ, or *acheiropoietai*, were used by defenders of icons to show that God himself approved of representational art. They also employed passages from Exodus and elsewhere in the Old Testament to prove that exceptions to the second commandment were permitted even at the time of Moses. The Jews were commanded to decorate the ark of the covenant with golden images of cherubim, spreading their wings above the mercy seat (Exodus 25:18–22). All of

Windows into the divine realm

The word 'icon' (*eikon* in Greek) simply means 'image'; in other words, a representation in any medium of the artist's vision of reality, whether concrete or imagined. In its more restricted sense, however, an icon has come to mean a religious image which plays a unique and important role in Orthodox Christian worship and doctrine. Anyone who has ever entered an Orthodox church will have noticed the icons, usually paintings of holy people or scenes on wooden panels, which are displayed prominently on stands both in the centre of the nave and on the screen in front of the sanctuary. Regarded in strict theological terms not as objects of devotion in themselves but as windows into the divine realm, icons are kissed and venerated at the beginning and at various points in the course of the service. It is important to recognize, however, that icons occupy a particular place in the hierarchy of holy objects within the church. It is incorrect, for example, to venerate an icon when the elements of the eucharist are being carried in or consecrated; at other times, however, the icon may occupy a central place within a particular sacramental act, such as confession or anointment with holy unction. The earliest icons were believed to have been painted at the time of Christ; the most famous example is the evangelist Luke's painting of Mary, the Mother of God. Later artists regarded the painting of icons as a spiritual act: they would prepare by fasting and prayer, having first completed a long technical training in the art.

Portable icons were usually painted on wooden panels, although they might also be fashioned in ivory, mosaic or enamel. Pigment was applied to a wooden panel, usually cypress, which had been strengthened with cloth and gesso to prevent splits or cracks. In the earliest icons, which survive at St Catherine's Monastery in Sinai, a wax encaustic has been used; this is the same medium that was used in the late-Roman portraits which have been uncovered in the Fayyum district of Egypt. Later pigments mixed with an egg tempera medium were more commonly employed in the manufacture of icons. Gold leaf was applied liberally to the background and the finished painting was protected with varnish.

these arguments were later taken up by defenders of holy images in the iconoclast controversy of the eighth and ninth centuries.

In addition to the literary evidence, material artefacts attest to the diffusion and use of icons in the seventh century. Many early icons were destroyed during the period of Iconoclasm, but some splendid examples survive at the remote St Catherine's Monastery in the Sinai desert. This spiritual centre, which continued to be inhabited by Orthodox Christian monks throughout the period of Arab rule, fell outside the jurisdiction of the iconoclast emperors. A few other early icons survive in Rome and elsewhere in the West: it is likely that these were made by Constantinopolitan artists or by their students.

Stories describing the miraculous intercession of icons in the lives of ordinary Christians began to proliferate from the seventh century onwards. Often these stories are embedded in the biographies of saints, miracle stories or religious chronicles. They suggest that icons were beginning to be regarded as the most accessible channels of divine power that could be tapped at times of need or peril. For example, a collection of stories compiled by a monk called John Moschos tells of a hermit who, before embarking on a journey, would light a lamp and pray to the icon of the Virgin and Child which he kept in his cave. He would ask the Virgin not only to keep him safe on his journey, but also to look after the lamp while he was away. On returning after a journey which may have lasted for as long as six months, the monk would invariably find the lamp well cared for and still burning. Another story in the same collection relates that a woman tried to dig a well on her property and failed to reach water. Eventually she had a vision in which she was told to take the icon of a local saint and lower it into the well. When this was done the water immediately began to flow, filling the well-shaft up to the halfway point. Many other stories of miracles involving icons reveal the increasing popularity of this cult in the centuries preceding the outbreak of Iconoclasm.

After the end of Iconoclasm, the Orthodox Church formally reaffirmed the validity of holy icons and relics. From the late ninth century onwards, these objects played a central role in religious worship. Certain standard types of icons began to appear; for example, Mary, the Mother of God, might be depicted in attitudes conveying such qualities as mercy and motherhood. Some churches in Constantinople possessed special icons which became the focus of special liturgical celebrations. At the Hodegon Monastery, for example, an icon known as the Hodegetria ('guide'), in which the Virgin holds the Christ child on her left arm and gestures to him with her right hand, was believed to have been painted by the evangelist Luke himself. This icon was regularly carried in processions around Constantinople. During a siege in 1187, it was taken up onto the walls of the city. According to an account by two Spanish diplomats who visited Constantinople in the early fifteenth century, a special ceremony took place at the Hodegon Monastery every Tuesday. Special bearers dressed in red, perhaps belonging to a lay brotherhood, carried the icon, which was large, heavy and covered with precious jewels, out into the assembled crowd.

Many icons and other precious artefacts were looted when the Latins stormed Constantinople in 1204, and ended up in the museums and treasuries of Western Europe. Destruction and pillaging took place again when Constantinople finally fell to the Turks in 1453, especially as these invaders did not approve of Orthodox religious art. Nevertheless, enough artefacts and literary records survive to prove the importance of icons and their role in private and public worship throughout most of the centuries of Byzantine rule. Apart from the period of Iconoclasm, which lasted for just over a century, icons featured prominently in this society as channels of communication, or intermediaries, between the divine and the created worlds.

> 'The icon is not just a simple image, or a decoration, or even an illustration of holy scripture. It is something greater. It is an object of worship and an integral part of the liturgy.'
>
> Leonid Ouspensky, *Theology of the Icon*, 1992

The world transfigured

One aspect of the formal defence of icons, which became known as the 'theology of images', was its stress on the sanctity of material creation. God created the world, argued the Byzantine theologians; therefore the world is good. God also chose to become incarnate, taking on a human body and thereby re-entering and saving the created world which had fallen away through the deliberate choice of our forebears, Adam and Eve. Iconophile theologians exposed the inherent dualism in the iconoclast position, which argues that man-made, or material, objects are incapable

> 'Through heaven and earth and sea, through wood and stone, through relics and church buildings and the cross, through angels and men, through all creation visible and invisible, I offer veneration and honour to the Creator and Master and Maker of all things, and to him alone.'
>
> Leontios of Neapolis, seventh-century defender of holy icons

of transfiguration. They argued the opposite point of view, which may be applied not only to icons, but also to holy relics and other material objects. This position is based not only on the biblical idea that creation is inherently good, but also on Neoplatonic philosophy, which teaches that the material world represents a copy of a higher, transcendent reality. Thus, while icons and relics may in themselves be permeated with divine power, they should never be understood as anything more than images or reminders of the figures they represent. Even so, icons, like the saints or martyrs they represent, may be transfigured by the presence of the Holy Spirit and may act as channels of communication between this world and the heavenly kingdom.

CHAPTER 7
THE KINGDOM OF GOD ON EARTH

Organized religious worship, which included the daily and weekly services in church, as well as the sacraments of Christian life, affected the lives of ordinary people in the Byzantine world. It is clear that every class of society, including the emperor himself, participated in one way or another in public liturgical life. Weekly church celebrations, festivals commemorating events in the life of Christ and other holy figures, and participation in the holy sacraments all provided structure and meaning to daily life.

The importance of liturgical worship, both public – and this includes not only the services held within churches, but also the numerous processions held outdoors in major cities and towns throughout the empire – and private, throughout the 11 centuries of Byzantine history can scarcely be overemphasized. Religious time, which was organized according to several different cycles, including annual, weekly and daily, gave deeper meaning to the ordinary passage of time. The Christian festivals of Christmas, Theophany (the baptism of Christ), Easter and the Transfiguration, to name only a few of the most important ones, represented liturgically the reliving of major events in the New Testament. By celebrating these feast days, Orthodox Christians felt a continuous sense of renewal and active participation in the life of the Church. In a broader sense, liturgical rites marked the important transitions in the lives of individual Christians, with the sacraments of baptism, confession, marriage, unction and burial. The sense of God's immanence and protection of Orthodox Christians was reinforced by special services of supplication at times of danger, such as siege, battles or earthquake, and of thanksgiving when these perils had subsided.

Historical development

The origins of the Byzantine liturgy, even after Constantine adopted Christianity as the official state religion, are unfortunately obscure.

The reason for this is that no liturgical sources, that is, the texts in which the order and words of religious ceremonies were set out, survive from this early period. The earliest surviving Byzantine liturgical text dates from the middle of the eighth century. Nevertheless, it is possible to draw conclusions about what went on from a number of sources, including sermons, a few surviving liturgical texts from other regions, the accounts of pilgrims and the architecture of churches. We know from these various sources that after the first three centuries of Christianity, during which a variety of liturgical usages developed in different parts of the Roman world, a slow movement towards the standardization of religious worship began to take place under the emperor Constantine and his successors. The Constantinopolitan liturgical rite was based most closely on the liturgies used in Syria;

The symbolism of the church building

In his commentary on the Divine Liturgy, the seventh-century theologian Maximus the Confessor sums up the significance of the church building to Orthodox Christian worshippers both then and now: 'God's holy church in itself is a symbol of the sensible world, since it possesses the divine sanctuary as heaven and the beauty of the nave as earth. Likewise the world is a church since it possesses heaven corresponding to a sanctuary, and for a nave it has the adornment of the earth.' To walk into a church is to enter symbolically the whole cosmos which includes the kingdom of heaven. All of creation worships the trinitarian God unendingly; in church the Byzantine faithful could feel they were participating in the heavenly celebrations, in company with the cherubim, the seraphim and all the other ranks of angels. This cosmos has a hierarchical structure, which is duly represented both in the architecture of the church building and in the ranks of both heavenly and earthly beings engaged in carrying out God's liturgy. In many Byzantine churches, a frescoed or mosaic image of Christ, the Pantokrator ('All-Ruler'), looks down from the central dome, while in the sanctuary, bishops, priests and deacons carry out the most secret and holy elements of the rites. The nave, which according to Maximos represents the created world, is filled with men, women and children, who experience the liturgical celebrations through all their senses: sight, sound, smell, touch and taste.

this is because most of the northern Byzantine territories originally had their closest links with the see of Antioch. The two main texts of the Mass, or Divine Liturgy, that survive in later manuscripts and are still used in Orthodox Church today, are attributed to Basil of Caesarea, who was based in central and north-east Anatolia, and John Chysostom, who came from Antioch.

Between the fourth century, when emperors were engaged in Christianizing the Roman empire, and the reign of Justinian (527–65), the Byzantine liturgy slowly became imperial. Not only were religious ceremonies carried out in the Constantinopolitan churches with increasing splendour and elaboration, but emperors played a central role in these liturgical rites. A tradition of religious processions from one holy site to another, or 'stational liturgies', often with services held along the way, had developed in Jerusalem at an early date. This custom spread to Constantinople and Rome at the same time that these cities were establishing churches and endowing them with relics after the Christianization of the Roman empire. In Constantinople every spectator must have felt involved in these splendid ceremonies, as the patriarch, emperor and clergy processed slowly around the city, probably ending up in the Great Church of Hagia Sophia.

After the splendid and dramatic processional liturgies of the early Byzantine period, however, it appears that religious rites began to move indoors from the eighth century onwards. Historians are not entirely certain of the reasons for this change, but it seems to reflect in some measure the difficult circumstances of the middle centuries of Byzantine history, when the empire was continually beset by both internal and external difficulties. What is noticeable is that after the end of the sixth century, much more attention was focused on the church building as the centre of Christian worship and (as we saw above) as a symbol of the heavenly and earthly cosmos. Liturgical rites which had originally taken place throughout the city now began to be performed within the confines of the church building itself. Thus, in the Divine Liturgy, the processions which introduce the two parts of the service, the Liturgy of the Word and the Liturgy of the Faithful, now moved merely between the sanctuary and the nave, instead of entering through the main doors of the church.

The cathedral and the monastic rites

Another development which seems to have occurred between the sixth and the ninth centuries is the introduction of two separate rites, one of which was intended for cathedral usage and one for the monasteries. The cathedral rite was an altogether more splendid affair: we may imagine the great spaces of Hagia Sophia echoing to the sound of antiphonal choirs singing highly elaborate musical settings of hymns. The monastic rite, which was developed especially at the important Constantinopolitan monastery of Studios, probably with influence from houses in Palestine, tended to be longer and more repetitive. These services, which took up a major portion of both day and night, especially in the more rigorous monasteries, required ever more hymns and readings to fill the daily hours. In the course of the ninth century, monks at Studios and other Constantinopolitan foundations undertook to compose hymns for every day of the year, commemorating saints and other holy figures.

Both the monastic and the cathedral Byzantine rites continued to be used until 1204, when the Latin crusaders sacked Constantinople in the course of the Fourth Crusade. After this date, the secular clergy appears to have found itself unable to maintain the complex sung office of the Great Church of Hagia Sophia. The rise in monastic power between the ninth and the eleventh centuries also contributed to the gradual supplanting of the cathedral rite by the monastic one. The monastic musical and liturgical tradition had the advantage that it could be performed by a few people as well as by many. During the centuries that followed the restoration of Byzantine rule in Constantinople in 1261, as Turkish domination of Asia Minor and mainland Greece slowly advanced and the empire shrank to a tiny enclave based in the capital, the monastic rite became the only viable method of liturgical celebration. This situation did not change after the fall of Constantinople to the Turks in 1453; while Orthodox Christians continued to carry out their religious rituals under Turkish domination, these offices belonged to the monastic tradition rather than to the elaborate settings of the old cathedral rite.

Liturgical time

The lives of Orthodox Christians were probably dominated most of all by their concept of liturgical time, which operated in various connected cycles, somewhat like the interlocking wheels of a clock. If we start with the smallest of these cycles, the daily one, we already see according to the monastic timetable a series of offices that fill up many of the hours in a 24-hour period. The monastic day began in the evening, according to the ancient Judeo-Christian method of calculating time. Thus Vespers would be the first office in the day, followed by Compline, Orthros (Mattins) and the First, Third, Sixth and Ninth Hours. It is impossible to know how much this monastic schedule would have affected lay Byzantine Christians, but the sources do tell us that many pious laypeople regularly attended morning and evening services, especially during Lent. Some, such as the mother of an eighth-century saint, Stephen the Younger, went to the all-night vigils which were held in some churches on the eves of important feasts or (in her case) in honour of the Virgin every Friday evening. A number of sermons from the eighth century onwards were preached in the course of all-night vigils and their audiences consisted of men and women of all ages and backgrounds.

After the daily cycle, an Orthodox Christian might think of the weekly cycle of services which culminates in the celebration of the Mass, or Divine Liturgy, on Sunday morning. Preparation for this holy rite was intense at all times in Byzantine history; if the faithful planned to receive communion they might fast all week on 'dry foods' – in other words, a vegan diet – attend the vigil that was held on Saturday evening, and perhaps also confession. We do not know how often Byzantine Christians received communion, but it is clear that this represented a most sacred 'mystery' in their lives; theologically, the eucharist represents the unity of all Christians and their participation in the body and blood of Christ. A seventh-century source which records what appear to be genuine questions and answers between laypeople and their spiritual leader reveals some common sources of doubt in relation to the eucharist. Some examples include, 'Should one receive communion if one has inadvertently drunk a cup of water the same morning?' and 'Should one communicate if one has had conjugal relations the night before?' After the seventh or eighth centuries, both literary and archaeological evidence suggest that the celebration of the Divine Liturgy came to be regarded more and more as a sacred mystery, consecrated behind the templon screen or, later, the iconostasis, and administered only to those who were prepared.

The annual liturgical cycle began on 1 September and finished at the end of August. This 'fixed' progression of feasts follows the solar calendar year and commemorates the major events in the life of Christ and of his mother, the Virgin Mary or *Theotokos* ('God-bearer'). Various feast days, especially those commemorating the Virgin, only gradually came to be added to the calendar, as church officials acknowledged her importance in Christian theology and recognized the need to remember important events in her life. Thus, the Nativity of the Virgin (8 September), introduced into the calendar in the late sixth century, is the first major festival in the calendar; this is followed by the Exaltation of the Cross (14 September), the Presentation of the Virgin into the Temple (21 November), Christmas (25 December) and so on.

'We who mystically represent the Cherubim and sing the thrice-holy hymn to the life-giving Trinity, let us now lay aside all worldly care to receive the King of All escorted unseen by the angelic corps! Alleluia!'

'The Cherubic Hymn', sung in the Divine Liturgy

The major festivals of the Church provided a defining structure in the lives of ordinary Christians. It was a happy coincidence that the Nativity of Christ was celebrated from an early date at about the time of the winter solstice, on 25 December. In 274 the emperor Aurelian

Iconography of the major Christian feasts

By about the tenth century, Byzantine religious art had evolved standard ways of depicting the major feasts of Christ and the Virgin Mary. Usually 12 scenes were chosen for the decoration of churches and icons. These were the Annunciation, the Nativity of Christ, the Presentation in the Temple, the Baptism of Christ, the Transfiguration, the Raising of Lazarus, Entry into Jerusalem, the Crucifixion, the *Anastasis* (descent into Hades and resurrection of the dead), Ascension, Pentecost and the death, or *Koimesis*, of the Virgin. However, the choice of scenes could vary, depending largely on those who commissioned these works of art. Each of these subjects represents a major feast in the Church, which would be celebrated by all-night vigils, a Divine Liturgy and feasting.

also chose this date for the pagan festival of the birth of the Sun god (scholars are still debating whether it was actually Christians or pagans who adopted 25 December for their nativity festivals first). In any case, Christians were able to appropriate much of the symbolism of the pagan festival: Christ was celebrated at this time as the Sun of Righteousness, representing the triumph of light over darkness. Imagery appropriate to the time of year could also be used at Easter, the most important of all Christian festivals. This celebration of Christ's resurrection and Christian rebirth falls at a natural time of renewal, in the early spring.

A second annual cycle, sometimes called the 'movable' liturgical year, centres around Easter, the most important of all the Christian feasts. Beginning with a Saturday in mid-winter, usually sometime in February, called the Sunday of the Publican and the Pharisee, the Easter cycle continues after Easter until the feast of Pentecost. This period is termed 'movable', in contrast to the fixed annual cycle, because it is calculated differently every year, in accordance with the lunar calendar. Easter originally followed the Jewish Passover, since according to the Gospels this is when Jesus entered Jerusalem and into the sequence of events that would lead up to his crucifixion. In the early centuries of the Church, however, Eastern and Western Christians disagreed over how closely Easter should follow the Jewish Passover and therefore exactly how the date should be calculated.

The sacraments

Finally, the lifetime cycle of a Byzantine Orthodox Christian, like that of most practising Christians today, was punctuated by a series of sacraments, or 'mysteries', which enabled him or her to participate fully in the life of the Church, as members of the body of Christ (Romans 12:4). It is interesting to note that unlike the Western Catholic Church, the Byzantines never formally committed themselves to a strict number of sacraments, or even to a formal definition of these mysteries. Whereas Theodore the Studite in the ninth century gives a list of six sacraments (baptism, communion, chrismation or confirmation, ordination, monastic tonsure and the service of burial), Nicholas Cabasilas, who wrote a commentary on the sacraments in the fourteenth century, listed only three: baptism, chrismation and communion. Other later liturgical writers listed as many as 10 sacramental acts within the Church. This lack of consensus suggests that the sacraments developed more out of the daily needs of the Byzantine Church than as a theoretical construct.

Baptism in the early period represented a truly significant event in the life of an individual who chose to become a Christian. After a three-year period of intensive training, which involved not only catechetical lessons in the mysteries and teachings of the Church, but also rigorous fasting and prayer, the initiate would be baptized on Easter night, thus experiencing in his or her whole being the true meaning of Christ's glorious resurrection. Infant baptism began to supplant the reception of adults into the Church in the sixth or seventh centuries and to some extent the spiritual significance of this most central sacrament in the Church was lost at this time. On the other hand, Orthodox infants and children were considered full, participating members of the Church from the moment of their baptisms, since their confirmation, or chrismation, was performed in the same ceremony. To this day, it is the babies and children in an Orthodox church who wait at the front of the queue to receive communion; if asked whether they fully understand the significance of the eucharist, an Orthodox will answer, 'Would I deny a child its spiritual food any more than its material nourishment?'

After baptism, chrismation and communion, which clearly represented the first three sacraments in the Byzantine Church, the role of confession as one of the 'mysteries' of the Church remained somewhat less clearly defined. The practice of public penance in the early Church slowly gave way to more private confession, followed by a prayer of absolution. The Eastern Orthodox Church differed from the Catholic West in that it never understood sin and salvation in a legalistic way; sin was viewed more as a disease than as a legal crime and absolution represented spiritual healing. A certain informality with regard to confession appears to have existed throughout the Byzantine period: individuals were free to choose their own spiritual guides and confessors. These 'spiritual fathers or mothers' might be lay monastic figures rather than parish priests or bishops.

Marriage

The idea that marriage between two Christians represents a sacred contract appears already in the writings of the apostle Paul: '"For this reason a man will leave his father and mother and be joined to his wife, and the two will become one flesh." This is a great mystery, and I am applying it to Christ and the Church' (Ephesians 5:31–32). This passage expresses two separate ideas concerning marriage. First, Paul reaffirms the Roman understanding of marriage as a legal contract between two consenting individuals. The consequence of this agreement is that they will establish a new home together, sharing everything as if they were one unit. Second, however, Paul suggests for the first time here a Christian view of marriage: the sacred contract between a man and a woman symbolizes the union between Christ and the Church. As a reflection of the eternal kingdom of God, marriage represents an eternal bond which will not be broken even by death.

After the Christianization of the Roman empire, the full involvement of the Church in sanctioning and blessing marriages came about relatively slowly. It was only by the early tenth century that the emperor Leo VI published a law which formally obliged the Church to validate *all* marriages. In spite of the Orthodox Christian belief in the eternal nature of the marriage bond, it was soon recognized that many Christians fell short in upholding this ideal. While not condoning divorce or remarriage after bereavement, the Church frequently allowed that such arrangements might be necessary. The marriage ceremonies of those who were entering into a second or third union were penitential in character and were not combined with the holy eucharist.

The final rites

The office of 'extreme unction', which is administered before every individual Christian's death, evolved out of a more general sacrament known as 'holy unction' delivered at the beds of those who are sick. Both services were composed of scriptural readings and prayers of healing, and would be performed by one or several priests. The ill or dying would also be anointed with holy oil, which symbolized divine mercy and liberation from human suffering of any kind. Along with the funeral service, which was considered a sacrament by many Byzantine liturgical writers, unction expressed also the continuing participation of the individual in the life of the Church. Even in illness and after death, Christians represented members of the living and resurrected body of Christ, into which they had been initiated through baptism and communion.

As we have seen in this chapter, the life of the Byzantine Orthodox Christian was regulated by various liturgical cycles, all of which helped to shape his or her everyday life. The daily practice of liturgical prayer, which lay Christians would carry out before the icons in their own homes, participation in stational liturgies or processions, attendance at church and finally, on a more personal note, participation in the major sacraments throughout their lives – all of these activities would have reinforced the sense of Orthodox Christian life as a structured and symbolic enactment of the kingdom of heaven on earth.

'The church is heaven on earth, where the God of heaven dwells and moves . . . It is prefigured in the patriarchs, founded on the apostles, adorned in the hierarchs, perfected in the martyrs.'

St Germanos of Constantinople (c. 634–c. 732), on the Divine Liturgy

CHAPTER 8

DOCTRINE AND THE SEVEN ECUMENICAL COUNCILS

Christianity, like Judaism, is a religion based on scripture. The early Church at first regarded the Old Testament, replete with prophecies foretelling the incarnation of Christ, as their scripture. In the course of the second century, the epistles of Paul, Acts and the four Gospels also gradually acquired the status of divinely inspired writings. Perhaps basing their accounts on oral traditions, the evangelists recorded for posterity what appear to be Jesus' actual words and teachings. But what do the Saviour's indications about himself actually mean? Jesus asks his disciples, 'Who do people say that the Son of man is?' Peter answers, 'You are the Messiah, the Son of the living God' (Matthew 16:13–16). Whatever these words may have meant to Jesus and his disciples, they were understood in many ways by later Christians.

It also may seem that various passages in the New Testament say different things about Christ. 'The Father and I are one' (John 10:30) seems to conflict with the sense of the statement, 'But about that day or hour no one knows, neither the angels in heaven, nor the Son, but only the Father' (Mark 13:32). Scholars today would explain the discrepancies in Jesus' own account of himself as reflecting the different intentions and backgrounds of the individual evangelists who reported his sayings. In the early Church, however, these statements had to be taken at face value and could only be understood as revealing paradoxical aspects of Christian doctrine. The more sophisticated interpreters of biblical texts could also resort to allegory, by arguing that the literal sense of a passage concealed a deeper, symbolic meaning.

The definition of an unknowable God

As we shall see in the course of this chapter, different understandings of the relationship of Christ the Son to God the Father, of the Holy Spirit in relation to both Father and Son, and of the way in which humanity and divinity come together in Christ, led to tragic schisms in the first five centuries of the Church. Nevertheless, it is important to recognize that these controversies did not result solely from intellectual speculations concerning the Trinity and the incarnation of Christ. As many of the early Greek Fathers reveal in their writings on these issues, Christian doctrine has a direct bearing on human salvation. In debating these matters, early Christians thus felt that the correct understanding of trinitarian and christological doctrine could affect their own destiny.

> 'If you ask for your change, the shopkeeper philosophizes to you about the Begotten and the Unbegotten. If you ask the price of a loaf, the answer is "the Father is greater and the Son is inferior"; if you say, "is my bath ready?" the attendant declares that the Son is of nothing.'
>
> **St Gregory of Nyssa, fourth century**

Human beings, since the fall from grace of Adam and Eve, have been separated from God by their participation in this ancestral sin, which also accounts for the difficulties of human existence. But God sent his Son to become one of us and to redeem us by his own death and resurrection. If Christ is successfully to bridge the gap between divinity and humanity, it is essential that he participate completely in both states of being. No one less than God can save humankind; Christ the Saviour therefore must be God. At the same time, however, humanity can only participate in the salvation offered by Christ's death and resurrection if he is fully human. The link between God and humanity can only be secured by a fully human and divine Saviour, the incarnate Christ. The early Greek Fathers took a further step by speaking of the possibility of the 'deification' (*theiôsis*) of humankind as a result of the incarnation of Christ. As Athanasius, bishop of Alexandria, expressed it in the early fourth century, 'God became human that we might become God.'

Sources of authority

The bishops engaged in resolving controversies concerning the nature of the Trinity or the humanity and divinity of Christ relied on various sources of authority to support their decisions. First and foremost, Christian scripture, or the books of the New Testament which had been accepted as canonical by the end of the second century, provided the firmest basis for an understanding of God and of Christ. As we saw above, however, many biblical passages appear to be contradictory; both spiritual knowledge and discernment were needed to make sense of the various evangelists' accounts of Jesus Christ.

Second, it is clear that from the second century onwards, bishops and teachers in the Church regarded both written and unwritten tradition as authoritative within the Church. The earliest Christian Creeds are probably based on local 'rules of faith' which were used in the instruction and baptismal initiation of new converts. Finally, Orthodox Christians believed then, and still believe, that God continues to reveal himself to us through the inspiration of the Holy Spirit. The ideas expressed in the seven ecumenical councils of the Church, which took place between 325 and 787, may go beyond biblical sources in their formulation of Christian doctrine; nevertheless, this reflects God's continuing involvement in human history and the gradual process of divine revelation. As Gregory Nazianzen argued in the fourth century, some doctrines, such as the divinity of the Spirit, were revealed only gradually since Christ's disciples and their followers were not yet capable of fully understanding them.

Negative theology

A branch of theology which seems to have been in use from the fourth century onwards, and which draws on Greek philosophical traditions which stress the unknowable transcendence of God, is known as 'apophatic'. This is sometimes translated 'negative theology' since it denies that any concept formulated by human beings can adequately express the mystery of divine being. It is clear that the apophatic approach remained deeply embedded in the Eastern Orthodox tradition throughout the Byzantine period. Whereas scholasticism, the idea that the human intellect may formulate systematic definitions of theology, gained adherents in the West in the course of the 11th and 12th centuries, Byzantine Orthodox theologians always regarded the apophatic approach as the best and deepest expression of our human apprehension of God. On the other hand, it was necessary to formulate doctrine in order to counter the heresies which continually challenged the Church. A tension thus existed in Orthodox theology between the affirmation that God is essentially unknowable and the need to formulate creeds in which the natures of all three members of the Holy Trinity are precisely defined.

'You perceive', writes Gregory, 'periods of illumination gradually enlightening us and an order of revelation which it is better for us to preserve, neither appearing in a single burst nor maintaining secrecy to the very end'.

The seven ecumenical councils

Controversy over the precise relationship of Christ the Son to God the Father, which initiated a long period of dispute concerning the Trinity, developed at the beginning of the fourth century. The timing of this debate and the repercussions that it caused throughout the Roman world (which in this period represented territories all around the Mediterranean Sea) are in fact no accident. Unity and shared definitions of doctrine became a high priority within the Church as soon as Constantine I adopted Christianity as the state religion of the Roman empire. Disagreements within the Church had occurred before, but had tended to be settled by local councils or by the rulings of individual bishops. Now that the Church acknowledged one emperor as its temporal head and as the ecclesiastical hierarchy came to be attached to five important sees, or patriarchates, the need for universal councils, whose decisions would be binding on the entire Church, arose.

Constantine I summoned and presided over the first ecumenical council, held in Nicea in 325, in response to the teachings of an Alexandrian priest called Arius. Either due to a literal understanding of scripture or because he wished to maintain the complete transcendence of God the Father, Arius taught that Christ the Son is inferior to God the Father. In one of his few surviving letters, Arius wrote that 'the Son, begotten by the Father, created and founded before the ages, *was not* before he was begotten'. In other words, although created by the Father even before the beginning of time, Christ the Son did not exist co-eternally with God; *there was a time when he was not*. Alexander, bishop of Alexandria, who seems to have been the first churchman to take exception to Arius' teachings, used passages from the Gospel of John to show that the Father and the Son are inseparable and of one being. He argued that by proposing a division between God the Father and Christ, Arius was suggesting that Christ was a mere creature. If this is the case, he no longer represents a link between humanity and divinity: thus, our chance of salvation through Christ does not exist.

At the Council of Nicea, the assembled bishops worked out a formula to express the divinity of Christ and his oneness with God. A new term, *homoousios*, which may be translated 'one in essence', was borrowed from Greek philosophy to express the indissoluble unity of Father and Son. The Nicene Creed stresses the co-eternal and uncreated being of Christ the Word: 'God from God, light from light, true God from true God, begotten not made, *homoousios* with the Father'. According to the historical and theological accounts written soon after the Council of Nicea, some bishops, although they may have signed the Acts of the council, remained uncomfortable with the expression *homoousios*. The term could be understood in various ways, but even more worryingly, it represented an innovation which departed from the purely scriptural definitions of Christ. Controversy over this word and the anti-Arian decisions of Nicea themselves rumbled on for nearly a century, especially under the pro-Arian successors of Constantine I. The debate was finally resolved at the second ecumenical council of Constantinople in 381, when the decisions of Nicea were reaffirmed and the term *homoousios* upheld.

The theologians who contributed most to the development of doctrine in the fourth-century East include Athanasius and the three Cappadocian Fathers, Basil of Caesarea, Gregory of Nyssa and Gregory Nazianzen. Athanasius, who spent much of his career as bishop of Alexandria exiled from his see under a succession of Arian emperors, defended the divinity of Christ in various works, including a treatise, *On the Incarnation*. In addition to their contributions to trinitarian doctrine, which were considerable, the Cappadocian Fathers helped to defend the divinity of the Holy Spirit against a new heresy which questioned his equal status with Father and Son in the Trinity. Basil of Caesarea wrote a treatise, *On the Holy Spirit*, in which he used the authority of both scripture and tradition to argue the equality of the three persons of the Trinity, Father, Son and Holy Spirit. The emended Creed, which was agreed at the second ecumenical council of 381, contained the longer definition of the Holy Spirit: '[I believe] . . . in the Holy Spirit, the Lord and life-giver, who proceeds from the Father, who with the Father and the Son is together worshipped and glorified.'

The Council of Constantinople also built on the work of the first ecumenical council in dealing with the external organization of the Church. It assigned a new order of precedence to the five administrative and spiritual centres of Christendom, or patriarchates. For the first time since Constantine's foundation of the city as 'the Second Rome' in 330, Constantinople was pronounced to be second in importance after Rome, followed by the more ancient sees of Alexandria, Antioch and Jerusalem. The continuing power struggles between the sees of Constantinople, Alexandria and Antioch played a significant part in the events leading up to the next great religious controversy, which dominated the fifth century. This was the debate over the two natures of Christ, contested mainly by proponents of the theological schools based in Antioch and Alexandria.

Trouble began when Nestorius, an Antiochene monk who was appointed bishop of Constantinople in 428, preached against the use of the term *Theotokos* ('God-bearer') for the Virgin Mary, arguing that she gave birth to the incarnate Christ, not to God. Nestorius was probably reacting to an already flourishing cult of the Virgin at this time, but he also based his arguments on christological teaching which he had assimilated in Antioch. The Antiochene school of theology interpreted scripture from a literal point of view, emphasizing the humanity of Jesus Christ and the reality of his historical existence. Cyril, the forceful bishop of Alexandria, on hearing of Nestorius' opinions, began writing letters to important figures in Constantinople, as well as to Nestorius himself. Cyril was informed by the Alexandrian school of theology, which stressed a more allegorical approach to scripture and which also traditionally emphasized the divinity of Christ, as the Word, or *Logos*, of God. Whereas Nestorius wished to uphold the diversity of the two natures in Christ, thereby safeguarding his true humanity, Cyril started from the position of unity, arguing that the divine and human natures are inseparable in the Son of God. Passages such as 'The Word became flesh' (John 1:14) and 'The Father and I are one' (John 10:30) justified the idea that the Virgin Mary, or *Theotokos*, in fact gave birth to God.

The emperor Theodosios II called the third ecumenical council, which was held in Ephesus in 431, in order to resolve this dispute. Cyril and the Alexandrian party dominated this council, which deposed Nestorius and upheld the Virgin Mary's title as *Theotokos*. The Council of Ephesus did not represent the end of the christological debate, however, as the emperor and his bishops struggled to reconcile the Antiochene and Alexandrian parties. Soon after the council, Cyril of Alexandria was forced to sign in 433 a 'Formula of Reunion', which had actually been drafted by the Antiochene theologian, Theodoret of Cyrus. This document, which incorporated the phrase 'a union of two natures' in describing Christ, seemed to Cyril's followers a wholesale sacrifice of Alexandrian theology. In the years that followed, influential clerics in both Alexandria and Constantinople pushed Cyril's Alexandrian theology even further, eventually declaring that there is just one, divine nature in Christ. Another council was held in Ephesus in 449, which was dominated by these hardline 'Monophysites', but which also alienated the eminent Pope Leo I, who had composed a doctrinal statement, or 'Tome', in which he expressed his adherence to a definition of Christ in two natures.

Eventually the need for unity and concord within the Christian empire as a whole decided the issue. After the death of Theodosios II in 450, his successor Marcian called for a new ecumenical council, the fourth, to be held at Chalcedon in 451. The decisions of this council represent a masterpiece of ecumenical compromise in the history of the Church. The Chalcedonian definition of christological doctrine succeeds in accommodating the divergent theologies of Antioch, Alexandria and Rome, as expressed by Pope Leo:

We all with one voice confess our Lord Jesus Christ one and the same Son, the same perfect in Godhead, the same perfect in manhood, truly God and truly man, the same consisting of a reasonable soul and a body, of one essence with the Father as touching the Godhead, the same of one essence with us as touching the manhood . . . born from the Virgin Mary, the Theotokos *. . . to be acknowledged in two natures, without confusion, without change, without division, without separation; the distinction of natures being in no way abolished because of the union but rather the characteristic property of each nature being preserved, and concurring into one person and one hypostasis.*

The Definition of the Council of Chalcedon, 451

Sadly, however, the first major schisms within the Christian Church were not averted by the ecumenical councils of the fifth century. A large group of Christians based in the Near East (modern Syria, Iran and Iraq) broke away from the wider Church. They could not accept the decisions of the Council of Ephesus, with its condemnation of Nestorius and other Antiochene theologians and its upholding of the title *Theotokos* for the Virgin Mary. This Church, which is often misleadingly called 'Nestorian' (it prefers to call itself 'the Assyrian Church of the East'), survives to this day, remaining out of communion with the Chalcedonian Orthodox Churches. A second schism occurred after the Council of Chalcedon, when adherents of Dioscorus and other 'Monophysite' followers of Cyril of Alexandria, felt betrayed by the definitions reached at that council. The so-called 'Monophysite' Churches, which still represent the majority in Egypt, Western Syria, Armenia and Ethiopia, also remain outside communion with the Western Catholic and Eastern Orthodox Churches which accepted Chalcedon.

Efforts at reconciliation

The development of doctrine within the Byzantine empire through the sixth and seventh centuries reflects a continuing effort on the part of both emperors and bishops to heal the schisms which had resulted from the councils of Ephesus (431) and Chalcedon (451). Efforts at compromise included the re-examination of the teachings of Cyril of Alexandria in the sixth century, the introduction of new ideas such as the 'Theopaschite' formula, which stated that Jesus as God suffered on the cross, and the reappraisal of terms such as *physis* ('nature') and *hypostasis* ('substance'). Eventually, the emperor Justinian called a fifth ecumenical council at Constantinople in 553, which officially registered such compromises in its formal definition of the faith. As so often happened at ecumenical councils, condemnation of one contending group, in this case a group of three Antiochene theologians of the fourth and fifth centuries, was also aimed at reconciling their opponents.

The compromises effected by successive ecumenical councils only had a limited effect in healing schisms within the Church, however. Some historians have argued that theological differences between the various groups were compounded by linguistic, ethnic and political separation. It is certainly true that the non-Chalcedonian Churches were largely based in the Eastern territories of the empire and composed of the non-Greek-speaking peoples of those areas. It is also possible that many of their members felt cut off and alienated from the bishops who represented the Church, who were based in the distant capital city of Constantinople. On the other hand, it is important not to underestimate the importance of 'right belief' or orthodoxy to Christians in this period. As we saw earlier, the doctrines concerning the humanity and divinity of Christ had implications for human salvation, both individual and collective. The fact that the differences between Monophysite, Antiochene and Chalcedonian christology seem in retrospect to reflect subtle variations in emphasis rather than major contradictions should not obscure the fact that their adherents held them to be matters of life and death. The separation of the Churches was further accentuated in the sixth century as rival bishops were ordained and separate ecclesiastical structures began to develop.

The doctrine of 'one will', or Monotheletism

Further efforts to reconcile the Monophysite and Chalcedonian Churches took place in the first half of the seventh century, especially during the reign of the emperor Herakleios. Sergios, Patriarch of Constantinople between 610 and 638, devised the 'Monothelite' doctrine, which he hoped would present enough concessions to draw the various Monophysite Churches back into the fold. According to the Monothelite teaching, which was published as an imperial *Ekthesis* (statement) in 638, Christ has two natures but only one, divine will. Although this formula seems to have worked for a time, enabling the agreement of various Eastern bishops to reunion with the imperial Church, two notable Byzantine theologians, a monk named Maximos the Confessor and Sophronios, Patriarch of Jerusalem, denounced it as heretical. Although Maximos did not live to see the success of his efforts against Monotheletism, the doctrine was eventually abandoned at the sixth ecumenical council of Constantinople held in 680–81.

Monotheletism represents the last attempt to heal the major schism within the Eastern Churches that had resulted from the Council of Chalcedon in 451. After the 630s, the imperial need to restore unity to the Church as a whole was rendered irrelevant by the unexpected loss of most of the Near East and North Africa to the Muslims. Christianity survived in these areas, both in Chalcedonian and non-Chalcedonian communities, but Byzantine emperors no longer felt the need to draw them back into the orbit of the Constantinopolitan patriarchate. It is thus correct to say that trinitarian and christological doctrines reached their full elaboration by the end of the seventh century and that no further attempts at compromise were made after that. Nevertheless, one more issue which was soon seen to have a christological dimension remained to be debated: this was the defence of holy images in the eighth century, in response to an iconoclastic imperial policy.

Iconoclasm as a theological issue

In the eighth century, a series of emperors, beginning with Leo III (717–41), introduced a policy of 'Iconoclasm' on the grounds that the Church was lapsing into idolatrous practices. The use of portable icons and the decoration of churches with images of Christ and other holy figures seemed to Leo and his supporters to contravene God's second commandment (Exodus 20:4). Although the arguments for and against religious images focused first on the charge of idolatry, they later began to move into the field of christological doctrine. The iconoclasts, as we know from the few surviving texts that they produced, charged the defenders of images with the heresies of both Nestorianism and Monophysitism. In creating an icon of Christ, they argued, one is guilty either of separating his human from his divine nature (Nestorianism) or of confusing the two (Monophysitism).

The defenders of holy images, or iconophiles, were fortunate in possessing several distinguished theologians who explored fully in their treatises the implications of the iconoclast charges. John of Damascus, a monk in the monastery of St Sabas near Jerusalem, could write safely from Islamic territories in the early eighth century on the subject of holy images within the Church. John defended icons on a number of grounds, using church tradition, Chalcedonian christology and even Neoplatonic philosophy to justify his arguments. The seventh and final ecumenical council, held at Nicea in 787, compiled a huge scriptural and patristic dossier in defence of holy icons, arguing primarily that their veneration could not be equated with idolatry in the light of Christ's incarnation and the inauguration of the kingdom of God. When Iconoclasm was reintroduced by Leo V (813–20), two more distinguished theologians, the monk Theodore of Studios and Patriarch Nikephoros, developed the christological and philosophical defence of images still further.

The doctrinal importance of the debate which took place in the period of Iconoclasm cannot be overemphasized in the history of Orthodox theology. This is one area in which the Byzantine Orthodox Church diverged significantly from intellectual and spiritual developments in the West. Although the popes who were asked to respond to this crisis supported the use of images, provided refuge for fleeing Byzantine iconophiles and signed the acts of the seventh ecumenical council, it is clear that they viewed icons from a very different spiritual perspective. Religious imagery had been used in the West for centuries, but was seen as fulfilling primarily educational purposes. The degree of cultural separation is indicated especially by the reaction of Frankish theologians to the Council of Nicea: at the Synod of Frankfurt (794) they stated that icon veneration was not an issue of true faith, worthy of discussion in an ecumenical council.

To the Byzantines, on the other hand, the 'theology of images' which developed in response to Iconoclasm represented the final stage in the definition of trinitarian and christological doctrine, which is summed up in the proceedings of all seven ecumenical councils. Precise definitions concerning God were of course inadequate, as he remains transcendent and uncircumscribed by either word or image. On the other hand, Byzantine Orthodox bishops and theologians recognized that the formulations agreed in ecumenical councils are necessary for two main reasons: first, one must define the faith in response to the heresies which threatened the integrity and meaning of the faith at various times in history; and second, the incarnation of Christ radically altered humanity's relationship with God. In taking on our nature, Christ, the Son of God, allowed himself to be circumscribed, thus forming a link between the divine and the created worlds.

The development of doctrine after 787

To Byzantine Christians the period of the seven ecumenical councils (325–787) represented the golden age of Orthodox theology in which trinitarian and christological doctrine were fully formulated.

The Bogomils

Like the Cathars in Western Europe, the Bogomils were dualists. Dualism is based on the idea that two opposing forces of good and evil are perpetually at war in the universe. Goodness is associated with an unseen, spiritual God who has nothing to do with the created world which we inhabit. A few individuals, called the 'elect', contain a 'spark' of divinity which separates them from the rest of creation. Matter and the physical body, on the other hand, are controlled by the forces of evil. The spiritual and the physical worlds are diametrically opposed and salvation consists in escaping the bondage of human flesh after death. Only initiates with a 'spark' of divine spirit, however, were believed to be destined for salvation. According to Byzantine accounts of the heresy, its adherents led a strict, ascetic life, eschewing meat, wine and sexual intercourse. Anna Komnena, the royal twelfth-century historian, described them as follows: 'Your Bogomil wears a sombre look; muffled up to the nose, he walks with a stoop, quietly muttering to himself – but inside he is a ravening wolf'. Reading between the lines of Anna's account, it is possible to detect that, as in the case of most other reforming religious movements, Bogomilism had a strong appeal for those who felt that the established Church had fallen away from the purity of its apostolic origins. The serious difference in doctrine between this sect and Orthodox Christianity, however, lay in their understandings of God and the created world. Whereas the Bogomils like other dualists believed that matter was essentially evil, Orthodox theology declared the whole of the created world to be the handiwork of a good and benevolent God.

This is not to say that further problems did not arise in subsequent centuries. What is clear, however, is that later doctrinal developments were concerned largely with finer points of definition, in response to challenges from both inside and outside the Eastern Church. After the restoration of icons in 843, called the Triumph of Orthodoxy in the Byzantine Church, differences in doctrine and practice arose between the Constantinopolitan patriarchate and the papacy in Rome. Ultimately these differences led to complete schism, formally initiated in 1054. Certain churches in the West had taken to inserting a short phrase, *filioque* ('and the Son'), after the statement in the Nicene–Constantinopolitan Creed concerning the Holy Spirit, 'who proceeds from the Father'. As attitudes concerning the *filioque* clause began to harden in East and West from the mid-ninth century onwards, Byzantine theologians such as the patriarch Photios wrote treatises elaborating the doctrinal significance of this issue. The Byzantines objected to the addition of the *filioque* on two grounds: first, that it represented an innovation that had not been agreed by the Church as a whole; and second, that the statement is false, since the Holy Spirit proceeds from the Father alone.

Other heresies emerged after the ninth century and helped further to define the boundaries of Orthodoxy. In the 10th and 11th centuries, a dualist sect called the Bogomils spread from Bulgaria through the Balkan peninsula and into Asia Minor, eventually reaching Constantinople itself. This movement may represent a link between earlier dualist heresies such as Manichaeism and the Cathar movements in Italy and Southern France, which appeared in the 12th and 13th centuries.

Palamism and the uncreated essence of God

In the fourteenth century, a new controversy arose concerning the nature of God and the ability of human beings to apprehend him mystically through prayer, as we saw in chapter 5. The debate between Gregory Palamas and his opponents, most notably a Calabrian monk named Barlaam, also touched on doctrinal issues concerning the nature of God. When Gregory, building on a long tradition of Byzantine mystical writings, asserted that it is possible for human beings to attain divine visions through prayer, Barlaam retorted that this is inconsistent with the doctrine of the transcendence and unknowability of God. Gregory Palamas responded that there is a distinction between God's unknowable essence and his energies. Citing Christ's transfiguration on Mount Tabor as an example, Palamas argued that what the disciples saw was a vision of uncreated light which represents the uncreated energy of God. The Christian mystic who experiences such a vision, both by means of his own efforts and by the grace of God, has directly encountered the living God. Another term for this experience is 'deification' (*theiôsis*); it is only possible because human beings are made in the image and likeness of God. The eventual acceptance of Gregory Palamas' teachings and the condemnation of Barlaam's point of view by the Byzantine Church represents an important stage in the development of Orthodox mystical theology. As in the case of religious images, the debate that accompanied this process helped to develop and clarify the dogmatic issues which were at stake.

Orthodoxy versus heresy

It is clear that the definition of doctrine in the Byzantine Church took place over many centuries and was beset by numerous controversies. The major definitions of doctrine, which took place in the course of the first five centuries of the Church and were ratified by a series of ecumenical councils, provide a dogmatic foundation which is shared by Eastern and Western Christendom alike. Such formal definitions of faith became necessary in response to intellectual challenges which arose within the Church. It is important to stress here that bishops would have preferred to avoid making such formal declarations about the nature of God if that had been possible. As questions arose concerning the nature of the Trinity or the relationship of Christ the Son to God the Father, Orthodox bishops felt that what they viewed as authentic Christian doctrine, based both on scripture and on the living experience of the Church, must be defended.

CHAPTER 9
FAITH AND WORLDVIEW

When we say that everyone was religious in the Byzantine empire or, for that matter, in the whole of the medieval world, it is important to understand exactly what we mean by this concept. Belief in one, transcendent God formed the basis of Orthodox Christians' belief, along with a basic understanding of scripture and trinitarian doctrine. However, Byzantine faith also encompassed an entire worldview. The formation of the universe, the playing out of history and humanity's final destiny were all understood from a Christian perspective which may seem alien in many ways to our modern, largely secular culture.

Other aspects of this medieval culture may also strike us as remarkable and deserve closer scrutiny. Byzantines of all periods felt that supernatural forces were present and active in everyday life. These included not only the power which came from God himself, channelled through holy people or objects in the created world, but also malevolent forces which usually took the form of demons. Perhaps because of the fragility of human life in a world which was threatened continually by invasions, epidemics and natural disasters, the Byzantines' belief in the afterlife was also strong. Finally, Orthodox Christianity, the dominant religion in this culture, provided people with a sense of belonging and identity. The perpetual castigation of minorities such as the Jews, heretics or external enemies such as Muslims in Byzantine texts reinforces the feeling of a tight-knit, well-defined group which is pitted against the rest of the world.

The cosmos

Early Christians inherited a number of different intellectual traditions, all of which had to be amalgamated somehow into a sensible explanation of how the world was created, why human beings were put into it and how their history would end. The Greek Fathers of the second through to the fourth centuries built mostly on Judaic tradition, using the biblical account in the first chapters of Genesis. At the same time, however, there were obviously problems with this account from a literal point of view. How, for example, could God separate light from darkness on the first day when he created the sun and the moon only on the fourth? A bishop called Theophilos of Antioch, writing in the second century, provided the first cosmological explanation of these verses. According to him, the universe was fashioned rather like a box: the earth (which is flat) represents its foundation and the sky, or firmament, is stretched out above it. The heaven which God made on the first day was not this visible sky, but an even higher one which lies above it and is invisible from the created world. This has the form of a roof or a vault, as suggested in the passage, 'It is he . . . who stretches out the heavens like a curtain, and spreads them like a tent to live in' (Isaiah 40:22). The suggestion here is that the visible world represents only a small part of God's creation; sources of light are therefore not confined to the celestial bodies that humans are permitted to see.

Origen, a Christian writer of the late second and early third century, ventured even more deeply into cosmology, constructing in his treatise, *On First Principles*, an elaborate explanation of the universe which was deeply influenced by Middle Platonism. Unlike Theophilos of Antioch and most later Christian theologians, Origen's system does not attempt to explain the physical universe. We find no box-like structures here: instead, the hierarchical structure which is topped by the transcendent God out of whom emanated the Word, or *Logos*, and all the angels and other created beings seems to exist in a purely conceptual framework. Origen's writings, especially *On First Principles*, fell into disrepute about a century after his death, owing to some unorthodox aspects of its teaching. The subordination of the *Logos* to God, even though Origen did affirm the Son's co-eternity with the Father, and the idea of restitution, or *apokatastasis*, at the final Day of Judgment for all, even conceivably the devil, were both ideas that seemed inconsistent with Christian doctrine as it was later formulated.

'To the Byzantine man, as indeed to all men of the Middle Ages, the supernatural existed in a very real and familiar sense. Not only did that other world continually impinge on everyday life; it also constituted that higher and timeless reality to which earthly existence was but a brief prelude. Any account of the Byzantine "worldview" must necessarily begin with the supernatural.'

Cyril Mango, Byzantium: The Empire of New Rome, 1980

Perhaps one of the best examples of a biblical view of the cosmos occurs in the *Christian Topography*, a book written by a sixth-century Alexandrian merchant known as Kosmas Indikopleustes. Kosmas had a wealth of experience with which to write about the physical universe. In the course of his career, he had travelled down the Red Sea and visited Ethiopia as well as many other countries. He does not appear to have sailed as far as India, but he had certainly seen more of the known inhabited world than most of his Byzantine contemporaries. Kosmas provides a strictly Christian picture of the universe, in which the created world (described in detail on the basis of his travels) is surmounted by the heavenly kingdom, according to the box-like structure suggested by earlier Christian writers such as Theophilos of Antioch. Like Theophilos, Kosmas creates his picture of the physical structure of the universe in accordance with a literal interpretation of the Bible, especially Genesis.

As we can see from the helpful diagrams which accompany the text of Kosmas' account, he pictures the cosmos as a three-dimensional box surmounted by a vaulted lid. The earth, which is rectangular, forms the base of this receptacle and is surrounded on all four sides by an uncharted ocean. A narrow strip of land encircles the oceans and it is to this that the four walls of the universe are fastened. These walls hold up the sky, which is rather like the ceiling of a house. Above this, the walls curve inwards, forming the vault which contains the heavenly kingdom. The whole structure replicates on a gigantic scale the tabernacle of Moses, with the earth representing the table for the Bread of the Presence (Exodus 25:30), and the firmament taking the place of the veil (Exodus 26:31).

It is of course impossible to know whether Byzantine Christians of all periods believed in such strictly biblical notions of the universe as this. It is clear, however, that Kosmas' *Christian Topography* was recopied and read by many Byzantines in later centuries. Intellectuals such as the ninth-century patriarch Photios were scornful of its content, but we may imagine that many pious Christians found this neat formulation of cosmology satisfying. At the same time, however, more scientific explanations of the structure of the universe were circulating throughout the Byzantine period. These were based on ancient Middle Eastern and Greek astrology and, although condemned by the Church, they must have informed the more educated members of the population. Ancient

Greek science pictured the universe as circular, with the earth forming a spinning core at its centre. The distant night sky was seen as the inside of a fixed sphere which revolved around the earth. The stars were attached to this surface and circulated with the sphere, keeping their characteristic groupings in the form of constellations. Meanwhile, within the space between the outer sphere and the earth, the planets, which included the sun, circulated according to their own specific routes. The Greek word *planetes* in fact means 'wandering', thus denoting 'stars' which followed their own paths.

The heavenly court

The heavenly and earthly realms mirrored the imperial Byzantine system in their strictly hierarchical structure. Christ, the incarnate God, is pictured in numerous Byzantine texts and images as an all-powerful ruler. He sits in majesty, surrounded by a court which is made up of such exalted figures as his mother, the Virgin Mary, cherubim and seraphim, archangels and angels, martyrs and saints. This very hierarchical structure replicates the imperial court on earth, except that God rules over the heavenly, as well as the earthly, cosmos. Byzantine texts vary in their depictions of God: he may appear as Ruler, Judge or merciful Father.

The angels who served God were infinite in number, but were also organized into a strict hierarchy. Some remained in the heavenly kingdom, endlessly praising God, while others were dispatched on missions to the created world, where they helped people in various ways: guarding them from danger, delivering messages or assisting their souls in the dangerous passage to the afterlife. Veneration of specific angels had been discouraged in the early Church, but the cult appears to have survived strongly into later centuries, judging by the numbers of churches dedicated to the archangel Michael throughout the empire. A theoretical and highly mystical treatise covering angelology was compiled by a

'The goal of a hierarchy . . . is to enable beings to be as like as possible to God and to be at one with him. A hierarchy has God as its leader of all understanding and action. It is forever looking directly at the comeliness of God. A hierarchy bears in itself the mark of God. Hierarchy causes its members to be images of God in all respects, to be clear and spotless mirrors reflecting the glow of primordial light and indeed of God himself.'

Pseudo-Dionysios the Areopagite, *The Celestial Hierarchy*, fifth century

shadowy fifth-century writer called Pseudo-Dionysios the Areopagite, who was influenced by Neoplatonic philosophy. However, it is unlikely that this difficult text was widely read, in spite of the fact that the Byzantines believed it to have been written by a disciple of the apostle Paul. Most Christians would have assumed the protection of a guardian angel who watched over them at times of danger. The archangel Michael, who was visualized as a military officer, was probably the most popular of all the angels among ordinary people.

Saints were also believed to be present in God's court, although the exact process by which they gained access to the heavenly kingdom after death was never fully explained. Most religious texts, including the *Lives* of saints and visionary accounts, suggest that these holy individuals were spared the long wait for the final Day of Judgment and taken straight to heaven after death. There they were pictured serving in the heavenly court or nestled in Abraham's bosom. From this privileged vantage point, a patron saint might intercede with God on behalf of human beings. Prayers and votive offerings to these holy figures thus played an important role in the everyday lives of Byzantine Christians. It is likely that the faithful felt a special bond with the saints because these were human beings who had crossed the boundary from the created to the divine world.

A large population of demons inhabited the created world, along with humanity and other living creatures. Byzantine texts, especially of the earlier periods, are unequivocal about the presence of these supernatural beings. They are subservient to their master Satan, but many seem to be harboured in pagan tombs and shrines. According to monastic treatises, the demons are usually invisible and work at tempting Christians to sin, gaining access through the five senses or the mind. Some demons are assigned to particular vices; thus there is a demon of pride and vainglory, a demon of fornication and so on. Demons also sometimes take on the form of a human being or an animal, such as a serpent, a dog or a dormouse. In this shape they may confront individuals, reserving their strongest attacks for the ascetic saints, seeking to distract, tempt or frighten them. Demons also frequently enter into the souls of people and animals, inhabiting them like parasites and driving them mad. Exorcisms similar to those recounted in the Gospels occur frequently in the early *Lives* of saints; by making the sign of the cross or laying his hands on

Stories of demons

One of the best sources of information on Byzantine demons is the seventh-century *Life of St Theodore of Sykeon*, an ascetic saint who lived and travelled in Asia Minor. On various occasions, according to this biography, Theodore was summoned by Christians villagers to help them exorcise or banish demons from their communities. As a man of God who had undergone rigorous ascetic training, Theodore was uniquely qualified to help in this endeavour. Once the citizen of a small village, while extending his threshing floor, levelled a small hillock in which a number of demons were lodged. The unclean spirits poured out of the hole and entered the animals and even some of the people in the village. The elders eventually sent for St Theodore, begging him to free their village of this infestation. He arrived and instructed them first to enlarge the hole in which the demons had been housed. On the following day he led a procession around the village and on reaching the site of the hole, prayed and commanded all demons to return to its shelter. He also exorcised them from the individuals who had been possessed. When the demons had re-entered the hole, it was sealed up and a cross was placed on top of the mound. The demons in the *Life of Theodore of Sykeon* represent a nuisance and threat to local populations, but they are easily subjugated by the saint. Interestingly, they appear to have local allegiances themselves – in one passage the demons in the region of Gordiane claim that they are tougher than those of Galatia. They appear in various forms, sometimes taking the shape of flies, sometimes as hares or dormice.

the afflicted individual, the saint expels the demon, who usually emerges with a loud, tearing sound.

Death and the afterlife

The Byzantine view of what occurs after death is not in fact a unified or consistent one. Many accounts emerge from different sources: it is clear that the Church's official line on this matter did not always agree with popular ideas. The prayers, hymns and homilies intended for use at funerals and memorial services generally convey the standard Christian belief that the soul is separated from the body after death.

After a period of waiting, the final Day of Judgment will arrive and every individual will be judged by Christ and sent to his or her final destination in heaven or hell. It is the period between death and the Final Day, however, that causes difficulties for most theologians. Does the soul go somewhere else when it is separated from the body and, if so, where? As we saw above, the souls of the saints were believed to go straight to paradise; does this mean that sinners waited in some other, less attractive place? The Byzantines did not at any period formulate an official doctrine concerning purgatory, as occurred in the West in about the twelfth century. In fact, this represented one of the issues of contention at the Council of Ferrara/Florence in 1438-39. Nevertheless, some kind of intermediate, third place between heaven and hell is implied in Byzantine texts from a very early period. This represents in effect a place of waiting, where repentance and the reversal of an unfavourable sentence may take place. The prayers of intercession offered by the living were believed to have an impact on an individual's final destiny.

Popular literature, that is, the texts that appear to have been written for and read by ordinary people, convey a somewhat different and occasionally amusing account of life after death. The idea that sinners were immediately punished for their sins was obviously an attractive one. A typical story of such punishment occurs in the seventh-century collection of miraculous tales compiled by John Moschos, a Syrian monk who travelled around Egypt and Palestine. In this account, John tells us that a monk was careless about carrying out the disciplines imposed on him by his superior. Some time later, the monk died and the elder prayed to God to reveal to him what had become of his disciple's soul. He went into a trance and saw a number of people standing in the middle of a river of fire. The monk was there too, submerged up to his neck. When the elder reproved him, saying that he had warned him repeatedly of the likelihood of this retribution, the monk responded, 'I thank God, father, that there is relief for my head. Thanks to your prayers I am standing on the head of a bishop'.

An even more remarkable idea concerning the fate of souls after death is that of the 'toll houses'. This concept was clearly not endorsed officially by the Church, but it appears in a number of sources, and is even hinted at in the highly reputable biography of St Antony, written by the patriarch Athanasius in the fourth century. According to these accounts, the human soul, after being detached from the body at the moment of death, was obliged to travel through the air, stopping at a number of toll houses along the way. The soul would be questioned about its actions during life at each of these staging posts. If the individual had sinned, he or she was obliged to pay an appropriate due, consisting of the good deeds performed during his or her life. According to the tenth-century *Life of St Basil the Younger*, there were 21 toll-houses in all, each of which represented a particular vice. These included pride, anger, avarice, lust and many others. Demons and angels fought at the moment of death for the right to accompany souls along this perilous journey. This is why the prayers of the living could play a pivotal role at this difficult moment.

Beliefs concerning the final Day of Judgment were based primarily on apocalyptic texts, especially the book of Revelation attributed to the evangelist John. Christ would sit in majesty, flanked by the Virgin Mary and John the Baptist, and surrounded by all of his angels, prophets and apostles. Seven angels (the number seems to vary in pictorial representations) would blow their trumpets and all of the dead would arise from their graves. This was the moment when the souls of the deceased would be rejoined with their bodies. According to the apostle Paul, this will not be a physical body, but a 'spiritual body' (1 Corinthians 15:44). To some extent the fate of these individuals had been predetermined since the day of their deaths: in images of the scene they are already lined up on the left or the right side of Christ as they await judgment. Each would then be weighed and dispatched to his or her appropriate destiny, whether this was the heavenly city or eternal damnation. This great event was thought to be imminent by many Orthodox Christians at various points in Byzantine history. Nevertheless, even after the fall of Constantinople to the Turks in 1453 (a catastrophe that some had predicted as heralding the advent of the anti-Christ), human history continued and Christians continued to wait for the Final Day.

> 'Grant her angels who will keep her soul safe from the spirits and beasts of the air, evil and unmerciful beings who endeavour to swallow up everything which comes into their midst.'
>
> **Prayer of the seventh-century saintly fool, Symeon of Emesa, at the death of his mother**

Illness and healing

Conventional medicine in the Byzantine empire was remarkably advanced for the period. The Greco-Roman tradition provided the background for Byzantine physicians, who drew on a number of treatises, including those of Hippocrates and Galen. The many copies of these medical texts which survive from the Byzantine period suggest not only that they were widely used, but also that doctors rearranged and added to them on the basis of practical experience. Many hospitals existed not only in Constantinople, but also in the provinces. It is clear that the use of drugs was sophisticated and that remedies could be prescribed for diseases of the chest, heart, digestive system and other organs. Surgery was also remarkably well advanced. Lists of surgical instruments suggest considerable scope in the number and variety of operations performed; we also have accounts of dissections and autopsies performed by Byzantine surgeons in order to advance their understanding of the human body.

At the same time, however, it is clear that many Byzantine citizens sought miraculous healing when conventional medicine had failed. Numerous collections of miracle stories survive, usually in association with the cult of a particular saint. Some saints specialized in healing certain types of illness and would therefore attract many people suffering from similar ailments to their shrines. Cures could be effected by means of pilgrimage to a holy site, for example the tomb of a martyr or saint, anointing with the holy oil that flowed from some tombs or icons, drinking oil or water associated with a holy site, or incubation. The last of these methods, which involved sleeping overnight at the tomb of a saint, may have links with the pagan cult of Asclepios, who also cured people in this way.

Judging by the accounts of supernatural healings and other miracles, Byzantine Christians believed strongly in the presence of both divine and demonic powers in the world. Faith in God played an important part in the efficacy of these cures: we hear of the failure of some individuals to receive divine aid because of their lack of belief. The power that came directly from God, even when channelled through saints, relics or icons, was infinitely superior to that of the demons. It was sufficient for a saint to make the sign of a cross, say a prayer or touch those who had

Miracle cures

A good example of a healing cult is that of St Artemios, a Christian official who had been martyred during the reign of the pagan emperor Julian, probably in about 362. A collection of miracles stories recounting the miraculous cures which occurred at the Church of St John the Baptist in Constantinople, where Artemios' relics had been deposited, was probably compiled in the middle of the seventh century. St Artemios specialized in diseases of the digestive and reproductive organs, especially those of the testicles. People suffering from hernias, tumours and other ailments, would come and sleep in the church. The saint would usually appear in a vision to these patients as they slept and cure them either by direct intervention or by offering medical advice. One man, named George, who had suffered from a testicular disorder for many years, had been advised to have these organs amputated. Instead he went to sleep in the Church of St John and dreamed that Artemios, in the guise of a butcher, pierced him with a knife in his lower abdomen. After removing and cleaning all his intestines, the saint rearranged them into one coil and put them back into George's body. When the sick man awoke, he realized that he was completely cured. Another individual was afflicted with a boil on his testicles which conventional doctors had been unable to treat. When he went to the Church of St John, the saint appeared to him in a vision and made an incision on the boil with a scalpel. Immediately the boil burst and the man was healed. It is interesting to note that in both of these cases St Artemios used the methods of conventional medicine to heal his patients, while at the same time drawing on supernatural power.

been possessed by these evil beings for them to be cured. The healings, exorcisms and other miracles described in Byzantine texts worked to restore the natural order according to God's plan. Disease and death both represented aberrations from this order, which God alone was able to remedy.

Orthodox identity in opposition to 'others'

Another aspect of the Byzantine worldview lies in the concept of collective identity. Orthodox Christians in every period of Byzantine history identified themselves above all by their religion. Obviously they were 'Romans', but that term denoted allegiance to a vast (although rapidly shrinking) political dominion inhabited by a multi-ethnic and multilingual population. In return for being citizens of the Eastern Roman empire and paying their taxes to the centralized, imperial government, Byzantines received military protection but not much else. The Christian religion, on the other hand, provided an entire worldview, encompassing both the earthly and the heavenly kingdoms, as well as life and the afterlife, as we have seen in this chapter. By reading scripture, attending church, praying before icons and visiting the shrines of martyrs and saints, Orthodox Christians participated in a community which shared a sense of collective identity and purpose.

The sense that this Christian identity was threatened both from outside and by forces within also emerges to a greater or lesser degree in every period of Byzantine history. Orthodox Christians felt that their beliefs and way of life were under threat by opposing ideological systems. The first step in combating these forces was to express what they believed in the doctrinal formulations which emerged from ecumenical councils and later in such documents as the *Synodikon* of Orthodoxy. The second was to castigate those who deviated from these doctrines both inside and outside the empire.

It is a striking, although unfortunate, fact that in many periods the group which was singled out for the most criticism was the Jews. There may be various reasons for this long-standing prejudice on the part of Byzantine Christians. Jews had been regarded from as early as the second century as the ideological adversaries of Christianity *par excellence*. Early Christians, many of whom were converted from Judaism, sought to distance themselves from their former brethren, who seemed to them to reject the new message which Christ had come to proclaim. Furthermore, the fact that Jewish communities continued to exist in most of the major cities of the Eastern Roman empire, and that they were allowed for the most part to govern themselves, meant that they appeared as 'outsiders' at the

'Arguing the Christian position through the condemnation of the Jews made perfect sense: over the centuries the process of Christian self-definition had always involved differentiating Christianity from Judaism, and the Christians often condemned their enemies by comparing them to the Jews.'

Kathleen Corrigan, *Visual Polemics in the Ninth-Century Byzantine Psalters*, 1992 heart of Byzantine society. It was especially during periods of military and economic pressure, such as the seventh and early eighth centuries, that Jews became scapegoats and were subjected to persecution of various kinds. It is clear both in Byzantine texts and images that Jews came to represent symbolically every ideological adversary. Thus, heretics such as Arians or iconoclasts are typically denounced as 'Jews'. Sermons and hymns, especially those associated with the services leading up to Good Friday and Easter, denounce the Jews for their part in the crucifixion of Christ.

Collective identity is constructed in every society not only from people's sense of who they are, but also who they are not. The Byzantines perhaps needed to identify themselves as a group more than do most societies, owing to their frequently precarious political and military situation. As we have seen in this chapter, this identity was based above all on their Orthodox Christian religion, which included not only an agreed set of doctrines and liturgical practices, but also ideas about the formation of the cosmos, the purpose of history and the close proximity of divine power in this world. The sense of belonging to a well-defined group also represented an important part of this worldview. It is unfortunate that this led to the oppression of religious minorities living within the Byzantine empire, but it also probably bolstered the confidence of a society that was frequently under threat of extinction.

CHAPTER 10

ART AS AN EXPRESSION OF FAITH

An important legacy of the Byzantine Church is the art it produced, much of which still survives in the former territories of the empire, especially Turkey, Greece, the Near East and the former Yugoslavia. Western tourists often visit these sites and are inspired by the wall paintings, mosaics and church buildings that they see. Many of the most precious Byzantine artefacts may be found in the art museums, libraries and treasuries of Western Europe. Some of these were stolen from Constantinople after the crusaders' sack of the city in 1204; others represent the purchases of later Europeans who travelled to the East. This chapter will explore the history of Byzantine art and architecture for two reasons: first, because these traditions represent an important expression of Byzantine spirituality; and second, because they remain probably the most accessible heritage of this extinct civilization for travellers and scholars alike.

Early Christian art

Assigning a beginning to Byzantine art is as difficult as determining a date of origin for the empire. Christian art in the early fourth century, when Constantine was founding Constantinople as his capital city, was still in its infancy. Although scholars still debate whether representational art of all kinds was banned during the first two centuries of the Church on the grounds that it was idolatrous, it is clear that very few images were created in this period. The earliest decorated Christian building, a baptistery at the site of Dura Europas (now in Syria), which is dated to before 256, contains paintings of Adam and Eve, Christ, the Good Shepherd, and the visit of the three women to Christ's tomb just after his resurrection. This monument suggests that a tradition of depicting carefully chosen biblical scenes symbolizing important Christian teachings was already in existence by the mid-third century. It is perhaps even more surprising that a Jewish synagogue contains many wall paintings of Old Testament stories at the same site. It is clear that both Jews and Christians living in this region at this time did not interpret God's commandment against religious imagery (Exodus 20:4) entirely literally.

Another important example of early Christian art may be found in the catacombs, which were used as burial places outside the city walls of Rome by Christians and pagans alike in the early centuries of the Church. The Christian catacombs are believed to date from the third through to the fifth centuries. What is perhaps most striking in the wall paintings that decorate these underground chambers is their ability to convey, in a striking and symbolic manner, a simple but fundamental message of Christian faith: salvation and resurrection in Christ. The choice of scenes, including Abraham's sacrifice of Isaac, Moses crossing the Red Sea, the three men in the fiery furnace and the raising of Lazarus, had all by this time become symbols of Christian resurrection. The catacombs in Rome reveal a fully developed ability to convey Christian truths by means of simple but effective pictorial images, expressing not a narrative, but a theological interpretation of events in the Old and New Testaments.

Another phenomenon which may be related to the rise of Christian art in the third and fourth centuries, but which also reflects a general shift in aesthetic values, is the movement away from classical realism towards abstraction in late-Roman art. Scholars have speculated that an abstract style is frequently used deliberately by artists and that it does not necessarily reflect falling standards in artistic technique. Sculptures such as the porphyry statue of the four emperors (tetrarchs) who ruled at the end of third century, which now stands outside St Mark's Cathedral in Venice, convey a deeper, symbolic message at the expense of a purely realistic image. The abstract, even primitive, style of this sculpture reveals key characteristics associated with these rulers: solidity, unity and military strength.

As Constantine promoted Christianity within the Roman empire, it became possible for the Church to build and adorn official places of worship. The decoration of churches soon got under way and various methods of depicting biblical scenes and holy figures developed. Two very different systems of monumental church decoration are evident by as early as the fifth century. The first of these is the method, mentioned above in connection with the Roman catacombs, of portraying theological doctrine symbolically. The image of Christ seated on a globe, surrounded by angels, in the apse of the sixth-century Church of San Vitale in Ravenna, represents a good example of this trend. This mosaic conveys unequivocally the message that Christ, the All-Ruler, has come to save humanity.

The other style of decoration, which also seems to have developed early, is the more detailed, narrative scene, whose purpose is to tell the biblical story by means of a picture. We find examples of this style of decoration in the fifth-century Church of Santa Maria Maggiore in Rome, which contains detailed scenes from the Old and New Testaments. We know that the Church recognized the educational value of religious imagery and that this may indeed have been seen as the primary purpose of church decoration of this type. Various early Fathers extol the educational value of religious imagery, which they see as useful for the many Christian faithful who were unable to read or who lacked access to books.

Mosaic decoration of church walls and ceilings was widely in use throughout the empire by the fifth and sixth centuries. Ever more fragile and expensive materials were used for the individual tesserae as this artistic technique was perfected. A mosaic mural might be made up of pieces of terracotta for the darker sections, but also translucent glass and even semi-precious gems. Gold and silver tesserae were created by fitting thin wafers of these precious materials between layers of translucent glass. The tesserae would be cut to different sizes, with the finest and smallest being saved for the depiction of human faces and other important details. Artists, as they planned and executed mosaic images high up in churches, would carefully consider the issues of perspective and light. A mural was planned so that it would look realistic from the ground, even if this meant foreshortening individual figures. The most splendid examples of sixth-century Byzantine mosaics survive in the areas of the empire that were not affected by Iconoclasm. The beautiful image of the transfiguration of Christ in the apse of the church in St Catherine's Monastery, Sinai, or the various churches established by fifth and sixth-century rulers of Ravenna, including Justinian, probably represent the finest examples of this 'de luxe' form of monumental decoration.

Portable icons

Between the fifth and eighth centuries, especially in the Eastern half of the Roman empire, still another form of representational art was becoming increasingly popular in both public and private worship. These are the holy icons, images usually painted on wooden panels, although they could also be fashioned by means of a number of other media, such as ivory and enamel. The earliest examples of painted icons are dated no earlier than the sixth and seventh centuries. The largest collection to survive from this period, which consists of about 27 icons, is preserved at St Catherine's Monastery in the Sinai desert, now in Egypt.

A famous icon from the Sinai collection, which is usually dated to the sixth or early seventh century, depicts the Mother of God holding the Christ child on her lap, flanked by two saints, St George and St Theodore. Behind them stand two angels, half turned away and gazing up towards heaven. The different artistic styles evident in this icon have been noted by scholars and are generally thought to be deliberate on the part of the artist. The Virgin, while appearing as a solid, human figure, looks slightly away from the viewer as if to convey her association with divinity. The two angels, who are painted in an impressionistic style, reveal an ethereal quality which is appropriate to their status as 'bodiless' ones. The soldier saints, on the other hand, gaze fixedly at us since they represent the most immediate point of contact between the divine and the human worlds. The severe frontal pose and abstract style revealed here is typical of depictions of saints in this period. It is likely that this was used in order to convey a sense of the spiritual detachment from worldly society of these holy figures.

'Represent a single cross in the sanctuary . . . Fill the Holy Church on both sides with pictures from the Old and New Testaments, executed by an excellent painter, so that the illiterate who are unable to read the holy scriptures may, by gazing at the pictures, become mindful of the manly deeds of those who have genuinely served the true God, and may be roused to emulate their feats.'

St Neilos of Sinai (died c. 430)

Art after the end of Iconoclasm:
the 'Macedonian Renaissance'

Byzantine art experienced a revival after the end of the period of Iconoclasm, when religious imagery had been suppressed for just over a century. Churches were again decorated with mosaics and wall paintings; icons were produced, and manuscripts illustrated with miniatures and other decoration. This is the period when standard methods of depicting certain biblical themes, called iconography, began to be formulated and employed. At the same time, original and creative artistic approaches are visible in many different media. In this section we will confine our discussion to just two of these categories: the illustration of manuscripts and monumental wall decoration, especially in mosaic.

The production of manuscripts increased markedly after the early ninth century. This is the period in which a new, more cursive script, known as the minuscule, was invented. The defeat of Iconoclasm and increasing importance of monasteries in the Byzantine world may also have spurred on this enterprise. Although most surviving Greek manuscripts are not illustrated with miniatures, those that were commissioned by rich patrons or emperors often contain beautifully executed images decorated with gold leaf. Gospel books and collections of biblical readings called lectionaries are the most numerous among these illustrated manuscripts. Many of these contain full-page illustrations of the evangelists writing their books, as well as images of individual scenes in the life of Christ. Another liturgical book which was frequently illustrated was the Psalter, which contained the 150 psalms attributed to David. Some of the earliest examples of illustrated Psalters are dated to the ninth century. The images which accompany individual Psalms appear in the margins of these manuscripts; interestingly, they refer not only to the content of the verses that they accompany, but also to contemporary events such as Iconoclasm.

The illustrations in some ninth and tenth-century manuscripts suggest a return to the classicizing style of Hellenistic and late-Roman art. The modelling of the figures, the depiction of the folds of drapery, attempts at perspective and the use of pagan personifications in these images have led to these works being viewed as products of a cultural renaissance.

The use of the term 'renaissance' is perhaps somewhat misleading, however. The pagan, classical past was always present in the Byzantines' memories and was never in need of deliberate revival. It is perhaps more helpful to view classicizing images and literary texts as representing a particular branch of Byzantine culture which never ceased to be important. It was quite acceptable to portray a Christian message by means of pagan rhetorical or artistic techniques. Indeed, these may even have provided a stamp of legitimacy for those readers and viewers who were capable of appreciating their background.

Church decoration in the Middle Byzantine period

The cathedral of Hagia Sophia, designed and constructed early in the reign of the emperor Justinian (527–65), became the ideal model for all subsequent ecclesiastical architecture in the Byzantine empire. Hagia Sophia is a domed basilica which is built on a square foundation. This provides a huge central area in which the eye is drawn upwards by means of a series of arches to the great dome at the top. The eighth-century patriarch Germanos' statement that a church represents 'heaven on earth' was probably written with Hagia Sophia in mind, as he pictured the huge interior of the 'Great Church'. After the period of Iconoclasm, churches constructed in the Byzantine empire tended to be planned according to an architectural type known as the 'cross in square'. These churches, like Hagia Sophia are centralized in structure: the dome on top is supported by a series of pendentives and vaults which lead downwards towards a square foundation. Later Byzantine churches tend to be fairly small in size, however, compared to Hagia Sophia. This gives them a much more enclosed and intimate atmosphere than is found in the great cathedrals of Western Europe.

The decoration of Middle Byzantine churches is uniquely suited to their architectural structure. The wall paintings or mosaics convey by their choice of subject-matter the hierarchical structure of the universe. In the dome at the top appears the bust of Christ, the Pantokrator or All-Ruler, both the Judge and the Saviour of humankind.

The Virgin and Child usually appear in the apse, symbolizing the mystery of the incarnation, which is the central teaching of Orthodox

Christianity. On the upper walls and squinches that surround the dome we find scenes from the life of Christ. The choice of scenes usually reflected the important feast days in the Church. Such key feasts as the Annunciation, the Nativity, the Transfiguration, Palm Sunday and Easter were always included, but some flexibility was allowed in their choice and arrangement. On the lower walls of the church appear the portraits of individual saints, martyrs and other important figures. As in the case of the feast day scenes, the choice of saints varies considerably in individual churches. It is clear that the decoration of churches reflects to a large extent the wishes and specifications of their donors; each church is unique, representing the ideas of its patron, architect and painter or mosaicist, who have together planned its structure and decoration.

Later Byzantine art

Art and architecture continued to flourish in the later period of Byzantine history, in spite of the many vicissitudes experienced by the empire until its final destruction in 1453. A huge variety of artistic media, including not only wall paintings, mosaics and icons, but also manuscripts, ivories, enamels, silk tapestry and metal work, addressed religious themes. There is unfortunately no space in this chapter to treat each of these topics in detail; instead, it may be useful simply to provide a very general discussion of a few trends and issues in late-Byzantine art.

Returning to the field of wall paintings and icons, it is noticeable in the 11th and 12th centuries that a new, more realistic style was occasionally adopted. This contrasts with the more abstract style of many earlier representations. There is a reason for the choice of different artistic styles. More abstract renderings convey the sense of detachment and tranquillity which is appropriate for devotional art. The more realistic style which appears in some, although not by any means all, later icons seems to express narrative action or emotion on the part of the depicted figures.

This trend is apparent in a fine twelfth-century icon of the Annunciation which belongs to St Catherine's Monastery in Sinai, but which may have been created in Constantinople. As the archangel Gabriel approaches the Mother of God, his half-turned body in its swirling draperies convey his anxiety concerning the success of his mission; this idea also appears in a number of homilies commemorating the feast of the Annunciation. The Virgin herself is depicted as a humble young woman spinning her scarlet thread, according to the account in the *Protoevangelion* of James.

Another famous example of realism and emotion in the art in this period may be seen in the wall paintings of the monastery of St Panteleimon at Nerezi, near Skopje, in modern Macedonia. This monastery is dated by an inscription to 1164; its central church contains a number of wall paintings with about 20 scenes, including a detailed Passion cycle. The founder was a Byzantine, Alexios Komnenos, nephew of the emperor John II, who perhaps owned estates in the region. It is clear that he employed Byzantine artists to decorate the main church of the monastery; these highly skilled craftsmen provided a sure and delicate touch in their rendering of the story of Christ's passion. In the scene of the lamentation, in which the Mother of God clasps the dead Christ to herself and lays her cheek against his, her grief is strikingly rendered. Many scholars view twelfth-century monuments such as this as the direct precursors of the famous thirteenth-century Italian wall paintings by Giotto and others.

The period between the recapture of Constantinople from the Latins in 1261 and the final fall of the Byzantine empire in 1453 witnessed a flowering of culture which found expression in both literature and art. Icons proliferated, reflecting the continuing devotion of Orthodox Christians to these portable symbols of divine power. Exquisite mosaic icons, fashioned out of minute tesserae, represent a technical innovation of this period. Illustrated manuscripts, richly decorated with gold leaf and drawing on well-established iconographical traditions, also survive in great numbers. Churches and monasteries adorned with mosaic or frescoed wall paintings were built not only in Constantinople, but also in those outlying provinces which were still under Byzantine rule.

Wealthy private patrons were often responsible either for restoring or founding religious buildings. In Constantinople we hear of a number of such figures in the final centuries of the empire. A senior imperial official named Michael Glabas refurbished the monastery of Theotokos Pammakaristos, which still survives as a mosque in Istanbul known as the Fethiye Camii. Probably in the 1290s Glabas built a small domed

The nativity scene, Hosios Loukas

In order to appreciate the content and meaning of festal scenes in middle Byzantine art, it might be useful to analyse one typical example. The mosaic depiction of the Nativity scene in the late-tenth-century monastery church of Hosios Loukas in central Greece serves to illustrate a number of points concerning Byzantine liturgical art. First, it is important to note the economy with which the artist has constructed the scene: the Virgin Mary is shown sitting in a cave next to the Christ child. On her right are the shepherds adoring him and on the left, the three magi. Angels overlook the scene, while Joseph sits rather disconsolately some distance away from the central figures of Mary and Christ. Just to the right of the manger, as if in a separate scene, the child is being washed by two midwives. As we look at this scene it is immediately clear that it does not merely represent the illustration of a biblical story. Every element in the picture has symbolic meaning and may be drawn from a number of textual sources in addition to the Gospels. For example, the ox and the ass, who always appear in Nativity scenes, represent both the animal world and the uneducated classes who first accepted Christ's teachings. The presence of the ox and ass was seen as the fulfilment of Isaiah's prophecy: 'The ox knows its owner, and the donkey its master's crib; but Israel does not know, my people do not understand' (Isaiah 1:3). The story of the washing of the infant by the midwives comes from an apocryphal text known as the *Protoevangelion* of James. The scene is included because it conveys the true humanity of Christ and the reality of his birth as a baby. Many other aspects of the scene are inspired by Old Testament prophecy or by theological considerations such as this. Above all, however, the careful structure of the image and its focus on the symbolic meaning of the events is evident.

chapel with a mosaic of Christ the Pantokrator at its summit. Another important example of a late-Byzantine patron is the scholar and statesman, Theodore Metochites, who sponsored the restoration of an ancient monastery called the Chora on the outskirts of Constantinople. This refurbishment involved rebuilding and decorating the vaults of the earlier church with mosaics, building an inner and outer vestibule, or narthex, as well as an adjoining chapel called the *parekklesion*. The mosaics and wall paintings which decorate these various structures survive to this day and bear witness to the extraordinary ability of the artists who executed them. The economy and theological symbolism of earlier Byzantine iconography has been preserved, but in addition to these we see a sophisticated depiction of human bodies, emotion and movement.

The legacy of Byzantine art

Although much Byzantine art has been lost, a great deal survives throughout the Mediterranean region. Many modern tourists to these areas find the remains of the Eastern Roman empire as beautiful and inspiring as the more renowned monuments of classical civilization. What many Western travellers may not realize, however, is how widely the influence of Byzantine art and its craftsmen spread. The twelfth-century churches in Palermo and Cefalù, Sicily, for example, represent in many ways classic examples of middle Byzantine decoration. There can be no doubt that although commissioned by the Norman kings who ruled this area between the 1140s and 1180s, these churches were constructed and decorated by Byzantine workmen. The style and arrangement of the mosaics, from the figure of Christ the All-Ruler in the dome to the biblical scenes and figures in the nave below, are almost entirely Byzantine in their inspiration. At the same time, however, differences do emerge which probably reflect the wishes and perspectives of the Western patrons. In the Cappella Palatina in Palermo, for example, the placement of a second Pantokrator in the apse, with a seated Virgin below, is unusual in Byzantine iconography. Other variations emerge in the choice of scenes and their arrangement on the walls around the central nave.

In Venice, a city which had maintained close ties with the Byzantine empire even after the fall of northern Italy to the Lombards in the eighth century, the rebuilding of St Mark's Cathedral in the late eleventh century was strongly influenced and perhaps executed by Byzantine architects and mosaicists. The plan of St Mark's was based on the famous Church of the Holy Apostles in Constantinople, which unfortunately does not survive. The mosaics, like those of the small eleventh-century church on the nearby island of Torcello, are entirely Byzantine in style.

The influence of Byzantine art and architecture is thus evident not only in the areas which remained under Byzantine rule, but also in neighbouring states to the north, east and west. Many of the medieval churches of Macedonia, Serbia, Bulgaria, Romania, Russia and the Ukraine may have benefited by the skills of Byzantine architects and artists; others were built by local builders who had been taught by them. Byzantine influence also continued in Eastern territories, such as Armenia and Georgia, even after these areas were no longer governed by Constantinople. Cultural and religious influence brought with it the time-honoured traditions of church architecture and decoration; these arts were not abandoned, even after political influence had waned.

CHAPTER 11

THE LEGACY

Constantinople, the capital city of the Byzantine empire, was finally captured by the Ottoman Turks on 29 May 1453. On the night before this attack, the Christian citizens of the city, including both Greeks and Latins, gathered in the Great Church of Hagia Sophia for a final service. The assault on Constantinople began in the early hours of dawn. Eventually the Turkish troops succeeded in scaling the walls and storming the capital city. The Byzantine emperor Constantine XI died in the attack; his body was never recovered. For three days and nights, Sultan Mehmed II allowed his troops to plunder the city. During this period priceless works of Orthodox Christian art, including icons, manuscripts and ecclesiastical treasure, were destroyed. Finally Mehmed II made his triumphal entry into the conquered city and Constantinople became the capital of the Ottoman empire.

Did these tragic events mean the end of the Byzantine empire? Undoubtedly the fall of Constantinople signalled the end of political and military rule in the Eastern Roman empire. The last remaining territories of the Greeks fell shortly after this: the Ottomans soon captured the remaining Aegean islands, and the Despotate of Morea in southern Greece fell in 1460. Finally, Trebizond, on the northern shores of the Black Sea, which had been ruled by a Byzantine dynasty called the Grand Komnenoi, fell to the Turks in 1461. After this date the empire which had defended itself from enemies on all fronts for over 1,000 years finally came to an end.

The Orthodox faithful and their Church did not cease to exist after 1453, however. The Turkish Sultans in Constantinople were in fact tolerant of the Christian beliefs of their Greek subjects during the centuries of Ottoman rule. In accordance with the earliest traditions of Islam, Christians were viewed as 'people of the book', sharing with Muslims and Jews a common Old Testament heritage. Muslims also venerated Jesus Christ as a prophet, although they could not share Orthodox Christians' belief in his status as Messiah and Son of God. Soon after the fall of Constantinople, Mehmed II appointed the scholarly

Greek monk Gennadios patriarch of Constantinople. Gennadios was a determined opponent of the Roman Church and he soon overthrew the agreements which had been reached at the Council of Ferrara/ Florence in 1438–39. The Greek-speaking Orthodox Church thereafter maintained an independent existence from the churches of Western Europe, led by the ecumenical patriarch of Constantinople. Christians under Turkish rule were to a great extent allowed to govern themselves in what became known as the *millet* system. Since the Muslims did not make a formal distinction between religion and politics, their Orthodox Christian subjects were allowed to govern themselves independently in almost every sphere except the military. This system continued in Turkey until 1923 and in Cyprus until the death of Archbishop Makarios III in 1977.

In addition to Greek-speaking Christians in the former territories of the Byzantine empire, Orthodox Churches survived in the Slavic nations which had been converted from the ninth century onwards. Many of these nations, such as Serbia and Bulgaria, and eventually even Russia, had gained autonomy and self-governance for their Churches during the later centuries of Byzantine history. Whereas formerly the patriarch of Constantinople had appointed bishops and directed their church affairs, now these independent Churches possessed their own patriarchs or 'autocephalous' archbishops. Orthodox Christianity became closely entwined with a sense of national identity in some of these countries, especially as they began to win independence from the Turks in the course of the nineteenth century. None of these individual Churches ever lost the sense that their roots and traditions were based in the history of the Byzantine empire, however; as we have seen, their art, religious literature and monastic spirituality all reveal strong links with this medieval heritage.

All of these independent Orthodox Churches survive to the present day, now incorporating over 100 million adherents, not including the 27 million or so non-Chalcedonian Christians who make up the so-called 'Oriental' Orthodox Churches. Eastern Orthodox Christians are based mainly in Constantinople and Greece, as well as in the Slavic-speaking Churches of Eastern Europe including Russia, Bulgaria, Romania, the former Yugoslavia, including especially Serbia, and parts of the Ukraine. One important feature in the survival of the Orthodox Churches is their conservatism, which has led to the preservation of ancient liturgical services, doctrine and monastic spirituality. In contrast to the West's radical revisions of Christian worship, the Orthodox Churches have preserved and continue to use the liturgical texts which were mostly compiled for the universal Church in the fourth and fifth centuries. Many Christians today, including those from Protestant backgrounds, value the contribution which the Orthodox Church has made in preserving this early Christian tradition.

It is impossible in an account of this size to describe fully the development of Byzantine art, or indeed any other aspect of this society's beliefs, liturgical worship and institutional Church in adequate detail. It is hoped nevertheless that readers will have gained a broad understanding of these various legacies of the Byzantine Orthodox Church and that they will wish to continue reading in the field. As in the case of the medieval West, the best sources are those created by the people who actually lived through these centuries. Not only literary texts, but also artistic monuments tell us as much as we will ever know about how Byzantine Christians viewed the world, what they believed and how they expressed these ideas.

CHRONOLOGY

306–37 Constantine I, 'the Great' (sole ruler from 324).

312 Constantine's vision and subsequent victory at the Milvian Bridge, Italy.

325 Council of Nicea, first ecumenical (universal) Church council. This council formally rejected the teachings of Arius and stated that the Son is *homoousios* (of one essence) with the Father.

330 Inauguration of Constantinople as the 'New Rome'.

337 Baptism and death of Constantine I.

381 Second ecumenical council: the Council of Constantinople. This council again rejected Arianism as a heresy and affirmed the divinity of the Holy Spirit. It also established Constantinople as the second most important episcopal see after Rome.

431 Third ecumenical council: the Council of Ephesus, at which the title *Theotokos* ('God-bearer') for the Virgin Mary was approved.

450–51 Fourth ecumenical council: the Council of Chalcedon. This council affirmed 'two natures' in Christ, a doctrine which some bishops, especially in the Eastern patriarchates, felt that they could not accept. Major schisms

eventually developed as a result of the definitions formulated at the Council of Chalcedon.

527–65 Reign of the Byzantine emperor Justinian.

537 Dedication of the new Church of the Holy Wisdom (Hagia Sophia) in Constantinople.

553 Fifth ecumenical council held in Constantinople. Attempts were made to reconcile the Monophysite Churches.

614 The Persians occupied Syria, Palestine and Egypt (formerly Roman territories). The relic of the true cross was taken to Ctesiphon, the Persian capital.

622 Muhammad left Mecca for Medina. (Muslims call this journey the Hijra.)

622–27 Campaigns of the Byzantine emperor Herakleios against the Persians.

626 Failure of the combined siege of Constantinople by the Persians and the Avars. The Byzantines viewed this victory as divinely ordained, especially due to the help of Mary, the Mother of God.

626–28 Byzantine defeat of the Persians.

630 The relic of the true cross was restored to Jerusalem amid great rejoicing.

634–46 The Muslims conquered Syria, Palestine, Mesopotamia and Egypt.

638 The *Ekthesis*, a statement published by the emperor Herakleios and his ecumenical patriarch, Sergios, which attempted to reconcile Monophysites and Chalcedonians.

655 Pope Martin I and the Byzantine theologian Maximos the Confessor were found guilty of treason for opposing the imperial 'Monothelite' ('one will' in Christ) doctrine. Both were exiled and died shortly afterwards.

680–81 Sixth ecumenical council held at Constantinople. The doctrine of Monothelitism was officially rejected.

717–18 The Muslims besieged Constantinople. Leo III, formerly a general, seized power.

730 The patriarch Germanos resigned. This was due to the introduction of the imperial policy against holy icons, called 'Iconoclasm'.

741–75 Reign of the iconoclast emperor Constantine V. More active persecution of the defenders of icons (called iconophiles) began. Monks and monasteries especially were targeted.

754 The iconoclast Council of Hiereia, at which the policy against images was formally stated.

787 The seventh ecumenical council, held at Nicea, ended the iconoclast policy. The use and veneration of icons in Orthodox Christian worship was affirmed.

800 Papal coronation of the Frankish king Charlemagne, as Roman emperor in the West, took place in St Peter's Basilica, Rome. The Byzantines refused to recognize his claim.

811–13 Bulgarian victories over the Byzantines in the Balkans. The emperor Nikephoros was defeated and killed in battle.

815 Reintroduction of iconoclast policy under the emperor Leo V.

843 The Triumph of Orthodoxy. Iconoclasm was overturned for the second time; holy icons were reintroduced into the Church. The *Synodikon*, a document expressing the doctrines of Orthodox Christianity, was formally published.

860 Rus' (Viking) attack on Constantinople.

863 The Byzantine missionaries Cyril and Methodios set out to convert Moravia to Orthodox Christianity. They took copies of the Gospels and other religious texts which they had translated into the Slavonic language.

864 or 865 Baptism of Boris, khan of Bulgaria.

Early 900s Expansion of the Bulgars under Tsar Symeon.

922 Peace with the Bulgars.

954 or 955 Baptism of the Kievan (Rus') princess Olga.

963 onwards Major Byzantine campaigns in the East.

Reconquest of territory from the Arabs.

988 Baptism of the Rus' ruler Vladimir into Orthodox Christianity. He brought the new religion to the whole of the Rus' nation.

990–1019 Basil II ('the Bulgar slayer') overcame the Bulgar threat. Bulgaria was reincorporated into the Byzantine empire, with the Danube as the new frontier in the North.

1015 Death of the Rus' princes Boris and Gleb at the hands of their brother, Svyatopolk. They were revered in the Russian Church henceforth as 'passion-bearers' for their nonviolent response to his aggression.

1054 Official schism between the Western Church (led by the Roman papacy) and the Eastern Churches (under the patriarchates of Constantinople, Alexandria, Antioch and Jerusulem).

1071 The beginning of Seljuk Turkish domination of Central Anatolia. The Normans moved into southern Italy.

1081–85 Norman invasion of Western Balkan provinces.

1095 Beginning of the First Crusade.

1098–99 Jerusalem was captured; Latin principalities and a kingdom of Jerusalem were established in Palestine and Syria.

1146–48 Second Crusade.

1186 Rebellion in Bulgaria. After the defeat of Byzantine troops,

a second Bulgarian empire was established.

1187 The end of the Third Crusade, as Jerusalem was retaken by the Arab leader Saladin.

1203–1204 Fourth Crusade, ending in the sack of Constantinople.

1204–61 A Latin empire ruled over much of the former Byzantine territories. Independent Greek states survived, however, in Nicea, Epiros and Trebizond.

1261 Constantinople was recaptured from the Latins. The emperor Michael VIII became emperor, but was opposed by supporters of a rival emperor. Schism within the Church resulted from this, only to be healed by the death of the ex-patriarch, Arsenios.

1274 Second Council of Lyons, at which a union of the Eastern and Western Churches was agreed. However, this union was not accepted by most Byzantine Orthodox Christians.

1280–1337 The Ottoman Turks were taking the remaining Byzantine territories in Asia Minor.

1341 Synod in Constantinople discussed the complaints of the traditionalist monk Barlaam of Calabria against the Hesychast teachings of St Gregory Palamas. Palamas's doctrine was upheld.

1331–55 Height of the Serbian empire under its ruler, Stefan Dušan.

1347 The plague ('Black Death') reached Constantinople. A local council reaffirmed the decisions agreed at the Synod of 1341.

1365 Ottoman Turks took Adrianople, which became their capital city.

1389 Battle of Kosovo. The end of the Serbian empire and advance into the Balkans by the Ottoman Turks.

1393 End of the Bulgarian empire, as the Turks moved further into the northern Balkans.

1397–1402 Bayezit I, the Ottoman sultan, besieged Constantinople. He was forced to withdraw, however, when the Turks were defeated by the Turkic leader, Timur (Tamerlane), at the Battle of Ankara (1402).

1430 Thessaloniki was taken by the Ottoman Turks.

1438–39 Council of Ferrara/ Florence, attended by the Byzantine emperor John VIII, agreed union between the Eastern and Western Churches once again, in return for military aid against the Turks.

1444 Hungarian and Western crusaders, led by Vladislav of Hungary and Poland, were defeated at the Battle of Varna.

1451 Mehmet II became Sultan of the Ottoman Turks.

1453 Constantinople was conquered by the Ottomans under Mehmet II. The last Byzantine emperor, Constantine XI, died in the battle. The Greek Orthodox Church was allowed to continue under Ottoman rule, with a new patriarch, Gennadios II, appointed.

PART 2

FAITH
IN THE MEDIEVAL WORLD

INTRODUCTION

People today who are used to talk of globalism will find a 'globalism' in the smaller world of medieval Europe, too. The period known as the Middle Ages stretched for 1,000 years, from the end of the ancient world in the fourth and fifth centuries AD to the Reformation and Renaissance of the sixteenth century. In terms of people's values, priorities and interests, it is surprising how much stayed the same in all that time. The explanation lies in the culturally 'unifying' effect of the Christian faith.

Christianity was not a force for political unity. There has rarely been a period in Western Europe with so much war in it. In Northern Europe, the whole 'upper class' was dedicated to the profession of soldiery, with the exception of those who were church leaders. But Christianity did create a unity of fundamental ideas about the world, and of assumptions about its purpose. The result was a cultural stability remarkable in its powers to last throughout 1,000 years of social, economic and political change. The shared medieval culture went far beyond the obviously 'religious' aspects of Christianity, but it is impossible to understand that culture without first understanding something of the priorities Christianity imposed upon it.

Christians could go into a church anywhere in medieval Western Europe and find the same symbols, 'rites', or forms of worship, and the same religious language, Latin. Although the Western Church eventually stretched from the Atlantic Ocean to the borders of Greece, and from Scandinavia to the border with Islam in the south, almost everyone 'belonged' to this community and was consciously a part of it. In the Eastern half of the Roman empire, Christians worshipped in Greek, and the style of their church life was subtly different from that of worshippers in the Western half. However, the basics were the same, together with most of the symbolism in Christian art. The Christian faith of East and West was, in almost every point, identical.

This account is mainly about the medieval West, because Part 1 of this book, 'Faith in the Byzantine World', looks at faith in the East. But the Church – divided though it was by the Schism of 1054 into 'East' and 'West' – was a single community of faith throughout the medieval millennium, and some hints of the flavour of that Eastern world have a place here, too.

There were few people of other faiths in any part of Europe, except in southern Spain. Communities of Jews were to be met in the towns of Europe. In southern Spain, for some centuries, Islam held political control by conquest, and there Christians were in the position of 'subject people'. This is reflected in the surviving medieval architecture of Spain, where the great cathedrals tend to be of much later date than those in the north of Europe.

CHAPTER 12

THE WORLD THROUGH MEDIEVAL EYES

In 'Christian Europe' in the Middle Ages, the 'social' expectation was that people would regard themselves as Christians. It was almost unheard of for anyone to say that he or she did not believe in God at all, and the levels of 'popular' piety were high, even if they were sometimes little more than superstition. It is important not to lose sight of that contrast between an 'educated' understanding of the faith and a more diffuse 'religiousness' in the population.

> 'It had been my mother's custom to take cakes and bread and wine to the shrines of the saints on the saint's day of each. [Now] she learned to bring to the shrines of the martyrs a heart full of prayers which were much purer than any such gift. In this way she was able to give as much as she was able to the poor.'
>
> **Augustine, Confessions, VI.2**

Many of the ideas and principles which make up the Christian 'faith' are abstract and sophisticated. Most of the population was illiterate. There is evidence that it clung to its old 'gods', the little pagan deities who were local and familiar, and small enough to seem like family friends, by transferring loyalty to saints. Undoubtedly, there was sometimes confusion in the popular mind, and a tendency to revere these saints as though they were deities. Nevertheless, there were certain outward signs of a society of *practising* Christians. During the Middle Ages, almost every child was christened in infancy. Almost everyone went to church regularly. Almost everyone was married in church and buried in consecrated ground.

An outlaw religion

The early Christian period is a long story of persecution and exclusion, for the first Christians tended to come from the lower social classes and were not sufficiently powerful or privileged to make their faith socially acceptable. One of the most extraordinary features of the history of Christianity is the way that this 'outlaw' religion became so universally accepted in the medieval West. State approval came only in the fourth century, when the Roman emperor Constantine was 'converted' and declared himself a Christian.

Conversion in the Roman empire

We shall be looking at the 'political' consequences in chapter 17. The first thing to consider is how far the 'conversion' of the Roman empire meant that everyone had a clear understanding of the Christian faith or held it with real inner enthusiasm.

'Conversion' contains the idea of a 'turning'. This eventually came to be the word used when someone entered a monastery as an adult, because that meant a 'turning' (*conversio*) from the world to a fuller commitment to the living of a Christian life. But it was understood from the very beginning that there was another, more profound sense to conversion. Someone who had previously not believed in the God of the Christians at all, or who had held only a half-hearted belief, could suddenly become ardent in his or her convictions. The apostle Paul was first known as Saul, and he was famous for the zeal with which he persecuted the earliest Christians,

> 'Saul kept up his violent threats of murder against the followers of the Lord . . . As Saul was coming near the city of Damascus, suddenly a light from the sky flashed round him. He fell to the ground and heard a voice saying to him, "Saul, Saul! Why do you persecute me?" "Who are you, Lord?" he asked. "I am Jesus, whom you persecute," the voice said. "But get up and go into the city, where you will be told what you must do."'
>
> Acts 9:1–6

whom he saw as a threat to the Jewish religion at a time when they were growing in numbers. The New Testament (Acts 9) describes how he had a vision on the road to Damascus and was temporarily struck blind. It changed his life. It changed his attitudes. He became equally zealous to spread his new faith.

In many ways, Paul's experience was typical of that of other famous individuals who have been 'converted'. For a long time Paul resisted a belief which was forcing itself upon him – in his case, by persecuting those who held it. The change of mind (*metanoia*), when it came, was sudden and decisive. It was, says the story in Acts, as though 'scales fell from Saul's eyes'. He never looked back.

The impact of St Augustine's conversion

The conversion of St Augustine was immensely important to the future of the Christian faith in the West. Augustine was a great writer. He was prolific. For 40 years as Bishop of Hippo in north Africa, he was to pour out books, sermons and letters. In these, he explored for the first time, for Latin speakers and citizens of Western Europe, a number of key questions of the Christian faith.

> 'My inner self was a house divided against itself.'
> **Augustine, *Confessions*, VIII.8**

For example, he was the first to ask what it could mean to say that every human being since Adam and Eve is a sinner. His explanation of 'original sin' was based on his observation of small children. He describes in his *Confessions* how two infants behave like rivals at the breast, each jealous of the other's getting his share of the milk.

He also tells the story of an episode in his own childhood when he and a gang of other small boys stole pears from a tree, not because they were nice to eat (for they were rather small and bitter), but for the sheer devilment of the stealing.

> 'I have myself seen jealousy in a baby.'
> **Augustine, *Confessions*, I.8**

This kind of thing was proof enough for Augustine of an inherent tendency to do wrong, gratuitous wrong, habitual wrong, in every human from the moment of birth. The vividness of his account captured the Western imagination, and his picture of human sinfulness, which he expanded in a series of writings, became the accepted one, even though there were many who disagreed with him in his own day. Pelagius, for example, was a fashionable society preacher who led Roman families to believe that being good was simply a matter of trying hard. Augustine's more gloomy view was that it was beyond human power to overcome sin, and that God's help was essential. There emerged a doctrine of the need for 'divine grace', the 'free gift of God', if anyone was to overcome sin and become fit for heaven. We shall see how important this was to be in the centuries which followed.

> 'In an instant as I came to the end of the sentence, it was as though the light of confidence flooded into my heart and all the darkness of doubt was dispelled.'
> **Augustine, *Confessions*, VIII.8**

It is important, too, that Augustine was doing this in Latin. Early Christian civilization was predominantly Greek, and the Greek

The conversion of St Augustine

Augustine of Hippo (354–430) lived at a time when Christianity had become the official religion of Roman society, but there were still many alternatives open to an enquiring young man. Augustine's mother was a Christian, but his father was a pagan – and the young Augustine resisted his mother's attempts to bring him up in her faith. He found parts of the Bible crude in their contents and style. Christianity seemed an unsophisticated choice, and unsuitable for a budding professor of rhetoric.

Augustine spent his youth trying out the other religious options of his day: philosophy, magic and, especially, the system of the 'dualist' Manichees. The Manichees seemed to him to hold out a solution to the question of how the world began. They believed that there was both a good god and an evil god, who were at war throughout eternity for control of the universe. Matter, and the material world, was the creation of the evil god and the good god was responsible only for what was spiritual. Augustine remained an adherent of this sect for nearly ten years.

It was not until he had various disillusioning experiences, which undermined his respect for the Manichees, that Augustine grew restless. He left his native north Africa in search of career advancement, in Italy. He was impressed when he heard Bishop Ambrose of Milan preach.

Now he found himself 'pursued' by a Christian faith which eventually captured him in Milan. He had with him the New Testament book of Romans and he heard a child's voice singing in the garden next door, 'Take and read'. So he looked at the book and read the first passage his eye lighted on, and suddenly he found that the priorities of his life had shifted and he had become a Christian.

language was naturally better fitted than the Latin (which is much more 'concrete') for the exploration of ideas of a theoretical and 'spiritual' sort. Augustine stretched and enlarged the capacities of Latin as a theological language. His creation of a solid 'Latin tradition', covering much of the scope of Christian belief, was crucial at a time when the knowledge of Greek was beginning to die away in the West. Since the Roman empire had extended through Greek-speaking territories, educated Romans had been expected to speak Greek, too. Now that the empire was under pressure from barbarian invaders, and was beginning to disintegrate, that expectation was becoming less realistic. Augustine himself complained that he could never really master Greek. So one of the effects of his conversion, and the life and work which followed, was to make it possible for a strong and developed Western tradition of the faith to become established.

Conversion by mission

Once we move beyond the period of the late Roman empire, the question of what 'conversion' means begins to look different. It must be assumed that some still experienced these profound personal shifts of commitment and priority, but we do not hear from them for a few centuries.

The collapse of the old Roman political and social structures meant that Europe became fragmented. It was 'run' by a variety of tribes, each making its own compromise with the existing structures or sweeping them aside, as it chose. Some of the invaders were 'Arians', that is, Christian heretics who found it difficult to accept the divinity of Christ and his full equality as the Son of God with the other persons of the Trinity. That meant that the Christian faith was no longer a 'unity' in Europe for a time. Other invaders were not Christians at all, so the task at this time became one of the fresh conversion of territories which had been officially 'Christian' since the fourth century.

'Conversion by mission' is exemplified in the reconversion of the British Isles, where there is archaeological evidence that there had been Christians in Roman times. The Celtic Christians who persisted in Ireland favoured a 'charismatic' missionary method. They trusted themselves to frail boats and let the sea carry them where the Holy Spirit intended them to go. They then set about converting whoever they found when they landed. This resulted in conversion of the north of England to a Celtic Christianity.

St Columba landed in 563 on the island of Iona in the Hebrides. There, he founded a monastery, which was to be a powerhouse of Celtic influence. Missionaries went out from the monastery to Scotland and the north of England. It became a centre of learning and a place of pilgrimage.

Meanwhile, at the end of the sixth century, Pope Gregory I (Gregory the Great) is said to have seen fair Anglo-Saxons for sale as slaves in a Roman market. The story was that he cried, 'Not Angles but Angels', and was moved to send a mission to convert the people of their land to the Christian faith. His chosen missionary was Augustine of Canterbury (not a writer like his namesake). In 597, Augustine went to England and preached to the king of Kent, Ethelbert. Ethelbert was receptive, for his wife had been a Christian before she married.

Conversions of this sort may make a kingdom or state nominally Christian, but the accounts which survive of them are not as personal as those of the apostle Paul or Augustine of Hippo. They tell us very little about the degree to which a real understanding of, and commitment to, the faith penetrated into the minds and hearts of the people.

This kind of missionary activity continued, moving east across the European subcontinent during several of the early medieval centuries, until gradually the whole of Europe was brought into the 'fold'. Once Christianity was established and accepted as the 'official religion' once more, there was little by way of conscious objection. Hardly anyone would say, if asked, that he or she was an agnostic or atheist. There was, however, a good deal of argument about points of belief and practice, so there was no shortage of dissidence, as we shall see.

One example survives from the late eleventh century of an author who shows that there was still some understanding of the deeper meaning of 'conversion'. Guibert of Nogent wrote an autobiography, in itself a very unusual thing to do in the Middle Ages. In this, *On my Life*, he describes how when he was young his mother had found him a schoolmaster (again, an unusual privilege) and he had learned to love reading and writing poetry and reading under the bedclothes when he was supposed to be asleep. In due course, his mother followed a fashion of the nobility of that generation, and 'retired' to monastic life in maturity. This was a significant change from the many centuries in which the norm was for parents to place a small child in a monastery. It meant that the recruits to the religious life were making a real choice, and expressing a deepened faith. Guibert

'In this year Pope Gregory sent Augustine to Britain with very many monks who preached God's word to the English nation.'

Anglo-Saxon Chronicle, ninth century

realizes this, and he describes his own 'conversion', when he decided that he, too, would forsake these seductive literary pleasures and become a monk. So, for Guibert, there was a conscious choice between a lukewarm and an impassioned Christianity.

Conversion of the Jews

One more aspect of medieval 'conversion' needs a glance before we move on. There survive several 'dialogues' and other accounts of attempts to convert the Jews. Jews living in medieval Christian communities evidently fell into conversation with their neighbours, and the result was vigorous debate. Both sides were aware that they worshipped the same God and shared some of the same scriptures. The sticking-point was the Christians' insistence that Jesus was the Son of God. The Jews said that this made the Christians polytheists. There are no Christian records of Christians being converted to Judaism by these arguments, but there is a frank autobiographical account by a Jew called Hermannus of his conversion to Christianity.

The scheme of things: the cosmos

Faith in the West in the Middle Ages looked, just as it did in the Greek-speaking half of the old Roman empire, to an eternity beyond this life. Ideas of heaven were intensely real, and a comfort to those whose lot on earth was lowly or unpleasant. This 'heavenly mindedness' was an important factor in the comparative lack of interest in improving social conditions, which runs as an unbroken thread through most of the Middle Ages. Christianity taught ordinary people that acceptance and obedience to authority were virtues which would get them to heaven, where a far better life awaited them. The richer and more powerful learned that their duty was to use their wealth to help widows and orphans, and the rest of the poor and needy. The only groups of believers with any sustained interest in social reform were the dissidents, such as the Waldensians and the Lollards whom we shall meet later. Their concern was much more to challenge the 'establishment' than to replace it with a more egalitarian society.

The Bible gives one description of the kind of 'place' in which God intends his human creation to dwell. This is the Garden of Eden at the beginning of the book of Genesis. Adam and Eve were created to live in the 'garden' with the rest of creation. This was, above all, an orderly place, in which the first human beings were free to do anything which did not involve disobedience to the will of God, and in which there were no discomforts such as mosquitoes and thistles. (Those apparently came later, after the 'fall', when Adam and Eve sinned by acting against the divine will [Genesis 3:14–24]).

Adam and Eve were driven out of this garden after their first and decisive act of sin. This set in train in the Christian tradition a theme of exile and wandering, in which Christians could envisage themselves as living their lives in a search for the garden and in an attempt to deserve to be allowed to return to it.

This was also the Jewish legacy, of course, since the Jews also accepted Genesis as scripture. But the Jews had a different concept of the implications of the sin of Adam and Eve from that which developed in Christianity. For Christians, this was so central that it explained why God had sent his Son to be born as a man and to die on the cross. The Jewish tradition preferred to look forward to the coming of a messiah who would rule a better world, in which there would be peace and plenty, no war, and in which everyone would be righteous and law-abiding.

Three kinds of heaven

Anselm of Canterbury made an unusual contribution to the medieval collection of images of heaven in the last chapters of his *Proslogion*, written late in the eleventh century. This book contains his famous argument for the existence of God, and the theme of the end of a Christian's journey came in naturally at the close. Anselm reassured his readers that they would be able to go on enjoying in eternity every innocent pleasure of the present life. For example, if they enjoyed running in this life, they would be able to run faster than ever in heaven. This was a useful clarification of the role of the body in the life to come. It was the Christian belief that human beings were not just spiritual beings, but souls and bodies united, and that there will be a resurrection of the body in some form, so that they could spend eternity as 'whole people'.

The other useful lesson of Anselm's description of heaven in *Proslogion* was that heaven would be fun. It answered neatly the objection that heaven sounded pleasant, but dull. Anselm was confident that heaven was not merely to be a place of rest, but a place of strong enjoyment. This was his own idea, but it also echoed the more earthly picture, by the Roman author Pindar, of a heaven in which there would be pleasant surroundings, games, music and good company – a notion also found in the Qur'an and attractive to Muslims. There was also the 'heavenly Jerusalem', more easily 'pictured' by ordinary people, and sometimes apparently confused with the Jerusalem on earth to which pilgrims could actually travel.

Both these pictures of heaven were fairly easy for people to understand and to be attracted to. But the underlying idea was sterner, more cerebral, and also more profoundly spiritual. Ideas of what 'the blessed life' would consist of were also derived, in part, from ancient philosophy. The theme of the pursuit of happiness had encouraged a good deal of discussion about what true happiness was. Augustine of Hippo wrote one of his first books on this subject, *On the Blessed Life*, soon after his conversion, when he had retired with a few friends to spend time at Cassiciacum on Lake Como in northern Italy, thinking through the ways in which his new faith required him to revise his old ideas.

Augustine's was a rather intellectual heaven, whose pleasures would consist in conversation with one's companions about spiritual things, the contemplation of truth, beauty and goodness and, above all, the joy of gazing into the mind of God and meeting him personally in an exchange of mutual understanding which would raise the creature as high as it was capable of reaching, in an eternal rapture. A few Christians in the Middle Ages claimed to have had a foretaste of that rapture in brief moments of mystical experience, when they felt as though they had been snatched out of their bodies and carried beyond this life.

In Boethius's *Consolation of Philosophy*, written in the fifth century, Boethius wrote as a person facing the final crisis of his life. He was under house arrest, and condemned to death by his political enemies. As he awaited his end, he wrote a fictional conversation with Philosophy, who is personified as though she were a goddess. This is the more striking since there is good evidence that he was a Christian (he wrote several short books on Christian themes). A good deal of the conversation is about fate, fortune and the role of providence. It was a very interesting question to philosophers and Christians alike whether there was a power in the universe in control of the ultimate outcome of events. Christians were confident that their God was omnipotent and wholly good, and would bring all things to their perfect fruition and conclusion in the end.

Thinking about these things made Boethius concentrate on his prospects of eternal life. Boethius describes eternity as 'the complete possession of a life which does not end'. This, he explains, is quite different from life in time. In eternity, we do not have yesterday and tomorrow before us at the same time as today. God is not more 'ancient' than eternity in the sense that he comes before it in time; that is impossible, since there is no time in eternity. He is somehow 'prior' to eternity in the 'simplicity' of his nature. In other words, all created things which come from God are multiple and fallible. He alone is single and unchanging.

The characteristic medieval development of this rather 'philosophical' line of thought about eternal life was to shift the emphasis towards the Christian's relationship with God himself. This is to be found in the writings of such twelfth-century monks as William of St Thierry. William's God is intensely personal, but he also has these abstract and philosophical attributes. The monk, who gives up his whole life to prayer and to a special dedication to God, is portrayed as already in heaven, for that is what he will be doing for eternity. His cell is a microcosm of heaven itself. He may have a foretaste of that heavenly experience in moments of rapture, when he seems to be snatched out of his body and carried off to heaven to be, for an instant, in the intensity of the direct presence of God.

All these ideas of heaven were linked with the concept of a 'golden age', which pagan thinkers of the classical period had also shared. For the Christian, the golden age was to be the heaven of being back in the state in which God created Adam and Eve to enjoy, and eternally enjoying the loving presence of God and the companionship of other blessed beings.

Hell

Coupled with this 'heavenly mindedness' was a general assumption that the universe was arranged hierarchically by the God who created it. With heaven went a hell. In the New Testament, the story of Lazarus the beggar tells that when he dies he is carried to heaven by the angels. He is depicted as sitting 'beside Abraham at the feast in heaven' (Luke 16:19–31), from where both gaze at the rich man who is suffering in hell. The rich man is told that he has had his time of prosperity. Now it is Lazarus' turn. And, moreover, there is no passing between heaven and hell. The rich man is in hell, without hope, for eternity.

This story encapsulates the pervasive medieval attitude that the heavenly future was more important than improving social conditions (even if the rich man should have helped Lazarus). But it also creates a strong image of heaven and hell as places, one above the other, in a cosmic hierarchy. Both aspects are present in Augustine of Hippo's book, *The City of God*, towards the end of which he reflects on the pleasure that those in heaven will take in the contemplation of the sufferings of those in hell, for they will reflect on the extraordinary mercy of God in rescuing them from the fate which they also deserved as sinners.

Angels

In the Middle Ages, it was clearly understood that the angels were a separate creation of purely spiritual rational beings. Their creation is not mentioned anywhere in the Bible, and they were usually 'inserted' in the story in Genesis at the point at which the light was separated from darkness. Angels and archangels appear in several places in the Bible, and in chapter 6 of the book of Isaiah there is a description of the seraphim. These have six wings, two of which they use to cover their faces, two of which they use to cover their bodies and two of which they use to fly.

There was a hierarchy of nine 'orders' of angels, too, derived from the writings of the fifth-century Dionysius the Areopagite. The Greek word *angelos* means 'messenger'. Ordinary angels were at the bottom of the hierarchy – mere messengers to mortals. Archangels were above them, charged with delivering more important messages. The Archangel

Dante's heaven and hell

The most extensive medieval geography and sociology of heaven and hell is to be found in the thirteenth-century poet Dante's *Divine Comedy*. This narrative poem describes Dante's own journey through the cosmos, in a vision. It gives a clear hierarchical and moral 'structure' to the universe.

Dante's guide through hell is the Roman poet Virgil. The companions move onwards, travelling through different levels of hell until they reach a 'place' – an 'invention' of the twelfth century – called 'purgatory'. 'Place' should not have been used literally, since heaven and hell were believed in the Middle Ages to be 'in eternity' and, therefore, outside the world of space and time. But, in the case of purgatory, it was appropriate because the purpose of purgatory was to provide a waiting-room for heaven, in which time still existed. Most people died with sins on their souls. Even if they had confessed their sins and been forgiven by a priest, they had still not completed the penances imposed by the Church.

These penances were a token of repentance, and it was held very firmly in the Middle Ages that God had entrusted the Church with the authority to impose penances, and that God expected them to be discharged. A period in purgatory was seen as a method of discharging penances after death, so that the dead person became 'holy' and fit for heaven.

The last and highest place Dante comes to is heaven itself. Here, Virgil cannot accompany him as his guide, because he is not a Christian. Dante meets a new guide, Beatrice. Her name means 'blessed' and she is, therefore, a very suitable person to lead him into the realms where she herself dwells. But even Beatrice cannot take Dante to the highest levels of heaven. The levels of heaven empty out into metaphysics, a realm which is truly 'super'-natural.

Gabriel, for example, brought the news to the Virgin Mary that she was to be the mother of the Son of God, and Michael the Archangel is quoted in verse 9 of the book of Jude. At the top of the hierarchy were the seraphim, who spent eternity before the throne of God in adoring contemplation, and just below them were the cherubim. (Medieval cherubim were not simply the chubby babies of Renaissance art, but creatures of high spiritual dignity.) Between these highest and lowest ranks came five other ranks of angels: powers, dominions, thrones, virtues and principalities.

In some twelfth-century writings there is an attempt to equate these nine orders of angels with a hierarchy of humans. The idea was that, in eternity, human monks and nuns, who had given their lives to contemplation, could expect to be 'placed' in heaven alongside the contemplative angels. Kings could expect to find themselves with the thrones or principalities, and so on.

The fall of the angels

The relationship of people and angels as God's rational creatures was an idea which derived from the need to answer the puzzle of what happened to God's plan when some of the angels 'fell'. Their fall was not like the fall of Adam and Eve and, like the creation of the angels, it is not described in the Bible. It was a rationalization of a number of elements which required explanation. God could not be the author of evil, yet evil was obviously a very powerful force. We shall come later to the cluster of heresies which tried to struggle with this problem. But it was not difficult to point to the agent of evil in the world if it was suggested that one of the highest of the angels had turned against God and sought power for himself. The 'turning', said Anselm of Canterbury, consisted in wanting something which it was good to want (to be like God), but wanting it to a degree which was not appropriate for a mere creature. So there developed an understanding that Lucifer, or Satan, was a fallen angel, with a mission to seduce other spiritual beings and to deprive God of his people. One of the features of evil was that it twisted people and made them behave in irrational and destructive ways.

The fall of Satan and his followers could not be allowed to frustrate God's plan for the universe, for God is omnipotent. God intended there to be a heaven with a certain number of blessed spirits in it, so ran the medieval expectation. This gave a reason for the creation of human beings, to fill the gaps, and it also explained why Satan was so keen to frustrate this rescue attempt by seducing Adam and Eve. There resulted from this line of thought a picture of heaven in which the blessed were like living stones (1 Peter 2:5), forming the very fabric of the 'temple' of heaven, alongside the good angels.

The medieval hierarchy of the rest of creation ran downwards from the spiritual to the inanimate. Angels are pure spirit and capable of reasoning. Human beings also have rational minds, but their souls inhabit bodies. Animals are not rational, but they live and move. The vegetable creation lives, but it does not move. Stones and rocks simply exist. These facts about the world seemed so solid to medieval people that the reality and divine purpose of hierarchical arrangements in general seem to have been little questioned.

CHAPTER 13

WHAT DID MEDIEVAL CHRISTIANS BELIEVE?

When Christ died, Christianity faced the test which always arises when a great religious leader is no longer present in person. It had to become a system of belief and acquire some organizational structure, or it could not survive.

Medieval Christians got the 'content' of their faith from two main sources: the Bible, and that process of synthesis of a more or less systematic set of beliefs which took place in the Church in the early Christian centuries. This was a complex process. It involved debates, out of which some people emerged labelled as dissidents and heretics. It involved holding councils to take formal decisions about what was considered 'orthodox' and what was not, and about the influence of the underlying theology of the sequence of events in acts of worship (liturgy). It involved a great deal of subtle borrowing and adjustment, taking in certain elements from contemporary philosophy and from Judaism.

The Christian synthesis

Christianity was solidly resistant to 'syncretism' in the early Christian centuries. This meant that it would not compromise with the numerous polytheistic and 'philosophical' religions around it. It suffered persecution as a consequence. Resisting the intellectual trends of the day, however, was another matter, for these were not rival religions, but part of the cultural 'furniture' of the lives of educated people. For many generations, intellectuals 'doing philosophy' had taken 'philosophy' to include much of the area of discourse in which Christians were interested.

First, they saw philosophy as 'moral' philosophy. They tried to use their study of philosophical ideas as a basis for living a good life. Out of this emphasis, which was particularly influenced by the Stoics, came a tendency to value the preservation of tranquillity and moderation (or the avoidance of excess), and self-denial. These were especially Greek contributions. A conscientious attention to public service was expected by the Romans, and Cicero wrote in that vein.

Secondly, many topics with which the early Christians struggled were familiar ground in the philosophical debates of ancient Greece and Rome. This was the group of issues gathered together by Boethius in his 'theological treatises' in the sixth century, and they were most strongly influenced by Plato and his successors. They comprised, first, ideas about the nature and attributes of God: his transcendence, so high that he was perhaps to be thought of as beyond even 'being'; his beauty, truth, justice, mercy, so great that these were not really mere 'attributes' at all – they were of God's very substance.

Next came ideas about the triune nature of God – the Christian Trinity of Father, Son and Holy Spirit. There had been a good deal of discussion among 'Platonists' in the ancient world about the way in which a supreme being so high that he rose even above being itself could have any communication with the world we live in. It was suggested that there was a *logos*, or rational principle, somehow 'speaking' God's 'ideas'; and a 'soul of the world', which put them into action in the physical environment of the created world. The essential characteristic of this trio was that it was hierarchical. It formed a ladder leading down from God to the world. The *anima mundi*, or world-soul, was thought by some to be, itself, part of the world.

One of the most important tasks of early Christianity was to insist that the Father, Son and Holy Spirit, which bore some obvious resemblance to this triad of the philosophers, formed in fact a 'Trinity' of persons who were equal, co-eternal and divine. There was never a 'time' when the Father was not the Father of the Son. Although, in human relationships, sons are younger than fathers and junior to them, that is not the way it is with God. The Son is of the same substance with the Father, and in no way his inferior. When the Son was born as the man Jesus, he was already, eternally, the Son of the Father.

This is not at all easy to grasp, and throughout the early centuries and the Middle Ages attempts were made to find 'images' to help. St Patrick's famous comparison with the shamrock is one. He is said to have held up the three little leaves joined in one leaf and said that the Trinity was like that. A more abstract idea is to be found in Augustine's words, and adapted by Anselm. This compares God to a stream of water, where the water is all one 'substance', but there is a 'source' or 'spring' where the water begins, a stream and a pool into which the stream empties itself. These are compared to the Father, Son and Holy Spirit.

Third in the group of themes common to Christianity and ancient philosophy was 'creation'. Here the philosophers had contributed the idea of emanation, or overflow, in which God was able to make things by an overflow of his goodness.

This sort of thing had the attraction of being very interesting, and it had obvious relevance to the concerns of Christians. It is possible to see Christians in every century wrestling with their consciences about how much they should 'use' such ideas and read the books which contained them. Jerome, who made the Vulgate translation of the Bible, and who lived at the end of the fourth and the beginning of the fifth centuries, became famous for his admission in one of his letters that he had had a dream in which he was accused of being 'not a Christian but a Ciceronian' (*non Christianus sed Ciceronianus*). Boethius himself wrote a good deal more about philosophy than he did about Christian theology. When he found himself in a condemned cell as a political prisoner under house arrest in the stormy days of the end of the Roman empire, it was to philosophy that he turned in his reflections on the purpose of life and the ways of fate, in his *Consolation of Philosophy*. Medieval authors used the classics and the ancient philosophers where they could get copies of the books, but they generally tried to treat them as a less authoritative form of 'authority' than the Christian 'Fathers', and certainly than the Bible itself.

But there were still periods of 'crisis' about the use that a Christian could properly make of ancient philosophical ideas. For example, in the early universities of the third century, there were fierce disputes about the influence of the scientific works of Aristotle. Long lists of Aristotle's opinions were repeatedly 'banned' (which, of course, had the effect of making them more interesting still to students and scholars).

Jesus: God and man

There was, in addition, a 'body of belief' in the faith of Christians which was not easily identified as part of that set of religious themes already familiar to the philosophers of the ancient world. This concerned the historical events of the birth of Jesus, his life, death and resurrection, and the meaning of these events. The central difficulty in the centuries before our medieval period was to accept that someone who was fully human could also really be God. And yet, unless Jesus was both God and man, the Christian religion made no sense.

To begin with, the problem was that this seemed to demean God. Ancient philosophy had placed a strong emphasis on the idea that the supreme being was so high that he was almost above being itself. To bring him down to the level of contact with the physical world he had made was a distasteful idea. Yet the Christians said that he actually became man in Jesus, being born of a human female, like any other member of the human race. Some suggested that perhaps God, in the person of Christ, merely wore his humanity like a cloak or garment, so that he was only 'dressed up' as a man. Augustine's friend Alypius had that idea. The definition of Christian orthodoxy in the first centuries following Christ's death involved the systematic and determined rebuttal of ideas such as these.

> 'Alypius thought that Christians believed that God was clothed in the flesh . . . He did not think that their teaching was that Christ had a human mind . . . Later on he realized that this was the error of the Apollinarian heretics.'
>
> Augustine, *Confessions*, VII.19

An alternative view was to recognize that Jesus was an exceptional human being and no more. Augustine of Hippo says that, for a time, he himself thought of Christ in this way.

The 'grasping' of the meaning of the faith that Jesus was the Son of God was therefore something that each individual had to achieve for himself. It was not just a matter of the Church making a ruling.

Thinkers of the medieval centuries continued to struggle with this understanding. Anselm of Canterbury wrote the *Cur Deus Homo* (*Why did God Become Man?*) to try to show his generation why, logically, God must truly have become man. He assumes that the universe is like the kind of feudal kingdom with which he is familiar, where the king can be dishonoured by disobedience. He explains that when Adam and Eve disobeyed God they created a situation where honour required that something was done to put that right. For Anselm, this is a matter of the deepest 'order' of the universe. 'Right order' (*rectus ordo*) is a favourite theme of his.

The creeds

'Faith in Christ' began in the lifetime of Jesus, when he attracted the followers who were known first as 'disciples' (pupils), and then as 'apostles' (missionaries), because he sent them out on a mission to teach others. This was faith in a person.

A 'creed' is something different. It is a statement of faith. The word comes from the Latin *credo*, 'I believe', which was the first word of the creed, and which also gave it its name. But it was important that Christians said the creed together in worship, as they still do. It is really '*we* believe' (*credimus*). There was a strong emphasis in the early Church on the 'community of faith'. There was a single 'faith' which everyone held, and which distinguished true Christians from those of other religions and from those Christians who, from time to time, adopted 'erroneous opinions'. The faith of the community of Christians was set out in the creeds in a brief, but official form.

> '*I thought of Christ, my Lord, as no more than a man of extraordinary wisdom, whom none could equal. In particular, I saw his miraculous birth of a virgin mother . . . as an act of the divine providence which looks after us, so that by it he merited his special authority as our Teacher. But I had not even an inkling of the meaning of the mystery of the Word made flesh.'*
>
> **Augustine, *Confessions*, VII.19**

This was important in the late Roman world. The pattern of Roman conquest had always involved a simple 'amalgamation' of whatever religions were found in the conquered territories with the pantheon of Rome's pagan gods. So, in Greece, Zeus, the king of the gods, was identified with Jupiter. Hera was identified with Juno, the queen of the gods, and so on. Such syncretism was not, however, acceptable to Christians or Jews. While the Jews could 'know who they were' relatively easily, through family heritage, the new Christians had to 'define' themselves and discover their identity as a group of believers. They acclaimed their shared faith in Jesus and, in particular, their certainty that he had been resurrected from the dead.

This did not mean that the idea of faith as an individual's personal position, the commitment in trust of each separate person to Jesus, became secondary. There remained a moment of personal decision when a new Christian was baptized and, before that, a long process of study of the faith, which was known as the catechumenate. In the early Church, the catechumens would sit in a separate group in church and leave before the eucharist, so the Christian community was very conscious of them as not yet quite 'members'. But at the end of the fourth century, there was a change of practice, and it became usual in the West to baptize infants as soon as possible after they were born. The reason for this was a strengthening of the doctrine that baptism took away both the guilt and the penalty of original sin. Augustine taught that an infant who died unbaptized would be damned for eternity. So it became extremely urgent to make sure. As a result, this visible 'separateness' of those who did not yet 'belong' disappeared. There was, as a result, perhaps even a strengthening of the sense of community, for the members of a Christian family were also members of the Church from the beginning of their lives.

The balance between 'I believe' and 'we believe' was not a matter of controversy in the Middle Ages. When every child of a Christian family, which meant most of the population, was baptized in early infancy, it was taken for granted that individuals could join in the 'we believe', as well as say their own 'I believe'. That did not mean, of course, that they necessarily all believed it with the same liveliness and commitment. Instruction was patchy and worship was in Latin throughout the Middle Ages, long after Latin was the normal everyday language of ordinary people, so it is hard to be sure how much of their faith people really understood. We shall look at this question of the theological sophistication of the laity later on.

Alongside the idea of faith as a state or condition of the soul, a loving trust in God and a commitment to God, stands the question what exactly it *was* that Christians believed. What was the *content* of this belief? This was set out in the creeds themselves. The two most important versions of the creed in use in the Middle Ages (and still in use today) have quite different origins.

The Apostles' Creed

The 'Apostles' Creed' had the great attraction for medieval users of being thought to be the work of the apostles themselves. In its present form, it is first found in the eighth century, but it is certainly older, with versions in local use from at least the fourth century. It may go back to the first period of the Roman Church. It was known as the *symposium* because of a story, which was in circulation from about the end of the fourth century, that the apostles sat together around a table to make it up, each contributing a clause.

No council of the Church formally approved the Apostles' Creed. It gained its currency from its use and acceptance, and gained its authority from the belief that it was the work of Jesus' own apostles. It was used in the Middle Ages in the baptism service, and was thus important as a statement of the beliefs of the candidate for baptism.

The Nicene Creed

The Nicene Creed was approved by the Council of Nicea in 325, in a period of active controversy. It was amended by the Council of Constantinople in 381. Its main contents are really much older, and probably derive from the baptismal creed of ancient Christian Jerusalem, or something similar. In the late fifth century, the custom seems to have begun of reciting the Nicene Creed after the gospel had been read in the eucharist, or holy communion. Like the Apostles' Creed, it was regularly used in worship and became extremely familiar.

An ecumenical experiment?

A new clause, the *filioque* clause, was added to the Nicene Creed in the West in the eighth century. The line which reads, 'Who proceeds from the Father and the Son' originally read, 'Who proceeds from the Father'. The addition caused great offence in the Eastern half of medieval Christendom, because the Greeks would not allow any change to the original formulation. Their objection seems to have been more to the innovation than to the substance of the addition itself, though both became matters of fierce controversy for many centuries after 1054, when the two halves of Christendom became divided. Anselm of Canterbury was asked by the pope at the Council of Bari in 1098 to explain to the Greeks who were there why the Western view was 'right'. Anselm, Bishop of Havelberg, went to Constantinople in the mid-twelfth century and held 'ecumenical conversations' with Greek Christian leaders there. His *Dialogues*, reporting the results, still survive. They show how far apart the 'mindset' of East and West had now grown, as Anselm of Havelberg wrote his account in Latin for the Western readers who would understand 'Western' assumptions best.

The most significant official attempt to resolve the difference of opinion was the Council of Florence, which was held in a series of Italian cities – Ferrara, Florence and Rome – between 1438 and 1445. The Patriarch of Constantinople attended. Bessarion, Archbishop of Nicea, and Mark of Ephesus were the leading theologians from the East. Bessarion achieved something in tune with twentieth-century ecumenical methodology in his *Dogmatic Discourse*. He tried to show that the East and the West had always really taught the same thing. There was even a provisional agreement on the part of the Greeks at the Council to accept the pope as universal Primate.

The agreement foundered, however, when the Eastern bishops took it home and put it to their synods. The Greek Church 'on the ground' did not recognize the proposals as their own. This is a common phenomenon in ecumenical dialogue. Those involved in trying to reach an agreement gain one another's confidence and recognize all sorts of subtleties as a result of talking hard and cooperatively; those who have not been involved find it difficult to enter into what has happened and to 'own' the result.

There was another important 'structural' reason why the agreement of the Council of Florence did not mend the Schism between the Greek East and the Latin West. In the West, the Bishop of Rome, as pope, was head of the whole structure. However, in the East, each of the ancient patriarchs (of Antioch, Alexandria, Constantinople and Jerusalem) led an 'autocephalous' section of the Church – a section with its own head. Although these sectors agreed in one faith, they were self-determining in many ways. So when they said that they would not accept the outcome of the Council of Florence, this great medieval ecumenical experiment failed. Even today, this division is still not mended.

The development of theology

The problem caused by the *filioque* clause was one of the earliest medieval examples of the way in which a change of wording, or a sudden realization of what familiar words might mean, could throw up a challenge to belief. This could be a quite different matter from the heresy and dissidence we shall be looking at in a later chapter.

Debates about the faith developed in the Middle Ages as new areas of interest were opened up and new aspects of doctrine were fully defined for the first time. This made the Middle Ages an important period, particularly in the development of a doctrine of the sacraments and in the theology of the Church.

The beginning of academic theology is also to be found in the Middle Ages, with the rise of the universities. In the late eleventh century, there was a spurt of enthusiasm for advanced study. Young men began to travel Europe in search of the wandering teachers who would lecture to them not only on grammar (the theory of language), but also on logic (formal reasoning) and rhetoric (methods of putting arguments persuasively). These formed the subjects of the classical *trivium* ('three ways') and, together with what Boethius first called the *quadrivium*, the (less fully studied) mathematical subjects of arithmetic, geometry, music and astronomy, they made up the 'seven liberal arts'. They had been studied in a relatively elementary way since the fall of the Roman empire, but never before had more advanced study been applied systematically to the study of Christian beliefs, as now began to happen.

As an example, in logic, one of the Aristotelian textbooks was *The Categories*. In it, Aristotle lists 10 'categories' under which anything can be analyzed or defined, so that when it is referred to in argument there is no confusion about exactly what it is. He says that everything has a substance, which can have various attributes (quantity, quality, time, place and so on). One of these is 'relation'. The essence of this system is that everything about a given thing, except for its substance, can change. For instance, I remain human even if I get fatter or thinner (quantity), my hair turns

The Apostles' Creed

I believe in God the Father Almighty, Maker of heaven and earth:
And in Jesus Christ his only Son our Lord,
Who was conceived by the Holy Ghost,
Born of the Virgin Mary,
Suffered under Pontius Pilate,
Was crucified, dead, and buried:
He descended into hell;
The third day he rose again from the dead;
He ascended into heaven,
And sitteth on the right hand of God the Father Almighty;
From thence he shall come to judge the quick and the dead.
I believe in the Holy Ghost;
the holy Catholic church;
the Communion of Saints;
the forgiveness of sins;
the resurrection of the body;
and the life everlasting.

grey (quality), it is today rather than tomorrow that you are considering me (time) and whether I am at home or in the street (place).

The sole exception to this, said the Christian student, is God himself. In God, all these 'accidental' things are not accidental at all. They do not change. God's goodness and mercy (qualities) are of his very substance. God is infinite, and that is not a quantity – it is his very substance. He is eternal, and that is not a 'time' – it is his very substance. But, as Augustine of Hippo and Boethius both realized, there is one 'category' which poses special problems with reference to God, and that is 'relation'. If I am a father or a son, I am in 'relation' to my son or to my father. In that relationship, the son is not the father, and the father is not the son. In the Godhead, the Son is as old as the Father and their relationship never had a 'beginning'. This conundrum was studied afresh in the 11th and 12th centuries.

There was added to this another 'theological puzzle' arising out of *The Categories*. This concerned what happened when a priest consecrated the bread and wine in the service of the eucharist, or holy communion, in

The Nicene Creed

I believe in one God the Father Almighty,
Maker of heaven and earth,
And of all things visible and invisible;
And in one Lord Jesus Christ, the only-begotten Son of God,
Begotten of his Father before all worlds,
God of God, light of light,
Very God of very God,
Begotten not made,
Being of one substance with the Father,
By whom all things were made;
Who for us men and for our salvation came down from heaven,
And was incarnate by the Holy Ghost of the Virgin Mary,
And was made man,
And was crucified also for us under Pontius Pilate,
He suffered and was buried, and the third day he rose again according to the
   Scriptures,
And ascended into heaven,
And sitteth on the right hand of the Father.
And he shall come again with glory to judge both the quick and the dead:
Whose Kingdom shall have no end.
And I believe in the Holy Ghost
The Lord and giver of life,
Who proceedeth from the Father and the Son,
Who with the Father and the Son together is worshipped and glorified,
Who spake by the prophets.
And I believe in one catholic and apostolic church.
I acknowledge one baptism for the remission of sins.
And I look for the resurrection of the dead, and the life of the world to come.
Amen.

memory of what Jesus did at the Last Supper with his disciples. Did the bread and wine turn literally into the body and blood of Christ when the priest said the words, 'This is my body' and 'This is my blood'? Medieval Christians came to a clear belief that they did, once the doctrine of 'transubstantiation' had been worked out. Berengar of Tours, a controversial figure of the late eleventh century, had claimed that the change was merely 'spiritual'. That prompted the Church's apologists to react angrily and to insist on the most extreme literalism. This amounted to turning Aristotle's *Categories* on its head. Normally, a loaf grows mouldy; its 'quality' changes, but it is still bread. In the eucharist, the faith said, the outward appearance of the bread (its quality) remains the same, but its very substance changes from that of bread to that of the actual body of Christ. Whether this doctrine is correct has remained a subject of debate, but its importance here is that it illustrates the way in which academic study of secular subjects could affect thinking about the Christian faith.

The heated arguments generated by these debates created a certain competitiveness among the Masters, who were lecturing to a suddenly burgeoning number of students. The Masters favoured places which had an existing 'school' because these made natural centres for students to congregate. Here, one Master could woo another's students with comparative ease.

The cathedrals had all been required to have schools for their canons since Charlemagne's time (c. 742–814). Paris, in particular, was an attraction, because it had not only the cathedral school, but also the school attached to the House of Victorine Canons at St Victor. To Paris came teachers anxious to make their names, such as the ambitious Peter Abelard. As an arrogant young man who had proved himself as a logician, he was now intent on showing that he could apply these skills to theology. He had begun by attending the lectures of Anselm of Laon at the cathedral school at Laon. Abelard says in his autobiographical letter about these events that he expected a great tree of learning, but that when he came close he saw that old Anselm had nothing but bare branches to show. Abelard threw down a challenge. He said he would lecture the next day on Ezekiel, notoriously one of the most difficult of the Old Testament books to interpret. That gave him a taste for theology, and he went on to write a series of comprehensive works on the subject.

In such ways, above all under the pressure of interest in the ways in which the study of the liberal arts could throw light on theology, the demand for higher education grew throughout the twelfth century. By the beginning of the thirteenth century, there were recognizable 'universities' at Paris, at Oxford and Cambridge (neither of which began in proximity to a cathedral school), and elsewhere in Europe. Bologna, for example, developed a specialist interest in the teaching of law as a higher degree subject.

Robert Grosseteste, who died in 1253, spent a long life in and out of these schools, particularly Oxford. In the end, he became Bishop of Lincoln. His attempt to build serious science on the story of the creation in the book of Genesis is an example of the creative theological uses to which the new learning was being put. (The story of the creation of light, for example, prompted a study of optics.)

However, the application of the enthusiasms of higher education to matters of faith was not without its problems. A good deal more of Aristotle's work had now become available in Latin, particularly the scientific and philosophical writings, as a result of the labours of translators. With them came commentaries by the Arabic scholars who had possessed the Aristotelian materials in their own schools for some centuries. This led to a thirteenth-century university crisis about the dangers of Aristotle.

So, 'defining the faith' did not turn out to be something that could be done once and for all. The more Christians thought about it, the more they argued and, because of the almost universal recognition of its importance, they argued fiercely. These were not just academic debates. They were debates about life and death – indeed, about eternal life.

CHAPTER 14

BIBLE STUDY

Christ died on a cross, in a crucifixion, with all the grimness of the method of execution which was favoured by the regime of the time. But three days later, his followers claimed, he rose again. This located Jesus in history. That resurrection story became the foundation-stone of a Christian faith which would continue to look to a faith in a living person. Moreover, Jesus had promised that after his ascension he would send the Holy Spirit to be a comforter to his followers, so there was a further personal presence for Christian believers to turn to (John 14:16, 26). The Jesus of the fourth Gospel, the Gospel of John, is thus the 'sender' of the Spirit, who abides in the Church.

> 'They crucified Jesus there, and the two criminals, one on his right and the other on his left. Jesus said, "Forgive them, Father! They don't know what they are doing."'
>
> Luke 23:33–34

The Word of God

The early Christian community early adopted the idea that the Son of God was the *logos*, or Word of God, through whom God created the world. John's Gospel begins with the words: 'In the beginning the Word already existed. The Word was with God, and the Word was God. From the very beginning the Word was with God. Through him God made all things; not one thing in all creation was made without him. The Word was the source of life, and this life brought light to humanity.'

There was also a strong sense of the Word as literally a 'word' – indeed, the 'words' of the Bible. The Holy Spirit had a role here, too, because it was believed that it was the Holy Spirit who entered the world to give the actual words of scripture to its human writers.

The other Gospel writers concentrated on the life history of Jesus, and the teaching he gave was presented largely in that context. Although the author of John's Gospel may have known and used the other Gospels, and perhaps some of those which told the story of Jesus' life but did not find their way into the canon of the Bible, John's emphasis was different. He concentrated on Jesus as sent from God, doing miracles and making signs. The main focus is on Jesus the teacher, or rabbi (John 1:38), and on the teaching which Jesus gave in periods of withdrawal with his disciples, not on that which was given in his public ministry. There is a link with the theme of the *logos* here, too, because it shows the reader a Christ who is not only the source of the contents of the Bible as 'given' to its human 'authors' by the Holy Spirit but, somehow, also the very Word of God himself. So, one of the ways in which the early Christian community believed that it still had the living presence of Christ was through the writings which eventually formed the 'canon' of the scriptures, the books of the Bible in an agreed sequence.

The identification of Christ with the Word, and the belief that the whole text had come from God himself, lent the Bible a sacredness which no other writings could match. 'The sacred page' was studied minutely in the Middle Ages, every word weighed for significance. Bernard of Clairvaux is a particularly striking example of a writer who was almost incapable of writing a sentence without a scriptural echo in it. He was also conscientious about textual exactitude. In a 'retractation' to his treatise warning his monks how easy it was to go downhill on 'the steps of humility and pride', he says, 'I put down something by accident which I later realised was not as it is written in the gospel. The text simply says, "Nor does the Son know", but I, by mistake, forgot the actual words, though not the sense, and said, "Nor does the Son of Man know."' He explains that he built a passage of interpretation on this mistaken reading.

At the same time, the sense of presence of the Holy Spirit informed the reading of scripture. Ailred of Rievaulx, another twelfth-century Cistercian monk, and Bernard's contemporary, wrote in *The Mirror of the Soul* (II.8): 'The Holy Spirit, the very will and love of God, God himself, comes and pours himself out in our hearts . . . completely transforming our affection into something . . . which is not just a clinging to him . . . but becoming one spirit with him, as the Apostle clearly says in the words, "The man who unites himself to the Lord becomes one spirit with him."'

The language problem

The books of the Bible took their settled form in Greek and Hebrew, two languages which few Christians in the West could speak during the Middle Ages. The Roman empire had had two main 'centres': Rome itself, and Constantinople, the city of the emperor Constantine, which is now known as Istanbul. The language of the Western half of the Roman empire was Latin; the language of the Eastern part was Greek. As late as

The Bible takes shape

The Old Testament books which were accepted as part of the Bible were not new. They formed the Jewish scriptures. A New Testament was written during the first centuries following Christ's death. It consists of: four Gospels (though more were written), telling the story of the life of Jesus; a 'historical' book, telling the story of the earliest Christians and the way in which they gathered themselves together into churches (the Acts of the Apostles); a set of letters, mainly to these early churches and between the leading figures of this movement; and the Apocalypse, or book of Revelation, a prophecy about the end of the world.

The formation of the 'canon', that is, the list of 'approved' books which the Church accepted as scriptural, is a story in which it is apparent that the Bible and the Church cannot easily be separated as authorities. Judaism already had the idea of a set of texts which could be relied upon as a 'sacred literature'. The list was the subject of debate, for the books now known as the Apocrypha, or deuterocanonical books, never quite established their position incontrovertibly. But by the first century the list for the Old Testament was more or less fixed. Christians took this over and began to add books of their own. By the mid-second century, the four Gospels and 13 letters by Paul were generally accepted as part of the body of Christian sacred writings. However, even as late as the mid-fourth century, there was still uncertainty about other books which are now firmly part of the New Testament, such as Hebrews, Jude and the Apocalypse, or book of Revelation. Some other books (the Epistle of Barnabas and the Shepherd of Hermas) were accepted locally, but not by the Church as a whole. The texts which were admitted into the collection as 'sacred scriptures' were confidently believed to be inspired writings, divinely dictated word by word.

Jerome's Latin translation of the Bible

The most important version of the Bible for the West in the Middle Ages was the translation of the Bible into Latin which came to be called the Vulgate (the 'standard version'). It was translated by Jerome (c. 342–420), at the instigation of Pope Damasus. Jerome was a complex character, short-tempered and difficult to live with, but much respected as a spiritual adviser by the high-born ladies of late fourth-century Rome. Many of his letters of advice to them survive. He encouraged them to live like nuns in their homes, the widows refraining from marrying again and the daughters choosing not to marry, but to live as dedicated virgins.

Jerome's new translation was needed not only because there were already signs of a language gap, but because those who wanted to read the Bible in Latin were in danger of being confused by the existence of a number of different Latin versions, some more reliable than others. Jerome tried to equip himself to consult the Hebrew original. His version was not perfect, and he himself said very clearly that he did not consider himself inspired. Nevertheless, the Vulgate was treated throughout the West for more than 1,000 years with the reverence due to the very words of God, and fine points of his Latin wording were treated as though God had intended them exactly as they were. For example, at the beginning of the book of Job (1:1) Jerome chose the translation *vir unus*, 'one man'. Commentators puzzled over this. The sentence seems to mean that there was a man living in the land of Hus whose name was Job. Why say 'one man'? The 'one' must be significant. Interpreters therefore tried hard to find a reason for the 'one'.

the fourth century, educated Romans were expected to study Greek, but that expectation gradually diminished.

As the Roman empire decayed, and barbarian invaders destroyed its political structure, the old exchanges died away, and by the sixth century, few Latin speakers really had a command of the other language. It is uncertain whether Pope Gregory the Great (590–604) had any knowledge of Greek, even though he had spent time in Constantinople. This meant that even a highly educated Western European Christian, presented with a copy of the New Testament in Greek, had to ask for a translation. This language gap persisted until late in the Middle Ages.

For the Old Testament, too, there was the question of the Septuagint, itself a Greek version, which was, according to the story, made by 72 translators. In fact it is a work carried out over a considerable period and probably completed by the mid-second century. The text had substantial authority alongside the Hebrew original.

The lack of knowledge of Hebrew is more puzzling, in a way, because there were always communities of Jews living among the Christians in the towns and cities of Western Europe. In the Middle Ages, a few scholars went to the trouble of asking local Jews about the meaning of Hebrew words, but it was, again, not until late in the Middle Ages that it seems to have occurred to anyone to create formal courses of study so that students could learn Hebrew well enough to read the Old Testament in the original language for themselves.

'When I was a young man, though I was protected by the rampart of the lonely desert, I could not endure against the promptings of sin and the ardent heat of my nature. I tried to crush them by frequent fasting, but my mind was always in a turmoil of distracting thoughts. To subdue it I put myself in the hands of one of the brethren who had been a Hebrew before his conversion, and asked him to teach me his language.'

Jerome, Letter 125

What kind of book is the Bible?

Jerome's translation of the Bible, the Vulgate, did not resolve the problem of 'understanding' the Bible, which was faced by educated readers and simpler Christians alike in medieval times. The Bible is not a straightforward 'handbook to the faith'.

First, it is not one book, but a collection of separate books. That was very obvious to its readers; a complete *Biblia* in one volume was unusual. When Augustine was converted in Milan, he had just the book of Romans with him at the time.

Secondly, the Bible is a collection of many different *kinds* of books. There is history (the Acts of the Apostles), law (Leviticus), poetry (the Song of Songs) and prophecy (Elijah), as well as the Gospel stories, which describe the life and work of Jesus and his death on the cross.

But most importantly for the ordinary Christian reader, the Bible is not all written in a single tone of voice or style, or at the same level.

It is not a systematic 'textbook'. The medieval reader explained God's purpose in 'writing' the Bible in this way (as its divine author) in terms of the human state of sinfulness. Augustine was clear that one of the effects of original sin is to make the sinner lose the clear-headedness that God intended him to have as a rational creature. The illumination of divine reasonableness goes out of his life. He becomes confused and sees things in a twisted way. So the Bible is written to meet the sinner halfway in his darkness and confusion of mind.

The many meanings of scripture

The Bible is full of apparent contradictions. For instance, not all the Gospel stories match. This presented a problem in medieval times, if it was believed that every word had been dictated by God and was, in fact, the Word of God itself. God is truth and he is omnipotent, so there cannot be any mistakes. The possibility of errors was admitted in the course of the Middle Ages, but there was still no thought of criticizing the divine author. It was recognized that human scribes could make copying mistakes, and in the thirteenth century, there was a systematic attempt to tidy up such errors and restore the copies of the Bible then in circulation to a more accurate state. Even when that was done, the real anomalies remained.

The method of dealing with apparent contradictions, with obscure passages and with passages whose superficial meaning seemed unacceptable, was to look for different levels of meaning in the text. Medieval students of the Bible always approached it in the expectation that each passage would have many meanings. Earlier students of the Bible had done the same from early in the history of Christianity, with the recognition from the beginning that the books which were included in the canon were not uniform in their approach.

The key idea was that the text had both a literal and a figurative meaning. The literal meaning was simply 'what the text seemed to be saying' on a straightforward reading. (This was also called the 'historical' sense, but that can be misleading because *historia* meant 'story'.) However, when Christ was called 'the lion of Judah', no one thought that this meant that he was literally a lion. The expression was a metaphor, a 'transferred' usage. Similarly, talk of God reaching out a 'strong right arm' could be taken to be an image, and not literal. The great advantage of this division into literal and figurative sense was that contradictions could be made to disappear. A literal and a figurative interpretation need not meet head on; one could slide over the other.

There was the complication that the literal meaning of the biblical text could itself be figurative. As an example, when Jesus told his parables, he did not expect his readers to take the stories to be factual. The woman who lost the coin and searched hard to find it again, the wise virgins who made sure they had oil in their lamps, and the sower sowing his seed on different sorts of ground were clearly tales with morals. This raised all sorts of difficulties for biblical commentators in the Middle Ages. To them, it meant that Jesus was, in a sense, not telling the truth when he told these stories, because he was describing things which had not happened.

There was a more positive reason for looking for spiritual interpretations of biblical text than the 'emergency solution' to the problem of the Bible's obscurities. An idea which gained currency from the end of the second century was that the figurative senses were higher and finer, more spiritual, in the sense that they educated the soul more profoundly than the literal senses.

This led to a need to determine the number and kind of such figurative 'senses'. As late as Augustine (354–430), this was still an extremely vexed question, and Augustine himself placed a surprising reliance on the book of rules of Tichonius. Tichonius belonged to a schismatic group called the Donatists and, therefore, in Augustine's eyes, he was an enemy to the true Church. However, there was no other convenient guidebook at the time.

Two centuries later, Pope Gregory the Great had developed a fourfold system of interpreting the Bible, which was to become standard throughout the medieval West. He began with the literal sense, and included three figurative senses. The first figurative sense was the 'allegorical' sense, where a word or story was to be taken to mean something in a transferred way. The lion of Judah is, again, a good example. The reader is expected to 'take' from the idea of a lion those elements which are appropriate to a comparison with Christ (royalty and nobility) and to leave out those which are not (yellowness, being four-footed).

The second figurative sense was the 'moral', or 'tropological', sense. Here, the interpreter pointed to the lessons to be learned from the passage of scripture about how to live a good Christian life. The most famous and widely read example of this kind of interpretation was Gregory's own *Moralia in Job*, a long and detailed analysis of the lessons about living a good Christian life which are to be learned from the book of Job.

The third figurative sense was the 'prophetic', or 'anagogical', sense. Here, the reader searched the text for indications of God's future intentions. Some commentators were especially attracted to this kind of analysis. At the beginning of the twelfth century, the monastic scholar Rupert of Deutz created an immense framework for the whole of scripture and history. In it, the Old Testament represented the age of the Father and the New Testament represented the age of the Son. The age of the Holy Spirit stretched forward to the end of the world. Rupert was thus able to extend the comparison between figures in the Old and New Testaments into world history, and find analogies there.

A similar project, on a much smaller scale, was attempted by Anselm of Havelberg a decade or two later, when he wrote about God's providential purposes. Most notable of all, Joachim of Fiore interpreted from the Bible a symbolic system of threes and sevens. His attempts to move into the world of politics and to point a finger at the last world emperor made him the equivalent of today's 'sandwich-board man' in the last years of the twelfth century – for he was, in effect, crying, 'The end of the world is at hand!' He caused enough anxiety in respectable circles in the Church to be condemned by the Fourth Lateran Council of 1215.

Nonetheless, the prophetic enterprise was not, in itself, disapproved of by the Church. Far from it; it had the potential to focus the minds of faithful Christians upon their end and to make them test all their activities against their hopes of heaven.

The Glossa Ordinaria

Perhaps the most practically useful achievement of the Middle Ages in terms of biblical interpretation was the creation of the *Glossa Ordinaria*. This was the drawing together of the older commentary material on the books of the Bible into a 'standard' commentary. Some books had always been more popular with preachers and commentators than others, so there were gaps to be filled. The work of assembling a complete commentary was done mainly during the twelfth century, by a series of scholars, notable among whom was Anselm of Laon.

During the period 1230–35, when he was Regent Master in Paris, the Dominican Hugh of St Cher brought in material from the most recent scholarship in order to bring the *Glossa Ordinaria* up to date. He produced 'postils', or notes, on the whole of the Bible. These became, in their turn, a standard work of reference beyond the *Glossa Ordinaria*, acting as a supplement to it. Hugh of St Cher was born in about 1190 and ended his life in 1263 as a high-profile figure, a cardinal who had been Papal Legate to Germany (1251–53). He was the author of other works, in addition to his commentary on the Bible. His *Concordantia* of the whole Bible was still being reprinted in the 17th and 18th centuries. Even then, its orderly alphabetical arrangement of terms, by books and chapters of the Bible, made it both practical and accessible.

Early in the fourteenth century, another 'definitive' layer of commentary was added by the Franciscan Nicholas of Lyra (1270–1349). Lyra, who had some knowledge of Hebrew, completed a literal commentary on the entire Bible between 1322–23 and 1331. It was officially presented to Pope John XXII in 1331. Lyra intended it for the use of academic theologians, rather than for pastoral purposes.

This gradual accretion of 'layers' gave to the first printed Bibles the appearance of a set of concentric rings, or rather rectangles. A small square of biblical text was placed in the middle of the page and, around it, the *Glossa Ordinaria*, and these later additions and developments, working outwards.

Preaching the word

Preaching had, from the first, been one of the most important vehicles of biblical interpretation. Augustine and Gregory the Great both saw the bishop as a teacher. The *cathedra*, or seat from which the bishop taught, gives its very name to a 'cathedral'. Both Augustine and Gregory were highly successful preachers, who could hold a large audience for hours, in

Bernard of Clairvaux

Bernard of Clairvaux (1090–1153) was another great preacher, who revived or continued the tradition of live preaching on scripture. He never became a bishop but, as Abbot of Clairvaux, he travelled and moved in diplomatic as well as in ecclesiastical circles, and he had great influence. He made an intimate use of scripture in his sermons. In his long series of sermons on the Song of Songs, for example, he comes to the passage, 'My beloved is mine and I am his.' Bernard says, 'It is the Bridegroom whose words we have pondered until now. We implore his presence that we may worthily trace the words of his Bride, to his glory and for our salvation. For we cannot worthily consider and study such words as these unless he is present to guide our discourse. For her words are pleasant and lovely, bringing profit to the understanding, and they are deep in mystery.'

the noisy style favoured at the time, where the congregation would applaud a sermon they particularly enjoyed. Augustine preached long series of sermons, for example, his 'Narrations on the Psalms'. Gregory did so, too, in his sermons on the book of Ezekiel. For some centuries after Gregory the Great, live preaching became less usual, but sermons on books of scripture, which dated from the earlier centuries, were still read.

Preaching the word began to appear in a slightly different light in the later Middle Ages, with an increasing separation of the ministry of the word and the ministry of the sacraments. The founding of the mendicant orders of preaching friars, the Dominicans and the Franciscans, meant that, from the early thirteenth century, there were 'specialists' in preaching.

Meanwhile, the sacramental ministry, especially the saying of the Mass, tended to become something separate, with the focus on the action of the priest. In chapter 21, we shall see the problems that this caused in Western Christendom.

'While brother John of Penna was still a boy . . . a beautiful child appeared to him one night [and told him to go and listen to a friar who was preaching locally]. And he went to St Stephen's, and found a large crowd of men and women gathered there to hear the sermon . . . Then brother Philip stood up to preach, and spoke with the greatest devotion, proclaiming the kingdom of everlasting life not with words of human wisdom but with the power of the Spirit.'

Francis of Assisi (1181–1226), The Little Flowers of St Francis

Sermons in Latin on the Latin text of scripture were, in any case, an unsatisfactory way of bringing God's word to people who did not speak Latin. It is a puzzle that there is little surviving evidence of what went into sermons preached to the people in their own language. Those preachers who preserved their sermons tended to do so in the Latin version. Especially in the growing and prosperous towns of the later Middle Ages, people began to clamour for something they could use and understand.

Attempts at vernacular translations of the Bible were one symptom of this new need. Another was the return to an emphasis on the ministry of the word as a central part of the work of a priest, which was to be one of the great driving forces of the Reformation.

CHAPTER 15

DEFINING THE CHURCH

If the Bible was the inspired Word of God, what else did Christians need? Another way of putting this question is to ask: What was left to be completed after the resurrection of Christ? For even if Christ had paid the penalty for sin, that self-evidently did not mean that all those who had faith in him ceased to commit sins. There was obviously a great deal more to do, and by the early Middle Ages it was held that it was the task of the Church, which Jesus himself had founded, to do it (Matthew 16:18).

'Church' meant the buildings in which people met to worship, which grew more and more splendid as the Middle Ages wore on and they were built 'to the glory of God'. However, it also had deeper meanings, which were less easy to portray. Above all, the Church was the community of the faithful.

The Church as community

The person who becomes a Christian also becomes a member of a community. In the first Christian centuries, the emphasis was on the local 'churches', where people formed small groups. Far from having handsome buildings, they were often forced to live and worship in secret because of the periodical persecution of Christians by the state. When Paul wrote the 'letters' to the Colossians, the Ephesians and the Philippians – which survive in the New Testament – he was addressing such communities, at Colossus, Ephesus and Philippi. He warned them about the infighting which was hard to avoid in their closed-in small communities. However, it was also obvious from an early stage that it was going to be necessary to create a bigger organization or structure, if Christians were not to split up into warring factions, and if there was to be a sensible protection against 'charismatic' leaders with ideas of their own, who might lead people off into sects and divisions.

One major division in the early Christian community was between those who had formerly been Jews and those who had come from other races. Christians worshipped the God of the Jews, but with a new understanding of his intentions for humanity. It was, therefore, difficult for former Jews to know how much of their old observance they should be required to keep to.

In chapter 15 of the Acts of the Apostles, there is a description of an episode in which Christians from Judea were teaching the faithful that they must follow the old Jewish rules and submit to circumcision. Paul and Barnabas argued with them but could not persuade them. So it was decided that they should all go to Jerusalem to discuss the matter with the 'apostles and elders'. There, the argument continued, until Peter got up and addressed the meeting. He reminded them that it had been agreed that he should be 'apostle to the Gentiles', and he said that it was his experience that God converted non-Jews just as he did Jews, making no difference between them. Why, then, he argued, impose a yoke on their necks by making them observe Jewish rituals? He was supported by the apostle James. It was decided to write a moderate letter to the Christians in Antioch, Syria and Cilicia, where this was a matter of particular dispute. In the letter, they were encouraged to keep clear of idolatry and fornication, as the Jews did, but told that they were not expected to take on the whole burden of Jewish observance now that they were Christians.

This was not the end of dispute, by any means. The same chapter of the Acts of the Apostles describes how Paul quarrelled with Barnabas, and how each took a different companion before going off in opposite directions to preach. But it did suggest a way in which Christians could resolve differences and arrive at common decisions on points of faith and order. This method, of holding a 'council', became established. A series of general or 'ecumenical' councils was held in the first centuries, at which the Holy Spirit was believed to be present. At each, the assembled leaders of the Church formally ratified the decisions of those who had been at the previous council and declared themselves to be unanimous, thus preserving a continuity in 'the mind of the Church'.

'If any of you have a dispute with another Christian, how dare you go before heathen judges instead of letting God's people settle the matter? . . . Surely there is at least one wise person in your fellowship who can settle a dispute between fellow-Christians.'

1 Corinthians 6:1, 5

This raised other questions, about the authority of the leaders to decide 'for' the community, and how that was to be balanced against the right of the whole community to have its say. The community developed both patterns of leadership, and a recognition that Christians had a collective 'mind' and could form a consensus – the *consensus fidelium*, or 'agreement of the faithful'. There was always a tension between this strikingly modern and rather 'democratic' idea and the evolving formal leadership. The one thing almost everyone was able to accept was that there must be no division about the faith. There must be 'one faith' uniting Christians.

In the early Christian world there was another phenomenon which caused problems. Jesus had told his disciples to go out and preach and win disciples. That was what they did. But without centralized organization, such wandering preaching sometimes threw up wild, charismatic figures, whose teaching was not easy to control – people who claimed that they were 'led by the Spirit' and were, in effect, appealing to a direct divine mandate. Another debate of the early Church was, therefore, about the balance between 'charism' and 'order'. Requiring those who spoke for the Church to be given some sort of mandate was the natural response of officialdom in the Church to the threat posed by letting people say what they liked in the name of Christ.

> '*I saw [bishops] living in London . . . Some took posts at Court counting the Kings' money . . . Others went into the service of lords and ladies, sitting like stewards managing household affairs . . . I fear that there are many whom Christ . . . will curse for ever.*'
>
> **William Langland,**
> **Piers Plowman,**
> **mid-fourteenth century**

Ministers of the Church

The New Testament describes a variety of types of ministers: 'elders', 'apostles' and also 'deacons'. The deacons are the category whose functions we can be most sure of. They were the people who looked after the widows and orphans, and did practical good work. The others, 'elders', 'apostles' and so on, were the leaders who were also teachers, and who united the community 'under' them, with the apostles naturally the most respected in the first generation, because they had actually known Jesus.

By the Middle Ages these shadowy early forms of ministry, about whose exact nature there is a great deal of modern scholarly debate, had become fixed. Eventually, certainly by the early medieval period, there was a ladder. There was ordination first to the diaconate (the office of deacon), then to the priesthood and then to the episcopate (the office of bishop). A deacon could not say the Mass. Only a priest or a bishop was able to declare forgiveness when a penitent confessed. Only a bishop could ordain new priests.

In the West, monks were not necessarily ordained, and their 'hierarchy' should not be confused with that of the deacons, priests and bishops. Monks in Benedictine houses had abbots, usually of the higher social classes, who were the targets of satire, just like the wealthy bishops, like Chaucer's 'hunting, shooting and fishing' monk. Though they might see bishops (and abbots) passing on fine horses (and there was a good deal of critical comment about that), most people did not have much to do with the higher reaches of this clerical hierarchy in the Middle Ages.

In ordinary people's lives in the later Middle Ages, the ministry was likely to be represented by the local parish priest. Chaucer's 'Poor Parson of a Town', from his *Canterbury Tales*, was a learned man, a clerk, 'that Christ's gospel truly would preach; his parishioners devoutly would he teach'. He was patient in adversity and charitable to his parishioners.

The responsibilities of a parish priest were pastoral. The parishioners' children had to be baptized, and there were marriages to be celebrated. But above all, from at least the twelfth century, there was a penitential role.

Confession

The defining moment in the evolution of the sacrament of penance in the Middle Ages was the requirement of the Fourth Lateran Council of 1215 that everyone, of either sex, should confess to a priest at least once a year, in Lent. But well before that, and leading up to it, had come a natural development of penitential practice in response to pastoral need. Baptism was believed to wipe away all original and actual sin completely. When everyone was baptized in infancy, it was inevitable that a catalogue of

'Well ought a priest ensample for to give; By his cleanness, how that his sheep should live.'
Chaucer, *Canterbury Tales*, Prologue (1387–88)

actual sins would follow. Yet baptism could not be repeated. It was held firmly, from the earliest days of the Church, that a person could be baptized only once. The reason for this was Christ's saying that someone who put his hand to the plough and looked back was not fit for the kingdom of heaven (Luke 9:62).

In some 'rigorist' early communities, those who sinned after baptism were cast out for ever. Others allowed penitents to return, but only after a considerable period of public penance, during which they were dressed in special clothing and separated from the rest of the congregation. This 'public penance' was usually imposed for serious sins, such as murder, adultery or apostasy (renunciation of faith), and the restoration to the community required the bishop to declare the penitent forgiven.

During the early Middle Ages, it was realized that this was not going to meet everyone's ordinary needs for cleansing from more everyday sins, and the practice grew of confessing privately, not to the bishop, but to a priest. This created a need for instruction manuals for priests, so that they could judge fairly what penalties it was appropriate to impose for particular sins. It was accepted that something more was required than merely to admit the sin and repent of it. The priest should expect the penitent to demonstrate the sincerity of the repentance by some action, such as almsgiving or fasting.

None of this penitential practice affected the work of a parish priest directly, but it did so indirectly, partly because it made for immense complications in the Christian lives of the population. It bred anxiety and a sense that it was necessary to work extremely hard to earn a place in heaven. One of its most visible effects was to give a disproportionate prominence to the importance of 'saying Masses'. It was held that saying a Mass could 'apply' the effects of the sacrifice of Christ – that is, his death on the cross – to the spiritual needs of individuals. The emphasis moved, therefore, from the participation of the faithful in the eucharist, or holy communion, because these Masses could be said by a priest alone, and pious laypeople might

'There was also a Pardoner . . . He produced a document covered with bishops' seals, and claimed to have power to absolve all the people . . . The ignorant folk believed him and were delighted. They came up and knelt to kiss his documents while he . . . raked in their rings and jewellery with his roll of parchment.'

William Langland,
Piers Plowman,
mid-fourteenth century

Indulgences

An indulgence was not part of the penitential system, but it depended on that underlying structure of assumptions. An indulgence was the remission by the Church of the temporal penalty of forgiven sin (the punishment imposed by a priest, not the eternal consequences). So, it was a 'letting off' of the acts which would otherwise have had to be done in penance. The idea was that God recognized the Church's 'sentences' on penitents, because he had given the Church authority to impose them. This was based on Jesus' grant of the power to bind and loose in heaven and on earth, which came to be known as 'the power of the keys' – that is, the power to use, or refuse to use, the 'keys' to let someone into heaven (Matthew 16:19 and 18:18). It was expected that God would require penances to be discharged before the person on whom they were imposed could be admitted to heaven.

The Church – this required a bishop or the pope himself – could relax these penalties. Pope Urban II did this when he granted a 'plenary indulgence' (that is, a remission of all their penances and direct entry into heaven) to those who went on the First Crusade and either died on the way or got as far as Jerusalem. In the course of the later Middle Ages, it occurred to the Church's authorities that they could charge money for indulgences, and the system became corrupted, with anxious relatives trying to buy freedom from the penitential burden for those who had died.

pay for a certain number of Masses to be said for them for a particular purpose.

Preaching or teaching his parishioners (the ministry of the word) was the other main part of a parish priest's duties, but the effect of the concentration on the 'sacrificial' aspect of the eucharist or Mass was often to diminish, or almost eliminate, the ministry of the word. In any case, simple homilies about how to be a good Christian were all an unlearned priest might manage. The level of education of the parish priest was usually not high. Because of the 'ignorance of priests', Archbishop Pecham held a provincial Council at Lambeth in 1281, at which a plan of 'instruction for the laity' was drawn up. This was turned into verse for use in the province of York in 1357, on the orders of Archbishop Thoresby. An indulgence of 40 days was given with it, to encourage people to learn it and teach it to other people. It was still in Latin, however, though in 1425 it was translated into English at the instigation of the Bishop of Bath and Wells. He had it put in every church in the diocese, and he told his archdeacons to sell all the clergy copies at sixpence each. These are striking advances, but they are patchy and spaced over a considerable period of time, and they do not suggest that the clergy generally were always delivering a very high standard of pastoral ministry.

Really good, sophisticated preaching with a sound theological basis needed an expertise and education which few parish priests had. From the thirteenth century, there were 'experts' about, who could deliver powerful, exciting sermons to stir people up to stronger faith and deeper understanding. These were the friars, whom we shall meet in a later chapter.

The medieval papacy

Jesus said to Peter that Peter was the rock on which Jesus would build his Church (Matthew 16:18). Already in the period after the end of the Roman empire, there was debate about which of the ancient patriarchates was the most senior. Pope Gregory I (Gregory the Great) was one of the main protagonists of the argument that Rome should come first. In the late eleventh century, Pope Gregory VII began to enlarge the claims of the papacy, not only over against the other leaders of the Church – including the bishops of the West – but also in relation to the state.

A document known as the *Donation of Constantine* was relied upon for much of the Middle Ages, although it eventually turned out to be an early forgery. It suggested that the first Christian emperor, Constantine, had, as a gesture, 'given' authority over the state to the Church. Gregory VII strengthened that position, claiming that 'at the knee of the pope every king should bow'.

This was a period in which Church and state were engaged in a dispute known as the Investiture Contest. Every time a bishop died and had to be replaced, there was a complex process in which the local king or emperor handed over the lands of the diocese (the 'temporalities') and the Church consecrated the new bishop for his office (the 'spiritualities').

A handbook for priests

There are indications that the Church was sufficiently concerned to try to educate the parish clergy better, which is in itself an indication that there was a problem. William of Pagula wrote an *Oculus sacerdotis*, or 'Priest's Eye', in the early fourteenth century. It was an immensely practical handbook, divided into three sections. In the first, the priest was told how to hear confessions. This included suggesting what questions to ask in order to ascertain which of the seven deadly sins his penitents had committed, so that priest and penitent alike should have a clear framework. The second section gave the priest help with catechesis and the general instruction of laypeople in the way to live a good Christian life. The last part was full of resource material for the priest on theological and sacramental matters. This was only one of a considerable number of such works in use in the last medieval centuries.

Royal patrons had been intruding on the Church's part of this process, giving the new bishop his pastoral staff or the ring which symbolized his 'marriage' to his diocese. This dispute reached an uneasy settlement in the Concordat of Worms of 1122, but it prompted still more determined self-aggrandisement on the part of the Church. Bernard of Clairvaux wrote a series of letters to Pope Eugenius III, called *On Consideration*, in which he spelled out for the pope the position in the universe which set him above everything on earth.

The consequences of this rebalancing of the powers of Church and state, and of the pope within the Church, were enormous. The following medieval centuries saw a growing papal monarchy, and less and less awareness of the Church as a community.

One of the great medieval difficulties was to keep the live and individual experience of a personal faith in Christ in balance with the enormous growth of the institutional structure of the Church, which was associated with the rise of the papacy to such a position of monarchical power. That was, perhaps, the chief development of Christianity in the Middle Ages; it was certainly the most conspicuous. It set up tensions which led, in the end, to a lasting division of the faithful from the period of the Reformation of the sixteenth century.

CHAPTER 16

LAYPEOPLE

In a hierarchical society, in which the social strata were 'fixed', most educated people were likely to be from the classes whose members were at least free and not in poverty. The educated in the Middle Ages were mostly the clergy. The word 'cleric' and the word 'clerk' come from the same source, and a priest was for a long time known in English as a 'clerk in holy orders'. These two social and educational factors encouraged a division in most people's thinking between those who ran the Church and the bulk of those who made it up.

The people of God, the *laos*, were really the whole 'people', including the clergy. However, that sense of the term was easily lost sight of, with clergy and people alike falling into the habit of thinking that only the ordinary people were the 'laity'.

In these circumstances, there was a natural tendency for theologians, and the Church's own hierarchy, to regard laypeople as 'children' in the faith, and to expect less of them theologically. This was reinforced by the gulf which opened up after the end of the Roman world between those who knew Latin and those who spoke only the local vernacular. Several of those vernacular languages – Italian, Spanish and French – remained close to Latin for some centuries, and it is not easy to say when they ceased to be Latin and became new languages. If people could not read, they were largely cut off from the finer points of what was written, in any case.

How far could laypeople be expected to understand the subtleties of the faith, where the arguments and the teaching were being conducted in Latin? The answers to that question are sometimes surprising. In the twelfth century, there arose groups known as the 'Poor Men of Lyons', led by a man called Waldes, or Valdez. They were also called the 'Waldensians', after this leader. They questioned the role of the clergy as they knew it. There was a mounting resentment of the claims that no one could get to heaven without the assistance of the Church, when some of its leading ministers were manifestly taking advantage of their position to swagger about in fine clothes on expensive horses, and leaving the pastoral care of their people to curates.

The Waldensians belonged to the early 'middle classes'. They were townspeople, tradesmen, people of enterprise, who set about gaining an understanding of what was in the Bible by reading it for themselves. Theologically, they were not unorthodox, except in this one respect of their challenge to the need to rely on the Church for one's salvation. When attempts were made by the Church's apologists to bring them to order by quoting scripture at them, they answered smartly back, using their own quotations.

The same practical method of self-help was adopted in the late fourteenth century by followers of John Wyclif, who were known as the Lollards. Surprisingly sophisticated Bible study was going on in Lollard 'house-groups' in the fifteenth century, with the same idea that ordinary people ought to be able to learn about their faith.

But oh, to see the Church so split
  Should cover all of us with gloom . . .
Consider now the latest sprout
  Which pride and envy have made grow
From schism, and to which we owe
  This recent sect of Lollardy.

John Gower, *Confessio Amantis*, mid-fourteenth century

John Gower was born in about 1330, of a solid country family which gave him enough social standing to gain an entry to court circles. He was an enemy of the Lollards, but he himself, writing within a different framework of conventions, exemplified some of the understanding of the issues of faith which the Lollards also demonstrated. Like the Lollards, Gower showed that ordinary laypeople were not necessarily as ignorant of theology as the clergy sometimes liked to think. He wrote books in three languages, *The Voice of One Crying* in Latin, *The Mirror of One Meditating* in French, and *The Confession of Love* in English.

In *The Confession of Love*, Gower uses the device of getting Venus to appoint her chaplain to hear Gower confess his sins. The chaplain sets out the catalogue of the seven deadly sins. He looks at them first from a

Christian point of view and then from the satirical point of view of an adherent of courtly love. Courtly love was an artificial game of 'pretend' courting of an inaccessible highly born married lady, which was a fashion of the day. One of the questions Gower raises with his confessor is whether a Christian is allowed to kill. No, God forbids it, says the confessor, and gives a little homily on the virtues of peace:

And when his Son was born, he sent
  Down angels, through the firmament,
Whose song of peace the shepherds heard.

John Gower, *Confessio Amantis*, mid-fourteenth century

Julian of Norwich is an example of a female mystic of the later Middle Ages, who was both formed and limited by certain expectations of the laity. She can have had limited formal education, but both female and male laypeople sometimes had the opportunity to discuss religious beliefs and perceptions with Dominican and Franciscan friars who came to preach locally. In 1373, Julian had a series of visions, which she called 'showings'. She reflected on these for two decades, and then, in the 1390s, she wrote her *Revelation of Divine Love*. The writing, like the experience, is vivid. 'I saw the bodily sight of the dying Christ,' she claims. She describes 'the plenteous bleeding of the head' and the way 'the great drops of blood fell down from under the garland'.

The reputation of such a mystic could spread through tales of her wonderful experiences, and also through reading her writings. Julian was visited in Norwich by Margery Kemp, whose own book, *The Book of Margery Kemp*, is another example of this type of lay female writing. Margery herself certainly had opportunities to hear Dominicans preaching in local pulpits.

It was possible for popular religious movements to remain 'within the fold', but it was not easy. The establishment tended to regard them with suspicion precisely because the laity was not under obedience in the same way as were members of conventional religious orders, or priests (who owed canonical obedience to their bishops). In other words, there were fears that they would get out of control. Among the popular movements which preserved a degree of 'respectability' were the 'third orders' of friars, who formed the 'confraternities' of the thirteenth century.

Hildegard of Bingen and Mechthild of Magdeburg

Hildegard of Bingen (1098–1179) was a child who had visions. In 1141, she reported that she had been given a knowledge of scripture which others achieved only by patient reading. Ten years' work followed, at the end of which she had completed her *Scivias*. In about 1158, Hildegard began to travel on preaching journeys. The Lollard women preachers had not yet made an 'issue' of women engaging in this kind of ministry. Hildegard delivered apocalyptic sermons at Cologne and Trier. Hers was not a call for radical reform; nor was it millennarianism. Nevertheless, in her old age, Hildegard became something of a controversial figure.

A fourteenth-century female figure who invited comparison with Hildegard was Mechthild of Magdeburg. She lived in community for a time, as a Beguine. These were groups of women (though groups of men were formed, too) who lived together, caring for the poor and sick, without taking the formal vows of a nun. She, too, had visions, which she wrote about in Low German. Mechthild's themes are of the overflowing of the Godhead upon creation, and of the love which was the essence of that outflowing.

Like Hildegard of Bingen, Mechthild grew bold. She became a critic and social commentator. She won both admiration and opprobrium. She had the spiritual counsel of a Dominican friar, Heinrich of Halle, who was a pupil of Albert the Great, Thomas Aquinas' teacher. That helped to bring her into the mainstream. With the assistance of Dominicans, collections of such writing began to be disseminated in fourteenth-century Germany. Lay spirituality, especially that of women, could become associated with social comment in this way, partly because of its association with the active work of the friars among the people.

These associations had the authority of the bishop, and their members were bound together by rules. The Flagellants were a more dangerous manifestation, because of their inherently 'extreme' common interests. They would march naked through the streets, bewailing their sins and encouraging public confession of sins and crimes. This was an Italian movement in origin, although it spread some distance across Europe in the course of the thirteenth century before it subsided. In twelfth-century Italy, 'singing gilds' arose, which evolved into more formal organizations with chapels. They held processions and met in piazzas and sang hymns in vernacular languages.

Not all the ordinary laity took such an intellectual, spiritual or energetic interest in their faith. Many were content, and were encouraged to be content, with 'pictures' on the church wall.

Popular piety

The cult of the Blessed Virgin Mary flourished in the West from the twelfth century. It was not that there had not been reverence for Mary earlier than this, especially in the East. But a series of Western writers now drew attention to her, and encouraged Christians to focus their thoughts and prayers upon her. Anselm of Canterbury wrote a prayer to Mary in the new tradition of personal private prayer which he encouraged.

Bernard of Clairvaux played a part in the reform of the Cistercian liturgy, which helped to bring to prominence the act of worship associated with the relatively new Feast of the Assumption of the Virgin (the belief that Jesus' mother Mary did not die in the ordinary way, but was taken up into heaven at the end of her life). In the Cistercian form of service, there is a strong association of Mary with the Song of Songs. In the form of worship ('office') for the Nativity of the Virgin there is an antiphon, 'Behold you are beautiful my love, behold you are beautiful. Your eyes are doves . . .'; and another at Vespers, 'You are most beautiful, my beloved . . . come and you shall be crowned.'

A 'cult' of the Virgin developed, which had a strong popular attraction. Mary was a figure to whom ordinary people could 'relate'. It was easy to pray to her to ask her to intercede with her Son, Jesus.

There was also a strengthening in the medieval West of the cult of the saints, which was always a powerful element in popular religion in the East. In the East, it had long been customary to revere the very 'icons' of the saints, to a degree where, in the eighth and ninth centuries, there was a period of active controversy, in which one party (the 'Iconoclasts') pressed for the destruction of these icons. In Byzantine churches, medieval and more recent icons can still be seen, hung with votive tablets. These show, for example, an eye, an arm or a leg, hung there by the faithful in the hope of a cure for an ailment.

The Western controversy about this came much later, at the very end of the Middle Ages. At this time, the reverence of ordinary people, not only for pictures and statues of saints, but also for 'relics', such as fingernails, bones and the hair of saints, began to seem to some critics rather like idolatry. There was a fine line between asking God to help for the sake of the goodness of his saint and attributing to the saints themselves, or to physical objects associated with them, semi-divine powers close to magic. It was expecting a great deal to hope that ordinary people would stay on the right side of this line and not become confused, and reformers began to express serious concerns as the Middle Ages came to an end.

Christian goodness for ordinary people

What was a good person? In his book, *The Perfect Righteousness of Man*, Augustine had come to the conclusion that there was only one good man – Jesus himself. For ordinary people, there was no hope of being truly good. Augustine wanted to emphasize the need for God's help ('grace'). Some medieval thinkers, such as Peter Abelard, went so far as to argue that the main purpose of Christ's coming was to show what man was created to be.

There was a dilemma here. On the one hand, the Church's teachers wanted to encourage people to trust in God and to rely on him as their only means of rescue from sin. On the other hand, they wanted people to strive to be good. This balance between 'faith' and 'works' was to become important in the last medieval phase, when reformers began to complain that the Church had allowed – even encouraged – a 'pastoral drift' towards an emphasis on 'good works' and 'earning your way to heaven'. Like the questions about the excessive devotion to the saints, this became one of the 'Church-dividing' issues which brought the Middle Ages to a close.

CHAPTER 17
POLITICS AND THE CHURCH

The earliest Christians often came from the lowlier parts of society, and some were slaves. The Christian religion was, at first, a minority religion, of which the state disapproved. From time to time in the first Christian centuries, there was active persecution against Christians. All that changed when the emperor Constantine himself became a Christian in the early fourth century, and the Roman empire adopted Christianity as the 'state' religion. His 'conversion' was probably as much political as religious. He wanted to win a battle, and he thought that the cross of Christ might be the 'sign' under which he would conquer. Symbolic of Constantine's attitude to his new faith was the fact that he built a ring of Christian churches around the edge of Rome, leaving the pagan temples of the inner city untouched.

The transformation of old pagan temples into Christian churches ought to be a useful indicator of the degree of penetration of Christianity into the pagan Roman world. It was more common in the East than in the West, but in Rome the Pantheon was converted to a church in the seventh century. Yet the evidence is not easy to interpret. Many ancient temples were excavated in the past by classical archaeologists who were not looking for Christian remains and did not preserve what they found, so it is hard to be sure that evidence was not destroyed. To build a Christian church on the site of a temple as soon as the temple was abandoned made a statement. But to use a convenient platform, two centuries later, when the local people had half-forgotten what the temple had stood for, shows only that public observance of the old religion had ceased. Between the fifth and the seventh centuries, much changed in the world of Western Europe. There seems to have been some lingering sense of the grandeur of the old buildings, and it was not unknown for a temple façade to be preserved so as to maintain a fine vista, even when the temple behind had vanished.

This uncertainty about the 'temple-to-church' transformation reflects a similar difficulty in being sure how far Christianity had really penetrated into ordinary people's lives and minds at the beginning of the medieval period. Augustine of Hippo's mother seems to have maintained a simple peasant's reverence for the shrines of the saints that was little different from the old worship of the gods, and she was far from untypical. It was not unusual for someone who had become a Christian to go on being a pagan, too – just to be on the safe side.

Citizens (or subjects) have to live in a community and under its laws. This recognition was central to Christianity from the beginning. Jesus was asked whether it was right to pay taxes (Matthew 22:15–22). He asked to be shown a coin, and then asked whose head appeared on it. 'Pay the Emperor what belongs to the Emperor,' he said. So, the Christian was to keep a separation in his loyalties between his duty to God and his 'civic' duty, but he was also to be an obedient citizen. There was a similar theme in the advice of the apostle Paul (Ephesians 6:5) that slaves should obey their masters. Christians were not social revolutionaries in any active sense, revolutionary though their ideas were in their potential for changing society from the inside. The only note of violent disagreement with society's norms was struck by Jesus himself, when he threw the money-changers out of the Temple in Jerusalem (Matthew 21:12). He was objecting to the intrusion of secular values into the place where God was to be worshipped. There was sufficient potential 'nuance' in these passages to afford many centuries of debate in the Christian West about the balance which ought to be struck by a faithful Christian between his duty to God and his duty to the state.

In his *The City of God*, Augustine of Hippo brought things up to date for Christians at the end of the ancient world. He emphasized that the 'city' of which Christians are citizens is eternal. It is God's City. Its members include people who have already died and people not yet born. Similarly 'eternal' is the 'other' city, made up of those who are not God's people. Looking around the faces to be seen in this life, one may not know who belongs to which city. Asking whether they belong to the Church is not a reliable way to tell. They may be regular churchgoers and still not be among God's 'chosen'. Only God knows who are his own. Even the individual himself does not know. This way of thinking encourages citizens to look towards the next world.

> 'God's City lives in this world's city, as far as its human element is concerned; but it lives there as an alien sojourner.'
>
> **Augustine, *The City of God*, XVIII.1, c. 420**

There is a further complication, in that the idea of the 'state' did not always have its modern connotations. The way it was envisaged depended on the structures of government involved, and also on an ideology. In the late Roman period, the head of state was an emperor, and there arose a cult of the emperor himself. Good citizens were expected to 'worship' him.

Because the transition to the Middle Ages involved the collapse of the old Roman political and social structures, there were immense and radical changes in the patterns of life for ordinary people and also for their leaders. Augustine's broad, and essentially other-worldly, picture made it easier to carry over Christian ideals of a 'heavenly' citizenship – where the citizen's first loyalties were to God – through centuries of change, upheaval and reconstruction, leading to the development of the feudal system in Northern Europe and big changes to the old city states in Italy.

This kind of event is a useful reminder that religion always has a place in society. For the Middle Ages, the social and political role of Christianity was to be central. In medieval Europe, a nominal 'Holy' Roman empire persisted, but the dominant pattern in most of Northern Europe was the feudal system, with a royal figure at its head.

The 'king' became idealized, not because anyone who had dealings with actual kings had any illusions about the royal realities, but because he retained, with appropriate Christian modifications, something of the aura of semi-divinity which used to be attached to the Roman emperor. In the Christian version, the king was 'anointed' by God, rather than being 'divine' himself. This did not give him priestly powers or functions. It was always clear that a Christian king was not a 'priest-king'. But it did make him God's 'favourite', and the recipient of a divine 'authority to rule'. There was a good deal of self-consciousness about the importance of this distinction. That assumption is reflected in the coronation ceremonies in which the Church 'made' the king the legitimate vessel of an authority which comes from God.

At a more modest and human level, all this made it important that a king should be seen to be a good Christian, to set a religious example as the leading layman. Kings are praised in medieval narratives for their piety, as well as for their courage and competence on the battlefield.

Conflicts of loyalty

In feudalism, a king owns the lands of his kingdom and he allows his 'vassals' to 'hold' portions of his lands at his pleasure. In return for the lands, the vassals swear an oath of allegiance to their king, kneeling and placing their hands between his. In their turn, these vassals become the 'barons' of the kingdom. They owe the king so many days of knight-service a year; in other words, they have to find him soldiers to serve in his armies. Their own people work on their lands as farmers, in a further relationship of subservience. These serfs might, in some circumstances, hope to be emancipated, but room for 'social mobility' is extremely limited in a feudal environment.

> 'This world is chiefly ruled by the sacred authority of bishops and the power of kings . . . But the episcopal dignity is greater than the royal, for bishops consecrate kings, but kings do not consecrate bishops.'
>
> **Hincmar of Rheims (c. 806–82)**

This had various implications for Christians, as well as for the Church and its institutions. Land could not be 'held' outside the feudal system. So churches and especially bishoprics and also monasteries, which all needed lands, held land of the king, like everyone else. In return they, too, had to provide their days of 'knight-service' and other feudal dues. Bishops were, in effect, barons themselves, and that was, to some degree, also true of abbots. When kings granted charters, the barons who were present would attach their names, and the names of bishops and abbots appeared alongside those of secular lords. In fact, they came first in the order of precedence because they were spiritual, not secular, lords. So, this was a society in which the leaders of the Church had a clearly defined 'place' in the secular world, and also certain duties there.

There were, naturally, conflicts of loyalty. Anselm, Archbishop of Canterbury in 1092–1109, went into exile twice, seeking support from the pope, because of problems with two successive kings of England, William II and Henry I. On the first occasion he found himself in conflict with the king, it was over exactly this question of where his first loyalty lay. This was one of the numerous periods when there were rival candidates for the papacy, and Anselm had given his loyalty to Urban II before he became

> 'The Prince is the public power, and an image of God's majesty on earth . . . For all power is from God . . . Whatever the Prince has power to do comes from God.'
>
> **John of Salisbury, *Policraticus*, mid-twelfth century**

archbishop. For political reasons, William II favoured Urban's rival, and he did not want his Archbishop of Canterbury on the opposite side. Anselm could not bring himself to abandon his honest commitment. To whom did he owe obedience? He believed it was to Urban; the king said it was to him, as feudal overlord.

The whole question had become even more complicated at this time, because kings and emperors had fallen into the habit of 'investing' new bishops with the ring and staff of their office. It took three principal steps to make a bishop. First, a name had to be chosen. That was, in theory, a matter for the people of the diocese, but it had, in practice, long been accepted that it lay with kings to nominate candidates. Family connections could be important. Bishops could function as barons best if they were the brothers and cousins of other barons and came from the same noble families. Then the king or emperor invested the new bishop with the lands or 'temporalities' of the diocese. And the Church performed its quite distinct 'sacramental' part, in which the secular authorities had no role. This was what made the bishop into a bishop. The 'investment' with the ring and the staff were tokens of this part of the making of a bishop. The ring symbolized the marriage of the bishop with the people of his diocese; the pastoral staff his role as their shepherd.

When Anselm of Canterbury was made archbishop, he had been reluctant to accept the office which was being (literally) thrust upon him with these symbols. It was a convention from the earliest Christian centuries that new bishops should pretend that they were unwilling to be given high office in this way. But in Anselm's case it was genuine enough. This meant that he had, in fact, resisted the 'investment' with the ring and staff which the king (who had no authority) had attempted to perform in person. In later years, when he had a better understanding of the significance of this part of the ceremony, he was glad that he had done so.

But it is of considerable interest that Anselm, one of the most learned men of his day, was so ill-informed about the rules which gave Church and state separate roles in the making of a bishop, and which kept the secular authority of the king strictly out of the sacramental part. He was able to get a better understanding of the issues during his

The tale of the Fisher King

The belief in the divine authority of kings is vividly reflected in the tale of the Fisher King, in the Arthurian legends. In the story, the Fisher King (who was sometimes understood to be Joseph of Arimathea), was sick. He could be cured only with the aid of the Holy Grail, the chalice used at the Last Supper, and also the legendary vessel used to catch the blood and water which flowed from the side of Christ when he was on the cross and was 'pierced' by the lances of soldiers (John 19:34). The story mainly concerns the search for this Holy Grail. But it also describes how the whole kingdom was sick because of the sickness of the king. The crops were failing and the cattle were dying. In a way, the Fisher King *was* his country.

own time as Archbishop of Canterbury, because this was the period of the Investiture Contest.

Church versus state

Troubled by the encroachment of the secular powers upon the areas where he felt the Church's authority should be supreme, Pope Gregory VII (1073–85) began to make a bid to gain the upper hand in the Church–state relationship. The pope had one supreme weapon for bringing royal personages to heel, and that was excommunication. An excommunicated monarch was cut off from all the sacraments, and this was believed to mean that not only would he himself go to hell if he died while he was under this 'ban', but so would all his subjects. (This was on the principle which shapes the 'Fisher King' legend that a king *is* his kingdom and people, and that they sink or swim with him.)

The pope did not hesitate to use this method of bringing the emperor to submit, and the emperor had only his armies with which to respond. This passage culminated in a meeting between the pope and the emperor at Canossa, North Italy, in 1077. Here, the pope made the emperor wait for three days in the snow and then kiss his stirrup, as a vassal would a feudal lord, in order to have his excommunication lifted. The humiliation of the secular authority was not so great as this made it seem;

there were sophisticated politics behind, and the emperor was able to use the situation to strengthen his position at home.

But one result was a determination to clarify not only the particular question of who could make a bishop, and which parts of the process belonged to the Church and to the state respectively, but also the wider issue of the relationship between Church and state. The Concordat of Worms of 1122 made a distinction between 'temporalities' and 'spiritualities'. The Church was to have authority over the 'spiritualities', and the state over the 'temporalities'. But the two 'arenas' were not so easily separated in real life, and for the ordinary Christian a bishop was still to be seen simultaneously as a great lord in the king's retinue and as a high figure in the Church.

So, one question had not been settled by the device of trying to separate the spheres of jurisdiction of Church and state. That was the important question of which was the superior power in the world. Pope Gelasius I (492–96) had used the image of the two swords (Luke 22:49–50) as a convenient way of posing the problem. When Jesus was arrested just before his crucifixion, the disciples produced two swords to try to defend him. In the Vulgate version, Jesus said, 'It is enough' (*satis est*). This was taken literally, as though he had *approved* of the idea that there are two sources of authority in the world. The image was used again in this way by Bernard of Clairvaux, in the book *On Consideration*, which he wrote for Pope Eugenius III. It appears again in Dante's *Monarchia*. The immediacy of the sword as an image of power is characteristically medieval.

CHAPTER 18

THE REBELS

The Church spoke of itself from an early period as 'one, holy, catholic and apostolic' Church – that is, a unified Church with the Holy Spirit working in it, which was universal, and which continued in the tradition of Jesus' apostles and, therefore, of Jesus himself. Yet the claim with which this book began, that faith in the Christian world became one seamless robe, with almost the whole population becoming baptized and believing Christians, has to be modified to accommodate the various groups who, over the centuries, either declared themselves separate from the Church or were regarded by the Church as having cut themselves off from it.

In the period of the early Church, it would have been hard to say who were the 'rebels', because no one had yet defined orthodoxy. At first, all Christians were engaged in a common endeavour to establish a shared faith. Hints of early squabbles are to be found in the Acts of the Apostles (for example, Acts 15).

Heresy

The first main division, though it is a complex one, is between 'heretics' and 'schismatics'. The 'heretic' was out of step with the Church on a matter of faith; the schismatic made a 'Church-dividing issue' out of a point of disagreement. The heretic was not the same as the person with doubts. He adopted a belief which questioned, or was at variance with, the Church's official faith, and persisted in it when it was pointed out to him that he could not believe what he did and remain at one in faith with other Christians. The persistence was what made him a heretic. This was not an easy point to arrive at in the first Christian centuries, when much of the faith was still unmapped, and the Church might have to give time and debate to deciding whether the questioner was right or wrong. The topic of the divine and human natures of Christ, for example, caused immense confusion when questioners began to press for a really clear picture of what was involved.

A leading heretic, or 'heresiarch', could be dangerous in another way. He could become extremely noisy in his insistence that he was right. The 'Arian controversy', so called because it was begun by Arius, caused divisions across Europe during the latter years of the Roman empire. Arians did not accept the divinity of Christ and his full equality as the Son of God with the other persons of the Trinity. Some of the barbarian invaders were 'politically' Arian, as well as Arian in their beliefs.

Schism

A schism was a division of the Church. Schismatics did not, as a rule, set out to create division. They believed themselves to be the true Church. In their view, it was usually others who had gone astray, and when they stood firm against the existing community on a 'Church-dividing issue', schism resulted, with each thereafter holding itself out to be the Church. Schism was taken very seriously in the early Church, because the unity of the Church was itself an article of faith. That, in Augustine's view, made schism a heresy in itself; indeed, he considered it the worst heresy.

Such divisions arose in various ways in the Middle Ages. In Augustine's own lifetime, the followers of Donatus (the 'Donatists') of north Africa were the most pressing example. Between them and the Catholics there was a mutual conviction that the other had gone fundamentally astray. Each believed that it alone had the true succession of ministry in the Church. During times of persecution of Christians, priests and bishops were forced to apostatize, that is, to renounce their faith, and to hand over their Bibles. That made them *traditores*, 'handers-over', the original 'traitors'. Apostasy had always been a serious sin. Many thought it was the sin against the Holy Spirit which Jesus said was the one sin which could not be forgiven (Luke 12:10). Few in the early Church thought a person who had renounced his faith could ever serve again as a priest or bishop. This could present problems about ensuring the succession, because it also meant that a once-apostate bishop could not ordain priests. Augustine wrote many books and letters about the Donatists, who were creating difficulties because of an episode of this kind. They refused to accept the legitimacy of a bishop of Carthage, consecrated in 311, because his consecrator had been a *traditor*. The

Schism between East and West

The most notable medieval schism was that of 1054. The Greek East and the Latin West had long been estranged by a language division, which made it difficult for them to talk to one another with real mutual understanding. There were resentments about the claim of the Bishop of Rome to be the primate of the whole Church because he was the successor of Peter, the 'rock' on whom Jesus had founded his Church (Matthew 16:18). In the East, there were other primates – the patriarchs of Jerusalem, Antioch, Alexandria and the imperial city, Constantinople – who took the view that their primacy was not subordinate to that of Rome. Moreover, the Greeks complained, the Christians of the West had departed from the early tradition by making an addition to the Nicene Creed. This was the *filioque* clause, which said that the Holy Spirit proceeded from both the Father and the Son. It had been added in the West during the eighth century, for clarification, not because the Western Christians wished to alter what they believed had always been the faith of the Church. The Schism between East and West has proved a stubborn one. It was still a source of live resentments in the East during a visit by the pope in 2001, when he tried to make apologies on behalf of the West.

Donatists were, however, orthodox in their faith, if not on this point of 'order' in the Church.

The dualists

There was a third major category of 'unbelievers' visible alongside the Christians in almost every century, and these were the dualists. The earliest 'dualists' were the Gnostics, who existed before the time of Christ. Later came the Manichees, whom Augustine followed for nine or ten years, and then the Albigensians, Cathars and Bogomils of medieval Europe, who clustered in the strip of territory from northern Italy to southern France and northern Spain. They all had certain beliefs in common: there are two 'first principles', or divine originals, in the universe; the God of the Christians is not omnipotent, but is opposed by an evil god, who is his equal in power; matter is evil and is the creation of the evil god. The attraction of all this was that it 'explained' the problem of evil. This was a real difficulty for Christians, for a wholly good God cannot be the author of evil, and if he is omnipotent, why does he allow it? (The solution, devised by Augustine after he had left the Manichee sect in disillusionment, was to say that evil is 'nothing', an 'absence' of good, and that it gets its apparent power from the distance it sets between a person and God.) A feature of the dualist sects was their emphasis on the distinction between a body of the 'elect', who were specially favoured, and the rest of the sect, whose members were merely 'followers'.

Medieval anti-establishment dissidents

A phenomenon which was persistent in the medieval West from the late twelfth century was a challenge not to faith, but to order. Popular demagogues, such as Peter of Bruys and Henry of Lausanne, made the leaders of the Church nervous because they were like the charismatic figures of old. They were often calling for things which were orthodox enough in themselves, such as a return to New Testament standards, but they were not always doing it through the proper channels. They were out of control, and so they were seen as a threat.

In the 1170s, the wealthy merchant Waldes, or Valdez, of Lyons had a moment of vision or insight, which led him to think that a movement of renewal was needed in the Church. He and his supporters seem to have intended simply to call the Church back its roots, and to remind it of the example set by Christ and the apostles, the true 'apostolic ministry'.

The Church did not take kindly to this criticism. The Waldensians were excommunicated by the pope at the Council of Verona in 1184, and his movement became one of radical protest. The Waldesians went about in woollen habits, trying to show in their own persons and behaviour the example which they said the clergy should be setting. Waldes made every effort to ensure that it was not he, but Christ, whom his followers regarded as their leader.

The patterns of dissidence which can be seen in the Waldensians reappeared in other forms: in England, in the 14th and early 15th centuries; in the Lollard movement; and in Bohemia, in the Hussite movement.

Jan Hus

Jan Hus was born in the early 1370s in Bohemia. He was ordained priest in 1400, and taught at the University of Prague in the first decade of the fifteenth century.

In 1403, a list of already condemned 'Articles of John Wyclif' was sent to the office of the archbishop by a disturbed German master, together with 21 'articles' Hus had added. On request, Hus duly delivered up his own copies. He soon found himself under accusation as a Wycliffite heretic. The more vigorously and publicly he defended himself and his orthodoxy, the more insistent became the accusations.

Hus was now caught in the familiar trap of medieval 'heretics', from which he could escape neither by 'proving his innocence' nor by 'recantation'. As he attempted to 'explain himself', he was gradually drawn into clearer and clearer statements of positions which began to look very like Wycliffite heresies. He said that God ordered the preaching of his word throughout the world. He said that if the pope were to forbid this, then he was a false witness, and that this was a disobedience to God's will which ought to be punished.

In 1411, Hus was excommunicated by the pope. At the Council of Constance in 1415, Hus was brought to trial. He went there under a promised safe-conduct, but he soon found that again he was naïve in expecting that he would be given a fair hearing, or a hearing at all (there was an attempt to try him in his absence).

By this stage, the Czech nobility was now involved, and the battle over Hus had become tangled up with high politics and the power struggle between Church and state. Hus was condemned, and died at the stake in 1415. A martyr can be extremely influential after his death, and Hus became a national hero. His writings, especially those of the later period – when he had been thinking out, under challenge and threat, a body of now quite radical teaching on the nature of the Church – gained a lasting influence, notably on Luther.

John Wyclif was an Oxford master who argued from an academic point of view about a number of issues: the imbalance of power he perceived in the Church; the growth of monarchical pretensions on the part of the papacy; the unacceptability of some Christians thinking that they were 'better' than others (he meant the monks and friars, in particular); and the need to get back to scripture as the touchstone of Christian teaching. These ideas struck a chord with popular discontent and groups of ordinary Christians began to put about these so-called 'Lollard' ideas. Some of them met in house groups and studied the Bible in English. The conviction began to grow that laypeople could find their own way to a true faith simply by reading the Bible for themselves.

In reaction to this worrying trend, apologists wrote defences of the Church. Reginald Pecock's *The Repressor of Over Much Blaming of the Clergy*, written in about 1449, accepted that the clergy had some faults, but Pecock did not think that they were as bad as they were painted. He identified 'three opinions' as 'the cause and ground of many of the errors which many of the lay party hold, and by which holding they unjustly and overmuch blame the clergy'. The first mistaken opinion was that there was no legitimate government, except what was laid down in scripture. The second was that each individual Christian, reading scripture for himself, 'shall without fail and default find the true understanding of Scripture'. This notion rested on the confidence that the Holy Spirit would lead the reader safely to the right conclusions. It cut out the Church's teaching role and took away its control of what people believed, so it was an idea much frowned upon in the Church. This was coupled with the third dangerous opinion, which was that the individual who had read his Bible need not respect what the Church taught.

'I am accused by my adversaries before your Paternity's Grace as if I were a scandalous and erroneous preacher, contrary to the Holy Mother Church, and thus wandering from the faith. With God's help, I wish to refute the scandalous accusations of my enemies.'

Jan Hus (c. 1369–1415), *Letters*

Dissidents as dangerous

It is not hard to see why such attitudes were seen as dangerous, not only by the official Church, but also by the state. Among the political poems and satires which survive from the fourteenth century is one about the Council of London in 1382, which describes the whole kingdom as disturbed, because it is not spiritually 'right'. There are earthquakes and uprisings of the peasants; the 'ship of state' is foundering. The world is turned upside down.

In another poem, we read that the Church is God's garden, but that Satan fills it with weeds because he is God's enemy. These weeds are the Lollards. 'There has been no worse pestilence in the Church,' the poem continues. The traditional cry of a Church frightened by the sheer success of dissident movements is also in this poem: 'The simple are being led astray . . . The poison is getting everywhere.' But there is a new complaint in the poem, that heresies and schisms of the past have been guilty of a single error. These Lollards are full of errors; they challenge everything.

Returned to the fold by force?

It was accepted from the first centuries that if someone who had been a heretic or schismatic wanted to return to the Church, he or she could do so, provided that there had been a valid baptism. This meant baptism with water, in the name of the Father, Son and Holy Spirit. Baptism could, in an emergency, be carried out by someone who was not ordained, so there was no difficulty about the ministry. Valid baptism could be carried out in a schismatic or heretical sect. Baptism could not be repeated, so there was to be no question of 'rebaptizing' the convert. All that was looked for was repentance and the return to the fold, and then, in Augustine's view, the 'valid' baptism became 'efficacious', and the person's sins were forgiven.

'Nobility is in servitude and the peasantry rules.'
Anonymous,
fourteenth century

The responses of the medieval Church were more vigorous. The scene was different. Now the monolith of the unified Church in the West was sufficiently integrated to make it possible for the Church to act decisively. It did so in two main ways. The first took the form of a 'crusade' against the dualist groups called the Albigensians, in the south of France and northern Spain, in an attempt to convert by force. The second had an element of force, too. The 'Inquisition' was profoundly repressive. It used excommunication, confiscation of property and banishment to frighten people into 'returning' to the fold. It would even brand people who resisted. From 1157, perpetual imprisonment was a possibility.

Beginning in the 1230s in Langedoc and Lombardy, an inquisition was set up from time to time to 'examine' suspected heretics, a machinery created by Pope Gregory IX. Bishops were required to appoint people in each parish to inform the authorities about the local heretics. These were to be the witnesses to synods. Members of the mendicant orders of monks were 'used' by the papacy to help to 'run' the Inquisition system. Neighbours were encouraged to inform on one another. Terrified peasants were called upon to explain their views on complex theological questions.

The 'questions' used to test for heresy became quite standard. In a surviving text on Lollard inquiries, the *Fasciculi zizaniorum* ('Bundles of Weeds'), the repetition of certain points is striking. The reality may be that the witch-hunting of the heretics was creating a body of 'wrong opinion' by remorselessly putting it into the mouths of bewildered and uneducated people. It is not impossible that our picture of what heretics really believed is distorted in this way, for there is, in general, far more to read in the Middle Ages from the 'official' Church's side than from the side of the heretics and dissidents themselves.

There was an apparent pastoral intention in all this, for those who recanted would get a light penalty, such as wearing a yellow cross and going on a pilgrimage, and could be considered to have been 'saved'. But just as in the present day police forces may be encouraged to make arrests so as to increase their numbers of 'cases solved', so in this medieval policing of orthodoxy in the faith it is to be expected that offences were being artificially 'created'. A peasant who was unsure about what he was being accused of would be wise to 'recant', just to be on the safe side. There were distinctions here, however, because a good test of a real Waldensian or Lollard might be that he understood very well what he believed, and would not swear falsely or recant before the tribunal of the Inquisition.

It is not surprising that this kind of conduct on the part of the authorities led to a sense of persecution among the Waldensians and Lollards. Lollard literature is particularly eloquent on this subject.

Is there salvation outside the Church?

The presumption on which the Inquisition – and, indeed, all dealing with dissidence, heresy and schism in the medieval centuries in the West –

rested was that there was no salvation outside the Church (*nulla salus extra ecclesiam*). 'Interfaith dialogue' was not a possibility, unless it had the objective of converting the unbelievers to orthodox Christian faith, and those outside the Church, because they were Jews or Muslims, were deemed lost souls.

Another way of seeming to be 'outside the Church' was to engage in the kind of uncontrollable 'charismatic' preaching or writing which caused the early Church so much anxiety, because there seemed no way to ensure that such 'prophetic', and often extremely attractive, figures would not lead the faithful astray. One example from the East at the beginning of our period was Maximus the Confessor. He was born in about 580, and moved from a career in public life to become a monk. He eventually became a respected figure, partly for his writing about the importance of the correct formulation of the doctrine of the person of Christ. But he was put on trial, and his disciples were sent into exile.

> 'They dismissed the holy old man into prison . . . [His disciples were left] naked and hungry, having only God's help.'
>
> **Anonymous, seventh century**

Another example was Joachim, the Abbot of Fiore, who, at the end of the twelfth century, seems to have begun the later medieval fashion for describing the pope as Antichrist. The rabble-rousing flavour of his writing made him disturbing to ecclesiastical officialdom.

Who decides what is the true faith?

The phenomenon of the honest dissident raises an important question about the way in which it was 'decided' who was right. The Middle Ages recognized the same two ways for the Church to reach a decision as the early Church. One was by official pronouncements by a council or a pope, the other by the emerging of the *consensus fidelium*, or 'consent of the whole people of God'. In practice, these had been complementary. There have been striking examples of the Church officially ruling that something was unacceptable

> 'The divine plan I seem to understand in the scriptures, especially since some monks have most urgently advised me, that I have an obligation not to keep silent about the wrath of the Judge so soon to be revealed from heaven upon all the wickedness and injustice of men who are unwilling to do penance for their sins.'
>
> **Joachim of Fiore (c. 1132–1202)**

Attempts at conversion

There are instances of serious attempts at conversion. In the mid-twelfth century, Peter the Venerable, the Abbot of Cluny, arranged for a translation of the Qur'an into Latin to be made, so that Christians talking to Muslims could have a better sense of the differences of belief involved. In the same period, several dialogues between Jews and Christians were published, again so as to clarify the difference of belief. One autobiographical account of the conversion of a Jew survives, Hermannus Judaeus' *De conversione sua*. Hermannus described how he had resisted for a long time the conclusion to which he was now forced to come, that the Jews had been content with the rough outer husk of scripture, while the Christians had enjoyed its sweet kernel.

which, a few centuries, later quietly became accepted. Having the Bible in the language of ordinary people is one example. Allowing the laity to receive wine as well as the bread at the eucharist, or holy communion, is another. On the other hand, the *consensus fidelium* needed to be expressed through some 'official' channel, if everyone was to be clear what it was.

At the end of the Middle Ages, this was all becoming somewhat unbalanced by the increasing claims of the papacy to plenitude of power. In the mid-fifteenth century, Nicholas of Cusa wrote a *Catholic Concordance*, in which he made various suggestions for the solving of contemporary problems in the Church. Among them was discussion of the ways in which the opinions of the faithful as a whole, or at least of ordinary people, could be included.

Clues in the creeds

By the medieval period, the Nicene Creed of the fourth century was well established and, from the eighth century in the West, the Apostles' Creed was also in use. The clauses in these creeds which reflect the early controversies also helped Christian 'apologists', or defenders of the faith, to 'classify' heresies which reappeared in later centuries. The claim that heretics were preaching 'novelties' was very common, and yet the 'novelties' were also usually identified with the 'novelties' of other, earlier heretics.

Clauses in the creeds were used to argue against views which were considered heretical by the organized Church.

Dualism

Dualists, such as the Gnostics, Manichees, Cathars, Bogomils and Albigensians, believed that there were two opposed forces, or gods, in the universe, engaged in eternal warfare. They believed that matter was the work of the evil god. Clauses in the Nicene Creed (N) and the Apostles' Creed (A) counter this view:

> 'I think that qualified learned laymen should be included in making decisions since the common good of the Church is being sought.'
>
> **Nicholas of Cusa, _The Catholic Concordance_, 1433**

I believe in God the Father Almighty, Maker of heaven and earth. (A)

I believe in one God the Father Almighty (N)
Maker of heaven and earth (N)
And of all things visible and invisible. (N)

These clauses emphasize that there is only one God and that he is omnipotent and the maker of the physical world.

Christology

Some groups, such as the Arians, doubted the divinity and humanity of Christ. These clauses in the creeds emphasize Christ's divinity:

And in Jesus Christ his only Son our Lord (A)
Who was conceived by the Holy Ghost (A)

And in one Lord Jesus Christ, the only-begotten Son of God (N)
Begotten of his Father before all worlds (N)
God of God, light of light (N)
Very God of very God (N)

> 'How false it is when many learned theologians speak disparagingly about us Wittenberg theologians, alleging that we are disseminating novelties. They speak as though there would not have been people in the past and in other places who said what we say.'
>
> **Martin Luther (1483–1546)**

Begotten not made (N)
Being of one substance with the Father (N)
By whom all things were made (N)

The following clauses stress Christ's humanity:

Born of the Virgin Mary (A)

Who for us men and for our salvation came down from heaven (N)
And was incarnate by the Holy Ghost of the Virgin Mary (N)
And was made man. (N)

Some heretics over the centuries questioned the resurrection, which was of central importance to the Christian faith. Everything turned on this, because it showed the power of God in Christ, and gave assurance to the faithful that they were saved and could hope for heaven. Only if Jesus was really the Son of God, and was really human, and really died and was resurrected was the Christian faith not in vain. The following clauses emphasize these points:

Suffered under Pontius Pilate (A)
Was crucified, dead, and buried. (A)
He descended into hell (A)
The third day he rose again from the dead (A)
He ascended into heaven (A)

And was crucified also for us under Pontius Pilate (N)
He suffered and was buried, and the third day he rose again according to
  the Scriptures (N)
And ascended into heaven (N)

Questioning whether Christ was really to be the judge of mankind was also an aspect of this area of asking awkward 'heretical' questions which went to the heart of the faith. This point, too, is made quite clear in the creeds:

And sitteth on the right hand of God the Father Almighty (A)
From thence he shall come to judge the quick and the dead (A)

And sitteth on the right hand of the Father (N)
And he shall come again with glory to judge both the quick and the dead (N)
Whose Kingdom shall have no end (N)

Trinity

Questions about the Holy Spirit turned on his divinity, and on his equality with the Father and the Son. The area of dispute here tended to be whether the Holy Spirit was truly divine and not merely some sort of animating force in the world (the 'world soul'), as some 'late Platonists' had said. The creeds clarified this issue:

I believe in the Holy Ghost (A)

And I believe in the Holy Ghost (N)
The Lord and giver of life (N)
Who proceedeth from the Father and the Son (N)
Who with the Father and the Son together is worshipped and glorified (N)
Who spake by the prophets (N)

The full explication of the doctrine of the Trinity in the West came with Augustine, who stressed, above all, the equality and co-eternity of the three persons of the Godhead.

The Church

Questions about the role and nature and authority of the Church became much more complex in the West in the Middle Ages. At the time of the formulation of the creeds, the main thing which needed to be stressed was the fact that the Church was one – it was a single 'communion', or *koinonia*, a particular kind of community, which could also be thought of as the 'body', whose 'head' is Christ. It was 'universal', or 'catholic' (one Church throughout the world). It was 'apostolic', which meant that it was engaged in mission, as Jesus had said he meant it to be, and in continuity with his teaching. It was 'holy'. The creeds made clear these points:

The holy Catholic church. (A)
The Communion of Saints (A) [Note that 'saints' simply means those who are holy, that is, the faithful.]

And I believe in one catholic and apostolic Church (N)

Human destiny

Questions about sin and the forgiveness of sin, and the role of the sacraments, arose in much more complicated ways in the Middle Ages. However, at the time of the formation of the creeds, one key question was whether the Church had the authority to declare God's forgiveness of sins. The creeds set out the Church's understanding about these issues:

The forgiveness of sins (A)

I acknowledge one baptism for the remission of sins (N)

Questions about the purpose and end of human life were still in the early stages of consideration when the creeds were completed. However, there is an indication of the continuing importance of the battle to outlaw dualism, in that it had to be stressed that not only the soul, but also the material body, would be resurrected:

The resurrection of the body (A)
and the life everlasting (A)

And I look for the resurrection of the dead, and the life of the world to come (N)

CHAPTER 19

MONKS, SAINTS AND CHRISTIAN EXAMPLES

Time to spend thinking at leisure about philosophical matters in conversation with friends was highly prized in the ancient world. It was fashionable for figures in public life to express a wistfulness for such *otium*, or intellectual leisure. Sometimes, like Cicero, they acted this out and did, indeed, spend time in retirement writing on such themes as duty, friendship and old age. Augustine of Hippo had had the same wish as a young man, and when he became a Christian in 386, he left his professorship as a teacher of oratory, and acted on it. He retreated with a group of friends, his son and his mother, to Cassiciacum on Lake Como, to discuss and then to write about *The Happy Life*, *Order* and other such subjects, in which both classical philosophy and Christianity shared an interest. When he went back to north Africa, he set up a community in which he and his friends could lead a monastic life, apart from the world, studying scripture and praying. Augustine's contemporary, Jerome, the translator of the Vulgate version of the Bible, felt the same tug, and he, too, made a series of attempts to live apart from the world.

> 'Have no other occupation or meditation than the cry of "Lord Jesus Christ, Son of God, have mercy on me." Under no circumstances give yourself any rest. This practice prevents your spirit from wandering and makes it impregnable and inaccessible to the suggestions of the enemy.'
>
> **Nicephorus, Italian Hesychast on Mount Athos, fourteenth century**

In both East and West, the 'call' to the Christian version of this life of 'philosophical retirement' had a focus with an important difference from the old 'philosopher's version'. 'Reading' and 'thinking' remained central to the religious life in the West. Communities of individuals, and individuals on their own, chose from the earliest Christian centuries to set themselves apart from the world in this way.

The Jesus prayer

In the East, the emphasis was more strongly upon an affective and transcendental spirituality. Gregory Palamas, who wrote between 1338 and 1341, was approved by the Synod of Constantinople of 1368 as a Father and a Doctor of the Church. By this time, there was a strong hermit tradition in the East, known as 'Hesychasm'. Gregory helped to bring into focus and to defend the essential activity of the Orthodox monk-hermit. Such a believer was trying to achieve a permanent state of mental prayer. The prayer which was used was known as the 'Jesus prayer', and the hermit said the name of Jesus in his mind, day and night, throughout his life, putting into practice Psalm 34:8, 'Taste and see that the Lord is good' (Authorized Version).

Gregory Palamas was a monk himself, from the age of 20, in the Great Lavra on Mount Athos. He had to leave in 1341 because of the threat posed by Turkish raids on the Mount Athos peninsula. He sought refuge in Thessalonika in northern Greece, where he lived in a spiritual circle of friends, practising the Jesus prayer. From 1325 to 1326, he was an abbot, at the monastery of Esphigmenou.

Dispute and debate

Gregory then became involved in a dispute with Barlaam, who was rebuked by two Councils of Constantinople. Barlaam thought that monks were intellectually inferior, and that the practices of those who put the emphasis on spirituality were less impressive and less important than those of philosopher-theologians. Barlaam also accused the Hesychasts of many of the same offences as those with which the Lollards were charged in the West. He said that they rejected the need for social responsibility, they did not put a proper weight on the importance of the sacraments and they had charismatic tendencies.

Barlaam's debate with Gregory led to Gregory writing the *Triads*. They were arguing about the question of the extent to which purely spiritual effort and activity can bring a person to God, and whether the body as well as the mind can be transfigured by the divine illumination which is shed upon the devout and prayerful soul. Is this a way in which someone can truly 'know God', even if he does not have the intellectual understanding of a trained theologian? Many monks in the East had invested their lives in the trust that this was possible; indeed, for them, it was the best way to do it. Gregory explored the idea of *theosis*, the 'deification' by which man, 'made in God's image and likeness' (Genesis 1:26), returned to a communion with God in which he became truly 'like God'.

Baarlam had accused the Hesychasts of something close to dualism, and of being 'Messalians', because they were 'pretending' to contemplate the essence of God with their bodily eyes. Gregory discussed this in the *Triads*, too, explaining carefully the attitude of these monks to the body – always a difficult question for medieval Christianity, because it was so suspicious of the body as a vessel of temptation.

> 'As for us, we think the mind becomes evil through dwelling on fleshly thoughts, but that there is nothing bad in the body, since the body is not evil in itself.'
>
> **Gregory Palamas** (c. 1296–1359)

For professed religious people, such as monks, nuns and hermits, in both East and West, the crucial thing was the call to a way of life which would make it possible to 'go apart' and spend time with God in prayer and worship. Prayer was the *opus dei*, the 'work of God'.

The ascetic life

To try to become a monk, nun or hermit was to attempt to obey to the full the commandment to love God with all one's heart. It was also, especially in the Middle Ages, understood to be a fulfilment of the command to love one's neighbour, for the monk or nun was also praying for the world and for other people. It was even considered to be the special task of members of religious orders to perform this task for the world. There were those who prayed, those who ruled (ran things) and those who did the work, said Adalbero in the eleventh century, and the most important of these to society were those who prayed.

> 'Man has been created to praise, reverence and serve God our Lord, and by this means to save his soul; and the other things upon the face of the earth are created for man, and to help him in the prosecution of the end for which he is created.'
>
> **Ignatius Loyola** (1491/5–1556)

Nevertheless, there were fundamental differences in the structure and pattern of the lives of those who committed themselves to God in this special way in both the East and the West. In the East, the Desert Fathers set the pattern. They were hermits who adopted various extreme forms of life, and came to be regarded as powerhouses of spiritual influence and as authorities who could assist ordinary people with their problems. The Stylites, for example, lived on platforms on high poles, and were an object of reverence to those who came to ask their spiritual advice. Others, shut off from the world in caves or huts, sought to deny themselves any contact with the temptations of 'the world', especially with women. This was an aspect of the contemporary preoccupation with the dangers of the flesh, which was partly a legacy of the dualists' conviction that matter was evil and that only spirit was good.

In the East, there continued to be a preference for idiorrhythmic living, that is, a free choice by the religious as to the way he would plan his day. Monks lived largely in their cells, and met only at intervals to eat and pray together. Many of the early religious of the East were hermits, living entirely alone. Indeed, such figures can still be seen on Mount Athos, the holy mountain in northern Greece, living lives of solitude and prayer in cells high on the cliffs, on food lowered to them in baskets.

The crucial development in the West took place when, in the sixth century, Benedict of Nursia (c. 480–550) withdrew with a group of friends to try to live an ascetic life. This prompted him to give serious thought to the way in which the 'religious life' should be organized.

Benedict arranged, at first, for groups of 12 monks to live together in small communities. Then he moved to Montecassino where, in about 529, he set up the monastery which was to become the mother house of the Benedictine Order. The rule of life he drew up was a synthesis of elements in existing 'rules', particularly the 'Rule of the Master' (whose origins are uncertain). From this point onwards in the West, the Rule of St Benedict set the standard pattern for living the religious life until the twelfth century.

In the Anglo-Saxon period in England, nuns were already forming a significant proportion of the part of the population drawn to the religious life, and there were several 'double monasteries', where communities of monks and communities of nuns lived side by side. Certain abbesses proved to be outstanding figures in a way which was then difficult for women to achieve in their own right. Hilda, Abbess of Whitby (614–80), was of royal birth, in the kingdom of Northumbria. Her sister became a nun, and Hilda wanted to follow her. However,

The Rule of St Benedict

The Rule of St Benedict achieved a good working balance. It aimed at moderation and orderliness. Those who went apart from the world to live lives dedicated to God should not, he felt, subject themselves to extreme asceticism. They should live in poverty and chastity, and in obedience to their abbot, but they should not feel the need routinely to 'subjugate the flesh' with scourges and hair-shirts. They should eat moderately, but they should not starve themselves to the point of death. They should divide their time in a regular and orderly way between manual work, reading and prayer – the *opus dei*, or 'work of God', which was the chief activity and purpose of their lives. There were to be seven regular acts of worship in the day, known as 'hours', attended by the whole community. In Benedict's vision the yoke was to be sweet and the burden light. The monastery was a 'school' of the Lord's service, in which the baptized soul made progress in the Christian life.

Aidan, one of the principal figures among the Christians of the Celtic tradition, made her the abbess of a religious house in the north of England. In 659, she founded a 'double monastery' at Whitby, where she was able to exert an influence on Aidan's side at the Synod of Whitby in 664, when the Celtic and Roman Christians had a conference to try to sort out their differences.

Nobility and patronage in the religious life

Another common feature of monastic life in the West was also already evident, in Hilda's story. It was largely reserved for the upper classes. The serfs did not have the freedom to choose to become monks. The houses of monks and nuns became the recipients of noble and royal patronage. 'Spare' children of good birth would be given to the religious life by their families as 'child oblates', and would then be in a position to discharge on behalf of the family the role of 'pray-er' for the souls of their relations. Similarly, rich and powerful families would give monasteries lands and estates, for the good of the souls of their members. Rulers and soldiers were too busy to attend to their spiritual lives as they should, and 'professionals' drawn from their own families could help them by doing it on their behalf.

One consequence of this was that, in the later Middle Ages in particular, the abbot or abbess was usually a nobleman or woman. She was often chosen because of being the highest in birth in the monastery or convent, and not because of any natural powers of leadership or outstanding spirituality. Chaucer's cruel fourteenth-century caricature of a prioress depicts a woman who would have been much more at home in a country house playing with her lapdogs:

There was also a nun, a prioress
That of her smiling was full simple and coy . . .
Of small hounds had she, that she fed
With roasted flesh, or milk and stale bread . . .
Full seemly her wimple pinched was.

Chaucer, *Canterbury Tales*, Prologue (1387–88)

In these features of noble patronage of the religious life lay not only the stamp of society's approval, but also the potential for decay. Houses which became very rich, and which were filled with individuals who had not chosen to enter the religious life, but had been put into it in childhood, could also become decadent. The so-called Cluniac reforms of the tenth century were a consequence of the recognition that, from time to time, there would need to be a tightening up if the Benedictine religion was not to be lost sight of. At Cluny and the houses which imitated it, standards were high, although here, too, there was a danger of distortion of the original Benedictine vision. Cluniac houses had extra rules and a degree of rigidity which compromised the original simplicity of the Benedictine life.

Experimentation

At the end of the eleventh century, several developments radically altered the range of choice for those in the West who wanted to enter the religious life. The first was a change of fashion, which encouraged married couples of mature years to decide to end their days in monastic life. A knight who had fought his wars might make an agreement with his wife that they would go off into separate religious houses. Adult entry of this sort was entry by people who really did want to be monks and nuns, and it had the potential to alter the balance in favour of serious commitment.

We saw in chapter 12 Guibert of Nogent's comment on this issue, in his autobiography. The new emphasis was on a return to the concept of personal 'vocation' to the religious life, which made people see it as the 'divine call' it used to be in the first Christian centuries.

These mature adults were not the only category of the new 'volunteer religious'. Younger people were being drawn in, too. At Bec, earlier in the eleventh century, Herluin, himself an ex-soldier, had founded a new religious house. Lanfranc, a famous teacher, joined him there, and set up a school to which the sons of the local people were invited to come. They flocked there, according to the historian Orderic Vitalis, and some of them stayed. When Anselm, Lanfranc's successor, ran the school, it was for the actual young monks of Bec.

The same period saw a number of experiments in the religious life, some of them short-lived, or nothing more than the eccentric behaviour of one individual disillusioned with conventional provisions. Henry the Monk is an example of a former monk who became a popular demagogue in the early twelfth century. But so many were seriously

The Cistercians

Out of the period of experiment came one immensely important new order, the Cistercians. They used the Benedictine rule, but they had a different set of priorities. The first was a determination to protect themselves from the dangers which could come from growing too rich. They chose to build houses in remote places. They made a place for people from the lower social classes who had vocations. These were to be lay brothers.

The startling early success of this order was due to Bernard of Clairvaux. When he decided to enter the newly founded house of Cîteaux, he took with him a group of his relations and friends. He set a fashion, and so rapidly did recruitment proceed that more and more houses had to be founded in quick succession. He himself was made abbot of one of them, Clairvaux, at so early an age that, at first, the responsibility made him ill. But he went on to become a leading figure in the monastic world, and in the world of politics. He spoke so well and so movingly that he was useful as a diplomatic emissary, as well as a preacher.

engaged in pushing forward the boundaries of the religious life that one writer thought it would be helpful to review the available modes of living for the religious in the twelfth century. This *De diversis ordinibus* covered all the possibilities, from Benedictines and reformed Benedictines, to the canons – priests who did not live enclosed lives, but who were allowed to work in the world – and the various sorts of hermits.

The only real rival to the Rule of St Benedict was the 'Rule' of Augustine, which was adopted by 'regular canons'. These differed from monks, in that they were priests who could be active in the community, for example, serving in parishes. They were not living under the monastic rule of 'stability', which, in principle, confined a monk for life to the house in which he was professed. Canons of cathedrals, in particular, were encouraged to live in community under a rule, and the Augustinian rule was well-adapted to their needs.

The twelfth century saw the creation of new orders in a similar mould. The Victorines in Paris produced leading academic figures and teachers of 'spirituality', such as Hugh, Andrew and Richard of St Victor. The Premonstratensians were associated with their own leading figures, like Anselm of Havelberg, who made an attempt to sit down with Greek Christians and discuss the differences which were dividing them from the West. Anslem wrote an account of these early 'ecumenical dialogues' in his own *Dialogues*.

> 'Since . . . many kinds of callings have come into being, and particularly in own day, institutions of monks and canons differing in habit and worship are increasing, it is necessary to show, with God's help, how such servants of God differ and what the purposes of the different forms of callings are.'
>
> **Author unknown, *Book on the Different Orders*, twelfth century**

The rise of the mendicants

From the beginning of the thirteenth century there were orders of friars dedicated to preaching. These were the mendicants. The Franciscans were founded by Francis of Assisi, and they concentrated chiefly on preaching to ordinary Christians and trying to bring alive for them the spirit of the apostolic life, as Jesus had taught it to his disciples. The Dominicans were founded by St Dominic, specifically to preach against the heretics in the south of France and elsewhere.

The Franciscans faced a crisis when St Francis died, as many religious movements have done when they were begun by a particularly charismatic individual. The essence of St Francis's way was peculiarly dependent on his personality. On his death, some of his followers were anxious to keep to this extreme life of poverty and simplicity. Others recognized that the long-term survival of the order would require it to become 'institutionalized'. To the first group were attracted a number of individuals on the 'fringe' of religious respectability. There resulted a great debate about poverty.

Attitudes to the friars became extremely complex. Their sermons seem to have been popular with people starved of an adequate supply of preaching from the parish pulpit. Margery Kempe describes 'how fast the people came running to hear the sermon' when they heard that a famous preacher had come to King's Lynn. But people could also be choosy. Margery Kempe also notes how they would not sit down and compose themselves to listen, but would stand impatiently so that they could easily walk out if they did not like what they heard. Some, she said, came with their sins unrepented and, indeed, with no intention of giving up their bad ways. Some – and this is reported of sermon-goers in other centuries – went only to be seen, for the sermon was a local 'occasion', at which it might be fashionable to be present. Others, she said, were there not to listen to the content, but to sample the style.

On the other hand, because of their mendicant way of life, there was a risk that some friars would fall into corrupt habits. The resentment against the clergy, which mounted in dissident communities in the late-medieval centuries, was prompted most strongly by the sight of wealth and indolence among the higher clergy, but it was also difficult for ordinary people to feel respect for local clergy if they were ignorant and incompetent. Some of that resentment spilled over into criticism of the friars for similar, and other, faults. When these visible shortcomings were coupled with the Church's insistence that heaven was to be reached only 'within the Church' and with the aid of its sacraments, articulate laypeople were naturally resentful.

From the point of view of 'officialdom', the friars were unsettling. On the one hand they represented the Church: they were members of the clergy; the Franciscan and Dominican orders had had papal approval since the beginning of the thirteenth century, and they were highly

Jibes against the friars

There are jibes which suggested that the friars did, indeed, get a bad name. A 'Song Against the Friars', an anonymous fourteenth-century verse, put it satirically. There are those who claimed to be learned, who 'give themselves to great study'; and others who:

Men may see by their countenance,
*   That they are men of great penance.*

But the author had never, in the 40 years of his life, seen fatter men than these friars:

Priest, nor monk, nor yet canon
*   Nor any man of religion,*
Gives him so to devotion,
*   As do these holy friars.*
For some give themselves to chivalry,
*   Some to riot and ribaldry.*

educated preachers. Yet, partly perhaps because they wandered the countryside preaching, the friars sometimes became associated in the eyes of 'authority' with fringe movements, such as the Lollards.

The higher calling

The not-always-edifying story of the reality of living the monastic, or 'religious', life in the Middle Ages should not be allowed to detract too much from the central ideals. There is every reason to suppose that many, living quietly in religious houses, prayed, read and – if they were Benedictines – did hard manual labour, with the utmost devotion, throughout their lifetimes. There were spiritual giants among the mendicants, as well as thoroughly bad examples to their fellow men and women. This idea of setting an example was an important one.

After Augustine of Canterbury brought the faith to England it was said that it was as though the sun had come out. Also among 'God's athletes', Bernard of Clairvaux counts St Malachi, whose *Life* he wrote in the twelfth century, emphasizing its value as an example. One of the main attractions for medieval people of the cult of saints was the reassurance that some had managed to lead exemplary lives, and had shown others how to do it.

The requirements for sanctity were relatively easy to stereotype. In the *Life of St Erkenwald*, we read that he was 'perfect in wisdom, modest in conversation, vigilant in prayer, chaste in body, dedicated to holy reading, rooted in charity'. By the late eleventh century, it was even possible to hire a hagiographer, such as Osbern of Canterbury, who would come and write a *Life* of a dead abbot, in the hope that he would be canonized. It was usual to include a list of miraculous interventions by the saint, as indications that he or she had had divine approval. Here again, the corrupting effects of real life are evident. There was active competition to achieve canonization, because an abbey with a saint among its former membership could hope for pilgrims to come and visit the 'shrine'. There would also be relics and, with luck, stories of miracles brought about by those relics.

> 'After the passion and resurrection of the Lord, when the Catholic faith had been diffused throughout the world, there were "God's athletes" sowing the seed of the faith.'
>
> **Anonymous, Life of St Erkenwald**

This meant that there is about the phenomenon of the saints, both an inward and an outward aspect. A holy man or woman was thought to leave behind, in objects touched or places visited, a residual power, a 'merit', which pious people could acquire for their assistance in their own troubles by going on pilgrimage and praying at the shrine. A similar power inhered in the body of the saint, or in parts of the body, such as the fingernails or hair, which could conveniently be kept in little 'relic-holders' or reliquaries.

Simple people would use these, praying and touching the holy items, in the hope of miracles of healing – rather as people still visit the comparatively modern shrine at Lourdes or, in the Greek Orthodox world, go to the shrine at Tinos, where the 'saint' is the blessed Virgin, Jesus' mother. This, though mysterious and spiritual power, is outward in the sense that the consciousness of the devout was fixed on the material objects and in the places in which the power was believed to reside.

A better picture of what went on 'inside' a saint or an ordinary member of the religious orders trying to take his or her faith seriously is to be obtained from the comments of those whose writings survive, for here we have more evidence than can be got from stories of their activities and the miraculous consequences. The most frequent comment heard from those later rated 'saints' was the difficulty they had in keeping an appropriate balance between their active and their contemplative lives. We hear this from Gregory the Great, pope in the year 600; from Aldhelm, an abbot of Malmesbury, who was not canonized himself, in the seventh and eighth centuries; and so on until Bernard of Clairvaux wrote a book in five volumes for Pope Eugenius III, called *On Consideration*.

'Love flies, runs and leaps for joy; it is free and unrestrained. Love gives all for all, resting in one who is highest above all things, from whom every good flows and proceeds.'

Thomas à Kempis, The Imitation of Christ, c. 1418

The balance between the active and the contemplative life was, indeed, perhaps the core issue for those who aspired to be spiritual giants and examples to others, or for those who simply wanted to be good Christians (for a true saint is, of course, also humble). How much time should be given to God and how much to work in the world? Ironically, the idea that some people could be left to carry out the work of prayer for the world as professionals does not seem to have relieved them of this sense of the crowding demands of ordinary life. Anselm of Canterbury begins his *Proslogion* with the advice that the 'little man' (*homunculus*) who wanted to concentrate on God should withdraw into the chamber of his own mind, close the door and shut out the multitude of irrelevant thoughts which would otherwise crowd in upon him and distract him. There, a great liberation was to be found.

CHAPTER 20
HOLY WAR

Christ brought a message of peace and reconciliation. People of his time expected him to be a revolutionary, but he always sought to change things without violence, except on the occasion when he threw the money-changers out of the Temple (John 2:15). He taught his disciples to 'turn the other cheek' (Luke 6:29).

Yet the society of the Middle Ages was irredeemably warlike. In the feudal areas of Northern Europe, the whole social system depended on the maintenance of a military, or 'knightly', class, a permanent soldiery or noblemen whose only profession was fighting. In Italy, the city states were frequently at war – internally, with one another or with popes and emperors. In Spain, a line was drawn across the map for some centuries by the presence of the Muslim invaders. So even if Christians had wanted to create a peaceful society, it would have been socially and practically a difficult thing to do.

One way of dealing with this was to idealize the warfare. The idea of a war between good and evil is very ancient, and the first 'dualists', the Gnostics, who were interested in it at the time when Christianity came into being, presented an ideological challenge, because they thought in terms of two equal and opposed powers in the universe, locked in a real struggle for supremacy, in which the evil might possibly win. Christians had to insist, in opposition to this widespread view, that there was only one God and that his opponent was not another deity, but a fallen angel, a creature who had gone wrong.

In the Christian scheme of explanation, Satan is merely a fallen angel. He is still a powerful figure, working systematically and effectively for the possession of human souls, whom he wishes, in his destructive way, to seduce from God and to deny any hope of the heaven which is lost to him for ever. For most medieval people, Satan seems to have been a 'personal' threat, rather than an abstraction.

But the battle scenes were attractive. In the Middle Ages, a favourite way of retaining them without slipping into the error of believing that the powers of good and evil in the universe were two deities, was to describe battles between the Virtues and Vices, in which Prudence, Fortitude, Justice and Temperance, in personified form, did battle with their enemies in the form of their opposing vices. The model for this was Prudentius' *Psychomachia* (c. 348–410). It was imitated in the Middle Ages, for example, by Alan of Lille in his *Anticlaudianus*. This late twelfth-century poem describes an attempt to make a perfect man. The skills available to human knowledge can go only so far, and God has to be asked to provide a soul. However, when the 'perfect man' sets about his task of rescuing the human race, he does it by fighting just such a battle of the virtues and vices.

This kind of literature externalized the inward warfare of which all medieval Christians were encouraged to be aware – that between desires and longings prompted by 'the flesh', and the spiritual aspirations for which God created them.

The Christian knight

The 'soldier of Christ', the warrior for good, was not difficult to fit into the Christian scheme of things, even though the reality was that the pervasive fighting of the Middle Ages was far from merely figurative. In the feudal society of Northern Europe in the Middle Ages, the image of the 'soldier of Christ' was important. It enabled laypeople to experience a sense of living for Christ and 'fighting for the good' in their daily lives. It provided an image of great vividness:

In all the city no pagan now appears
  Who is not slain or turned to Christian fear.

Anonymous, 'The Song of Roland'

There was a good deal of doublethink, in the fact that the penitential system recognized that it was a sin to kill an enemy in battle, even if the battle was in a good cause. The tables of appropriate penances which survive make careful distinctions between the archer who has shot into the enemy line and does not know exactly how many he may have killed or injured, and the foot-soldier or knight who can remember with how many he had hand-to-hand combat, and whether he killed his enemy each time.

In the Holy Land, in the twelfth century, were 'military' religious orders, whose role was to give protection to pilgrims, and to provide care and support for Christians on crusade. The Hospitallers and Templars eventually became the subject of criticism and condemnation because some of their actions belied their ideals. Yet, at the beginning of the twelfth century, Bernard of Clairvaux could write a 'guided tour' of the Holy Places, drawing spiritual and practical lessons for such hybrid soldier-monks, and telling them how to divide their time between their duties of prayer and their duty to keep their weapons polished.

> 'Whenever a man desires anything inordinately, he becomes restless. A proud and avaricious man is never at rest; but a poor and humble man enjoys the riches of peace.'
>
> **Thomas à Kempis,** *The Imitation of Christ*, c. 1418

Just and holy war

It was therefore important for medieval Christians to be able to convince themselves that the war that they were fighting was at least justified. Quite a sophisticated system of identifying a 'just' war grew up. Augustine of Hippo had said a good deal about this, explaining that someone whose property or land has been stolen is entitled to get it back, but that this was different from warfare designed to enlarge one's territory. The underlying principle was that reasonable force could be used to maintain order.

But with the late eleventh century came a concept with a new importance – that of 'holy' war, war which God positively wanted his people to fight to restore to Christian control the holy places of the Holy Land. This was war which could not only be regarded as 'justified', and the sins committed in the course of it forgiven, but positively meritorious. God rewarded those who fought it. Guibert of Nogent, in his book *The Acts of God Through the Franks*, explains how to identify 'holy' war. It was not motivated by the desire for fame, money or conquest of lands. Its motive was the protection of liberty, the defence of the state and the protection of the Church. He makes it plain that he himself considered this kind of warfare a valid alternative to being a monk.

This idea was so engaging that, as the twelfth century went on, it had to be discouraged by apologists, who did not want everyone to see knighthood as spiritual warfare to such a degree. It was emphasized that crusading was special. Not all fighting came under the same umbrella.

Muslim literature reflects a similar heightened sense that war could be 'holy'. This period saw the revival of the *jihad*. After the fall of Edessa in 1144 in particular (the first of the crusader states to be regained for Islam after the First Crusade), Muslims increasingly came to see themselves as fighting the Christian polytheist infidels for the glory of God. It eventually became important to the Muslims to recapture Jerusalem itself, to banish the 'worshippers of the cross' from the mosque there. There emerged a 'spiritual *jihad* much greater than the actual battle'

'[He is] the most distinguished emperor of the Roman people, whose trophies and valiant deeds and stratagems against the barbarians the whole earth cannot contain.'

Anna Comnena (1083–c. 1148) about her father, the emperor, *Alexiad*

Crusading

The circumstances in which the Christian West came to engage with 'holy' war were political at the outset. The Turks were invading the Eastern empire. Romanus, the emperor of Byzantium, fought and lost the battle of Manzikert in 1071, and his successor Alexius called on the West to help. This was, in itself, a remarkable proof of how desperate things were. East and West had not been on friendly terms for centuries. The Greeks of the East rather despised the Westerners as barbarians, as is evident from the recorded remarks of Anna Comnena, one of the imperial family. It was as recently as 1054 that the formal Schism of the two Churches had taken place. Yet Alexius wrote to the pope with his plea.

Pope Urban II responded by preaching the crusade at Clermont in 1095. His doing so raised a number of important questions. Here was the primate of the Church, encouraging people to go to war and emphasizing that it was, if not a duty, certainly a meritorious act. He promised that those who went, and either died on the way or stayed the course as far as Jerusalem, would receive full remission of all their undischarged penances (a 'plenary indulgence').

It may be that Urban had an 'ecumenical' purpose. We know that he was keen to mend the breach with the Greek Church. At the Council of Bari in 1098, the matter was raised when Greek Christians were present. Urban called upon Anselm of Canterbury, who had come to him in exile for advice and help in his own dealings with the English king, to stand up at the Council and resolve the difference of opinion about the procession of the Holy Spirit. Anselm tried to do so, asking for a few days to collect his thoughts. Four years later, he published a book giving his opinion, which survives as his *On the Procession of the Holy Spirit*. So Urban's responsiveness to the Byzantine call for help may reflect his wish to reunify Christendom.

In his calling of the crusade, Urban took much the same line as Guibert. The knight who went on crusade was a penitent; he was serving God by bearing arms and he was acting out of sacrificial love, for he may be giving up his life. This was not the mere lending of assistance to a neighbour state in trouble. The 'enemy' were Muslims. The threat was to the holy places. It was a defence of the faith. The language of the Clermont 'decree' spoke of 'going to Jerusalem to liberate the Church of God', and Urban justified the crusade in a letter to the Franks.

> '*The barbarians in their frenzy have invaded and ravaged the Churches of God in the Eastern places; worse, they have captured the Holy City of Christ . . . And sold her and her churches into slavery.*'
>
> **Pope Urban II, *Letter to the Franks*, 1095**

Urban saw the Muslim conquest of these places as a contamination, and the task of the crusaders as one of purification.

The crusade, once called, had an immediate attraction for ordinary people, in an age when there were few opportunities for journeys. Itinerant preachers, such as Peter the Hermit, successfully raised armies of peasants. His group, mainly of Germans, was the second to leave. First was Walter Sans Avoir (Walter the Penniless), whose rabble of French peasants set off in 1096, disorganized and plundering as they went through Hungary. The alarmed Byzantines were quick to ship such groups across the Bosphorus into Asia Minor, where they could confront the Turks as they might.

Guibert of Nogent had a fine sense of the sheer scale of the thing. He described how, 'from almost every part of the West', 'innumerable armies' approached. Anselm of Canterbury, who knew and advised Guibert, according to Guibert's autobiography, would not have agreed with him there. Letters survive which were exchanged between Anselm and a young monk anxious for an excuse to leave his monastery and go and fight on crusade.

More senior and organized parties were conducted by leading nobles. Raymond of Toulouse was 60 years old and had fought the Muslims in Spain. Hugh of Vermandois, younger son of King Henry I of France, probably wanted to make a new life outside the unpromising circumstances of his prospective lack of inheritance at home. Godfrey of Bouillon and his younger brother, Baldwin, probably also had designs on lands in the Holy Land. One of the least highly motivated of all, in the kind of terms set out by Guibert of Nogent, seems to have been Robert of Normandy, eldest son of William the Conqueror, who set off with Stephen of Blois and Robert of Flanders.

There were mutual misunderstandings at Constantinople. The emperor exacted an oath of allegiance from Godfrey because he intended to remain in charge of the Western armies if he could. The armies moved off more or less at the same time across Asia Minor in 1097, to encounter in the Turks a formidable and quite unfamiliar style of fighting. The use of Arab horses and light swords, which could be used one-handed from horseback to slash an enemy on the gallop, set at a grave disadvantage the slow and cumbersome Western armies. They were experienced in the kind of battle where the opposing sides lined up and charged at one another, and where there was time to stand one's ground and wield a sword with both hands.

Nevertheless, partly with the aid of siege warfare, the crusaders were remarkably successful in this First Crusade, and they were able to establish kingdoms along the Mediterranean seaboard. They built 'crusader castles'.

The success of the First Crusade was acclaimed with a spiritual triumphalism, because it seemed that God must be pleased with the people of the West and what they had done for him. That did not last long. The situation in the Holy Land was inherently unstable even then, though the parties involved were different. The fall of Edessa in 1144 meant that a second crusade had to be called. Bernard of Clairvaux was, at first, reluctant to preach this crusade, because he believed that Christian effort was better directed at making Christendom itself more holy. He was eventually persuaded by Peter the Venerable, the abbot of Cluny who had

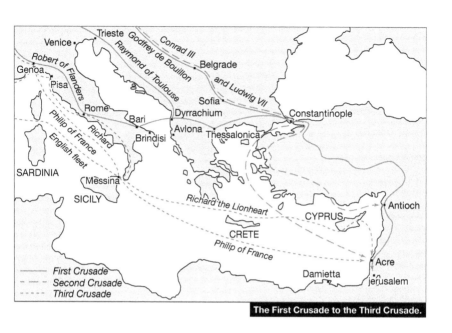

The First Crusade to the Third Crusade.

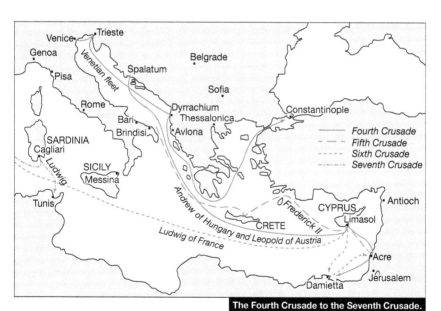

The Fourth Crusade to the Seventh Crusade.

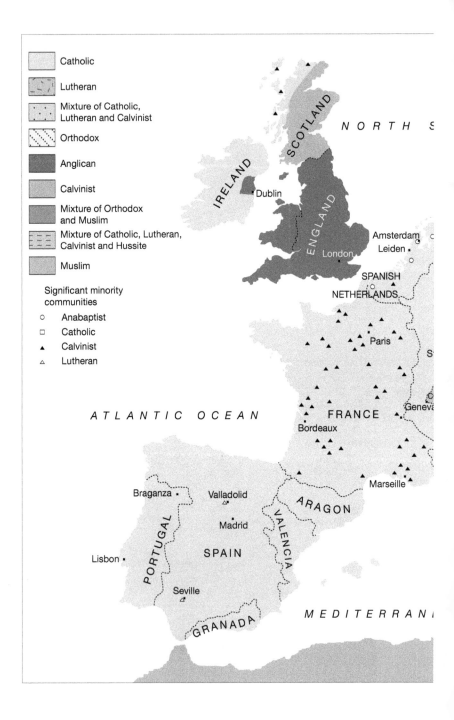

Legend:

- Catholic
- Lutheran
- Mixture of Catholic, Lutheran and Calvinist
- Orthodox
- Anglican
- Calvinist
- Mixture of Orthodox and Muslim
- Mixture of Catholic, Lutheran, Calvinist and Hussite
- Muslim

Significant minority communities
- ○ Anabaptist
- □ Catholic
- ▲ Calvinist
- △ Lutheran

IRELAND
Dublin
SCOTLAND
ENGLAND
London
NORTH S

Amsterdam
Leiden
SPANISH
NETHERLANDS

ATLANTIC OCEAN

FRANCE
Paris
Bordeaux
Geneva
Marseille

Braganza
Valladolid
Madrid
ARAGON
VALENCIA
PORTUGAL
SPAIN
Lisbon
Seville
GRANADA

MEDITERRANE

NORWAY

SWEDEN

LIVONIA

COURLAND

RUSSIA

E A

DENMARK

BALTIC SEA

Danzig

PRUSSIA

Hamburg

LITHUANIA

Warsaw

GERMAN
EMPIRE

Leipzig

POLAND

SILESIA

Frankfurt

Prague

BOHEMIA

Augsburg

MORAVIA

rasbourg

AUGSBURG

BAVARIA

AUSTRIA

Vienna

Budapest

Zürich

SWISS

SALZBURG

STYRIA

ONFEDERATION

TYROL

CARINTHIA

HUNGARY

CARNIOLA

VENICE

Venice

Genoa

PAPAL STATES

CORSICA
to Genoa

DALMATIA
to Venice

OTTOMAN

EMPIRE

Rome

NAPLES
to Spain

Naples

SARDINIA
to Spain

E A N S E A

SICILY
to Spain

The religious divisions of Europe in about 1560.

organized a translation of the Qur'an into Latin so that Christians could have a better idea what Muslims actually believed. Bernard was highly successful in winning people to fight, so much so that supplies of crosses for people to sew on their clothes ran out, and more had to be made by tearing up any cloth to hand. Yet the crusade was an ignominious failure. Instead of recapturing Edessa, the crusaders allowed themselves to be distracted into making a massive attack on Damascus, and thereafter it petered out. Bernard had to explain to himself and to others in the West what had gone wrong and why. His explanation was rather like that produced by Augustine after the fall of Rome in 410. God could allow what

Pilgrimage

Talk of pilgrimage may not seem to have a natural place in a chapter on holy war, but the pilgrimage context was important to the way in which the crusaders saw what they were doing. Pilgrimage to the holy places had been becoming popular during the eleventh century. There was an understandable conflation in people's minds between the journey of pilgrimage, the journey which was crusade and the journey which was a person's metaphorical travelling through life. Jerusalem was both 'heavenly' and 'earthly', and because it was so far away, it may not always have been clear to those who set out to go there that they were not really travelling directly to heaven. Many different Latin words to do with travelling were used, and almost all of them could apply equally well to literal or spiritual 'travelling' of the body or the soul.

The bringing together of the physical and the supernatural world in this way is visible in much earlier writing. Avitus, Bishop of Vienne (495–525), says, 'there is a place, far on the eastern side of the world' where winter and summer do not follow one another in succession. Gregory the Great, at the end of the sixth century, spoke of the fields where the sheep of Christ the shepherd fed, spending eternity in the presence of God and contemplating eternally he who was their spiritual food.

To be able to think of oneself as going to this place by the simple expedient of setting off on an expedition was a powerful idea. It was linked with the ancient Platonic and Christian idea that all creation is on a journey back to God. The 'region' close to God is the 'region of likeness'. Sinful humans have wandered off into the 'region of unlikeness' (regio dissimilitudinis), and their life's task is to return to God.

looked like a Christian enterprise (a Christian empire, a holy war) to fail because he had a far longer-term plan. He was looking to the long-term salvation of his world, and he needed to educate his people, to make them realize how high a standard of goodness was needed for things to work.

A third and a fourth crusade followed, both failures. The Third Crusade (1188–92) was precipitated by the fall of Jerusalem to the Muslims under Saladin. It drew in reigning monarchs to lead it: Frederick Barbarossa, the emperor of Germany; Philip Augustus, king of France; and King Henry II of England. The resulting political rivalries made the failure of the crusade almost inevitable.

The Fourth Crusade (1204), in particular, displayed a crude commercialism on the part of the Venetians, who required the crusaders to sack Constantinople first, in return for the use of ships for transport. The sight, in 1204, of Western Christians running about the streets of the great city, which was the capital of the Christian East, sacking, pillaging and raping was the ultimate betrayal of the ideal of the crusade as a holy war, although the crusading movement lasted into the thirteenth century, in a desultory way.

CHAPTER 21

TRADITION AND CONTINUITY: THE ROAD TO REFORMATION

Several things happened in the West in the 15th and 16th centuries to change the medieval scene so irrevocably that the period which followed could begin to be spoken of as the 'modern world'. As so often, the dividing lines separating what now look to us like distinct 'periods' were different in the Eastern half of Christendom. A detailed picture of this is available in *Faith in the Byzantine World*, another title in this series.

Another book in this series, *Luther and His World*, describes Luther's significant role in making people think differently and in opening up the lasting divisions in the Christian Church which can still be seen today in the numerous 'denominations', with their separate church buildings and their separated congregations. The ecumenical movement of the second half of the twentieth century did a good deal to mend these divisions, but it has not yet succeeded in putting the Western Churches back where they were in 1400, or in bringing together the East and West, which parted in 1054. It is probably still true that there is fundamentally one 'faith', but it is obvious that there is not, in any visible sense, one Church.

Renaissance

Alongside the changes in the Church ran an immense change of expectations among scholars, which was able to move with unprecedented speed because of the invention of printing. Printed books began to appear before the end of the fifteenth century, and during the course of the sixteenth century, printed versions were produced of a good proportion of the main works of the Middle Ages.

Medieval scholars invented the universities, and the universities, too, began to change, with 'alternative syllabuses'. The medieval method of study had gradually evolved into a system which is often labelled 'scholasticism'. There was a heavy burden of 'system', derived from the formal study of logic. Aristotle remained the basis but, in the medieval

Two Renaissance men

One of the first scholars to bring together the new 'Greek' learning and the transformation of the approach to the study of the Christian faith was Erasmus. He enjoyed the civilized wit of the Renaissance, which is reflected in his writings – for example, in *In Praise of Folly*, to which he gave a Greek title. An English contemporary and friend was Thomas More – lawyer, parliamentarian and scholar – who kept open house in London for Erasmus and his circle. More also wrote, notably, the famous *Utopia*, in which he imagines an ideal state and its drawbacks. These 'Renaissance men' were not always sympathetic to the Reform which was being called for in the Church. More was a staunch defender of the medieval Church while King Henry VIII was moving towards the breach with Rome, and he suffered for it politically. More was beheaded for treason in 1535 because he opposed the king's divorce. He wrote a *Response to Luther*: 'When I began to read – good God, what an ocean of nonsense, what a bottomless pit of madness presented itself.'

centuries, a 'new logic' was added. This built on Aristotle and dealt in a much more subtle and sophisticated way with the way in which language works. Given a problem, a teacher would divide it up for his students, and they would look at each part of it in order. This could have the effect of reducing all issues to the same level. It made it difficult to be inventive or to find new ways of approaching the framing and answering of questions.

Lorenzo Valla, in the late fifteenth century, began to point to drawbacks in the scholastic method. Peter Ramus, in the sixteenth century, took Aristotle and the 'new logic' by the scruff of the neck, and reduced it all to a simple introductory course. He did not do it very well, but his work was welcomed by students because this marked the end of the dominance of the medieval pattern of study.

At the same time, there was a reawakening ('Renaissance') of enthusiasm for the classics, not only for the Roman authors, such as Cicero, Livy, Horace and Seneca, who had been available all through the Middle Ages, but also the Greek ones. They were now becoming accessible to more readers because students were beginning to learn Greek. This trend was not separate from the moves which were leading to the Reformation. Melanchthon was a leading 'Renaissance' scholar and a close friend of Luther, working with him in running the University of Wittenberg.

The 'double life' of scholars who could write on secular themes and, at the same time, make a serious mark as theologians or writers on religious subjects was in evidence throughout the sixteenth century. John Donne, who became Dean of St Paul's, was able to write in jest, but not without seriousness, about holy things and theological ideas in a love poem, 'Air and Angels'.

So in a voice, so in a shapeless flame
Angels affect us oft and worshipp'd be . . .
And therefore what thou wert, and who,
I bid love ask, and now
That is assume thy body I allow,
And fix itself in thy lip, eye, and brow.

John Donne (1571/2–1631), 'Air and Angels'

Back to the sources

The last great medieval development in the study of the Bible, too, was the call to get back to the sources (*ad fontes*). Here, the reawakening of interest in the 'biblical languages' of Greek and Hebrew was important. In the twelfth century, a few scholars, such as Andrew of St Victor, asked the advice of Jews who spoke Hebrew when they were unsure of how they should 'read' a passage in the Old Testament. However, this does not seem to have led to serious attempts to learn the language for themselves. The late Middle Ages saw the founding of universities which specialized in teaching the three 'biblical languages' of Greek, Hebrew and Latin. Reuchlin (1455–1522), a German humanist, was one of the first individuals to tackle instruction in Hebrew systematically, by providing textbooks to help students to learn it.

In the same period, others – notably, perhaps, Erasmus of Rotterdam – were beginning to work seriously on the Greek. (Erasmus confessed that he could not manage to learn both languages at once.) Erasmus published a Greek New Testament in 1516, and made a fresh version of the Latin Vulgate to go with it. His notes on the New

Testament survive – a personal, witty, satirical commentary on the problems he faced. He was working on his *In Praise of Folly* at about the same time, and in something of the same comico-serious spirit. He was a humanist, and therefore conscious of classical comparisons and allusions. Considering the possible translations of the beginning of Matthew's Gospel, he observed that 'sometimes Homer used this word in the Odyssey, but that Matthew means something quite new when he uses it'. His intention was not to overturn the Vulgate as the Bible of the Western Church, but he could not help noticing its flaws. He is critical, but he 'pretends' that he cannot really believe that the Vulgate was the work of the great Jerome; perhaps the translator sometimes 'nodded off'? Erasmus, still learning Greek, nevertheless thought that he could usefully use the Greek New Testament in making his own Latin rendering.

One of the striking results of this kind of work was that it enabled scholars to look at the text in a new way and ask fresh questions. A quite different sort of early printed Bible began to appear, known as the Polyglot, because it set the text in various languages side by side for comparison.

Change in the Church

The Reformation idea of 'justification by faith' was largely a creation of Martin Luther. He had been disturbed by the growing elaborateness of the Church's expectations at the end of the Middle Ages, the insistence that no one could get to heaven without the good offices of the Church and its sacraments. He brought about an immense 'shake-up', by arguing passionately that God was interested only in the individual's personal faith, and that this was what 'justified' people in God's eyes. No one could get to heaven merely by doing good works, or through the penitential system of 'making up' for wrongdoing.

Luther's proposition undermined much of the structure we have been looking at in this book, because it threw into question what the Church was for and whether the faithful needed its 'official' help to be saved. The visible Church, with all its imperfections and corruptions, was actively contrasted in the sixteenth century with the spiritual and invisible Church.

Some reformers (the 'Congregationalists') argued that the Church as a whole was invisible, but that it had visible 'outcrops' in the form of local congregations. Much emphasis was placed on the self-government of these 'gathered churches', in order to weaken the stranglehold of the centralized and monarchical structure which had emerged in the Church in the West as a result of the mounting claims of the papacy to 'plenitude of power'.

This led other reformers to go back to the New Testament and to point to the apparent lack of authority there for the threefold system of ministry which was, by now, fixed in the structure and governance of the Church. Some of them (the 'Presbyterians') began to avoid the terminology of 'bishop' and 'priest', in favour of 'presbyter'.

A serious area of disquiet in the Reformation West concerned the traditional powers of priests. The trend away from the ministry of the word was being reversed by the new concentration on the study of the Bible. The cry was now *sola scriptura* ('scripture alone'). That left the ministry of the sacraments. There, the late-medieval tendency had been to treat the 'saying of the Mass' as something a priest alone could do, and not as an action in which all the worshipping community should be involved. We saw in an earlier chapter how the development in the 11th and 12th centuries of the doctrine of transubstantiation had led to a belief that, when an ordained priest said Jesus' words, 'This is my body' and 'This is my blood', the bread and wine of the eucharist, or holy communion, turned literally into the body and blood of Christ. So, the 'power' to say Mass became enormous, with the priests, some said, 'adding to' the sacrifice Christ himself made on the cross.

The question, 'What is a bishop for?' became sharper than usual in the second quarter of the sixteenth century, as dispute fastened on the theology of ministry and other aspects of theology which were turning out to be Church-dividing. In 1559, most dioceses were without a bishop, and it was unclear whether there would be any bishops in the future.

In England, the bishops were historically 'the king's men' as well as the Church's. The old battles of the Investiture Contest loomed again, with Archbishop William Wareham defending himself in 1532 against the charge that he had consecrated the Bishop of St Asaph in 1518 before the king had confirmed the grant of 'temporalities'. He made the striking claim that 'a man is not made bishop by consecration, but is pronounced so at Rome in Consistory'. The consecration gave him the 'rights of his order', but not its jurisdiction. This kind of thing was central to the discussion of whether the king could not take over part of the making of a bishop, which had hitherto fallen to Rome.

These structural questions about the exercise (or abuse) of power in the Church were enough to open up those 'divides' which have persisted so stubbornly. There were individuals in addition to Luther (notably, John Calvin and Huldrych Zwingli) who won personal support as leaders of the questioning, and as founders of new churches or communities of believers.

> 'We have learned from the grammarians that the words "This is my body" cannot correctly be turned into "In this bread the body of Christ is eaten."'
>
> **Huldrych Zwingli (1484–1531)**

Out on the edges were the charismatics again. The Anabaptists argued that there was no need for the sacraments, not even for baptism, nor for any ordained ministry. The people of God needed nothing more than the Bible and the help of the Holy Spirit.

Over against these changes, and replying vigorously to the awkward questions which were being raised, stood the continuing medieval Church. The Council of Trent, in the middle of the sixteenth century, took stock of it all and dug its heels in. The old literature and practice continued there, despite the Reformation and the Renaissance. Indeed, it was in the sixteenth century that the thirteenth-century *Summa Theologiae* of Thomas Aquinas finally became established as a standard authority for teaching theology.

Imaginative and risk-taking writing of great beauty was still possible in what was by no means a defeated Church. St John of the Cross wrote of Christ as a shepherd boy whose beloved (the soul as the bride of Christ) spurned him.

Time passed: on a season he sprang from the ground,
*   Swarned a tall tree and arms balancing wide*
Beautifully grappled the tree till he died
*   Of the love in his heart like a ruinous wound.*

St John of the Cross (1542–91)

Come ye to judgement.
  For now is set the high justice,
And the day of doom . . .
  when God shall examine, beware!
The truth alone he will hear
  And send you to heaven or hell.

Anonymous, *The English Passion Play*

The culture of the medieval world was steeped in the expectations and assumptions of the Christian faith to a degree which is not easy for the modern reader to enter into. Even taking East (the Greek Church) and West (the Roman Church) together, today's Christian believer is conscious of being in a cultural 'minority'. Those of other faiths are living openly, side-by-side, in the same communities. Those who are Christians are not always easily identifiable as such to colleagues and acquaintances. There are remnants of the cultural dominance of Christianity in the social expectations of the modern West, but the West itself is no longer uncontroversially 'dominant'. Nor should it be.

From the sixteenth century, the 'known world' grew bigger. Civilizations hitherto not in contact with the Christian West were 'discovered' (the American continent), became more active trading partners (parts of the East) or the fields of colonization (Africa). There

The last things

Still generally accepted without question in the sixteenth century was the habit of looking beyond this world to a better one, which the medieval picture of the cosmos had encouraged. This was reflected in medieval historical writing and in drama, as well as in theological and spiritual writings. Medieval historians often began with the creation of the world and went on to the present day, as though it were all one historical sequence. This gave their tales a great dignity and scale, which was important when historians were really chiefly interested in glorifying the small local subject of their story, or creating a 'myth' about their own people. Bede may have been doing that when he wrote *The Ecclesiastical History of the English People*. Whatever his local 'political' motives, he took it for granted that the proper place for human history was 'in the context of eternity' (*sub specie eternitatis*).

was a form of 'globalization' which was slower and more ponderous than is possible through modern electronic communication. Yet it nonetheless transformed the 'world' of the Middle Ages into something bigger and more diverse.

Today, the great 'test' is the capacity of the Christian religion to flourish in the immense variety of cultural contexts in which it is now found. We have watched it become 'inculturated' in a thousand years of the medieval period. Its modern integration is another story.

CHRONOLOGY

46–62 The apostle Paul goes on his missionary journeys, and new churches multiply.

By fourth century New Testament written, the Christian Bible created and approved by the Church. Donatism causing schism in north Africa.

325 Council of Nicea condemns heresy of Arius and creates the Nicene Creed; first ecumenical council.

337 Death of Constantine the Great, the first Christian emperor.

354–430 Augustine of Hippo.

381 Council of Constantinople confirms Nicene Creed, second ecumenical council.

Fifth century Conversion of Ireland by St Patrick.

431 Council of Ephesus, third ecumenical council.

c. 480–c. 550 Benedict of Nursia, founder of the Benedictine Order of monks.

451 Council of Chalcedon, results in separation of the non-Chalcedonian Churches of the East, fourth ecumenical council.

553 Council of Constantinople, fifth ecumenical council.

596 Conversion of England by Augustine of Canterbury, sent by Pope Gregory the Great.

c. 672–735 The Venerable Bede.

787 Council of Nicea seeks to end the iconoclast controversy and restore icons.

962 First monastery founded on Mount Athos.

1033–1109 Anselm of Bec and Canterbury.

1054 Schism between Greek and Roman Churches over papal primacy and the addition of the *filioque* clause to the Nicene Creed.

1090–1153 Bernard of Clairvaux, great Cistercian leader.

1096 First Crusade.

twelfth century Popular anti-establishment and dualist heresies flourish in France and northern Spain.

1204 Fourth Crusade ends the main crusading period.

1215 Fourth Lateran Council, creates more formal requirements in the penitential system.

thirteenth century Franciscan and Dominican Orders of friars flourish and largely take over the academic life of the new universities.

1274 Thomas Aquinas dies.

1309–77 Papacy in exile at Avignon.

1378–1417 Great Schism of the papacy in the West.

1384 John Wyclif dies.

1414–18 Council of Constance condemns Wyclif and Jan Hus for heresy.

1438–45 Council of Florence, attempts to mend the Schism of 1054.

1483 Martin Luther born.

FURTHER READING

Faith in the Byzantine World

The best way to learn more about Byzantine faith is to read texts written by people who lived in the period. The series *Classics of Western Spirituality* includes many Eastern authors. *Penguin Classics* and the translations published by St Vladimir's Seminary Press (Crestwood, NY), Cistercian Publications (Kalamazoo, MI) and Holy Cross Orthodox Press (Brookline, MA) also provide access to Orthodox writers. For spiritual treatises intended for both monastic and lay readers, see the ongoing translation of the collection known as the *Philokalia*, which contains extracts of writers dating from the fourth century onwards:

G.E.H. Palmer, Philip Sherrard and Kallistos Ware, *The Philokalia*, vols I–IV (London: Faber and Faber, 1979–95).

For translations of the biographies, or Lives, of saints, see especially:

E. Dawes and N.H. Baynes, *Three Byzantine Saints* (Oxford: Mowbray, 1948), and many subsequent editions.

A.-M. Talbot (ed.), *Byzantine Defenders of Images: Eight Saints' Lives in English Translation* (Washington, DC: Dumbarton Oaks, 1998).

A.-M. Talbot (ed.), *Holy Women of Byzantium: Ten Saints' Lives in English Translation* (Washington, DC: Dumbarton Oaks, 1996).

A collection of hymns by the great sixth-century hymnographer Romanos the Melodist may be found in:

Archimandrite E. Lash (tr.), *Kontakia on the Life of Christ by St Romanos the Melodist* (San Francisco, CA and London: HarperCollins, 1995).

The best introductory books on the Byzantine Church and Orthodox faith remain the following:

J.M. Hussey, *The Orthodox Church in the Byzantine Empire* (Oxford: Clarendon Press, 1986).

J. Meyendorff, *Byzantine Theology: Historical Trends and Doctrinal Themes* (New York: Fordham University Press, 1974), and subsequent reissues.

T. Ware, *The Orthodox Church: New Edition* (London: Penguin Books, 1993).

More specialized studies of the topics covered in this book may be found in the following bibliography:

D. Constantelos, *Byzantine Philanthropy and Social Welfare* (New Brunswick, NJ: Rutgers University Press, 1966).

R. Cormack (*Byzantine Art*, Oxford: Oxford University Press, 2000).

R. Cormack, *Writing in Gold: Byzantine Society and its Icons* (London: George Philip, 1985).

K. Corrigan, *Visual Polemics in the Ninth-Century Byzantine Psalters* (Cambridge: Cambridge University Press, 1992).

F. Dvornik, *Early Christian and Byzantine Political Philosophy*, vols I–II (Washington, DC: Dumbarton Oaks, 1966).

J. Herrin, *The Formation of Christendom* (Oxford: Wiley Blackwell, 1987).

J.N.D. Kelly, *Early Christian Doctrines*, fifth revised edition (London: A. and C. Black, 1997).

V. Lossky, *The Mystical Theology of the Eastern Church* (Crestwood, NY: St Vladimir's Seminary Press, 1998).

A. Louth, *The Origins of the Christian Mystical Tradition from Plato to Denys* (Oxford: Oxford University Press, 1981).

J. Lowden, *Early Christian and Byzantine Art* (London: Phaidon, 1997).

C. Mango, *Byzantium: The Empire of New Rome* (New York: Charles Scribner's Sons, 1980).

J. Meyendorff, *Christ in Eastern Christian Thought* (Crestwood, NY: St Vladimir's Seminary Press, 1975).

R. Morris, *Church and People in Byzantium* (Birmingham: The Centre for Byzantine, Ottoman and Modern Greek Studies, 1990).

R. Morris, *Monks and Laymen in Byzantium, 843–1118* (Cambridge: Cambridge University Press, 1995).

D.M. Nicol, *Church and Society in the Last Centuries of Byzantium* (Cambridge: Cambridge University Press, 1979).

J. Pelikan, *Imago Dei: The Byzantine Apologia for Icons* (New Haven, CT and London: Yale University Press, 1990).

P. Rousseau, *Pachomios: The Making of a Community in Fourth-Century Egypt* (California: University of California Press, 1985).

S. Runciman, *A History of the Crusades*, vols I–III (Cambridge: Cambridge University Press, 1951–54).

S. Runciman, *The Eastern Schism* (Oxford: Clarendon Press, 1955).

K.M. Setton (ed.), *A History of the Crusades*, vols I–IV (Madison, WI: University of Wisconsin Press, 1969–89).

A.-E. Tachiaos, *Cyril and Methodius of Thessalonica: The Acculturation of the Slavs* (Crestwood, NY: St Vladimir's Seminary Press, 2001).

R.F. Taft, *The Byzantine Rite: A Short History* (Collegeville, MN: The Liturgical Press, 1992).

L. Ouspensky, *Theology of the Icon*, tr. Anthony Gythiel, vol. I (Crestwood, NY: St Vladimir's Seminary Press, 1992).

J. Wilkinson, *Egeria's Travels* (Warminster: Aris and Phillips Ltd, 1999).

Faith in the Medieval World

The series *Classics of Western Spirituality* includes translations of the works of many medieval authors, from both the East and the West. Penguin's *Penguin Classics* and Oxford University Press's *World Classics* are also useful series in which to find examples of medieval writing. A few texts are given below in the 'Further Reading' lists for individual chapters, from which the reader may begin to get the 'flavour' of the Christian writing of the Middle Ages. But there is no better way to enter the medieval world of thought than to read as widely as possible in the original writings.

Chapter 12: The World Through Medieval Eyes

Augustine of Hippo, *Confessions*, tr. Henry Chadwick, *World Classics* (Oxford: Oxford University Press, 1991).

A.D. Nock, *Conversion* (Oxford: Oxford University Press, 1933).

Aristeides Papadakis and John Meyendorff, *The Christian East and the Rise of the Papacy* (New York: St Vladimir, 1994).

William C. Placker, *Theology: From its Beginnings to the Eve of the Reformation* (Philadelphia, PA: Westminster Press, 1998).

R.W. Southern, *Western Society and the Church in the Middle Ages* (Harmondsworth: Penguin, 1970, reprinted 1990).

John A.F. Thompson, *The Western Church in the Middle Ages* (Oxford: Arnold and Oxford University Press, 1998).

Chapter 13: What Did Medieval Christians Believe?

Peter Abelard, *Ethical Writings*, tr. Paul Vincent Spade (Indianapolis, IN and Cambridge: Hackett, 1995).

Thomas Aquinas, *Selected Philosophical Writings*, tr. T. McDermott, *World Classics* (Oxford: Oxford University Press, 1993).

Bede, *A Biblical Miscellany*, tr. W. Trent Foley and Arthur G. Holden (Liverpool: Liverpool University Press, 1999).

Henry Chadwick, *The Early Church* (Harmondsworth: Penguin, 1967).

J.M. Rist, *Plotinus: The Road to Reality* (Cambridge: Cambridge University Press, 1967).

Maxwell Staniforth and Andrew Louth (tr.), *Early Christian Writings: The Apostolic Fathers*, *Penguin Classics* (Harmondsworth: Penguin, 1987).

Chapter 14: Bible Study

H. de Lubac, *Medieval Exegesis* (two volumes), tr. E.M. Macierowski (Paris: Eerdmans and T & T Clark, 1998–2000).

G.R. Evans, *The Language and Logic of the Bible* (two volumes) (Cambridge: Cambridge University Press, 1984, 1985).

M. Simonetti, *Biblical Interpretation in the Early Church*, tr. J.A. Hughes (Edinburgh: T & T Clark, 1994).

Beryl Smalley, *The Study of the Bible in the Middle Ages* (third edition) (Oxford: Oxford University Press, 1983).

Chapter 15: Defining the Church

Tr. R. Davis, *The Book of Pontiffs (Liber Pontificalis): Ancient Biographies of the First Ninety Roman Bishops* (second edition) (Liverpool: Liverpool University Press, 2000).

Eamon Duffy, *The Stripping of the Altars* (New Haven, CT: Yale University Press, 1992).

Norman P. Tanner, *Councils of the Church: a Short History* (London: Heider, 2001).

T.F. Tentler, *Sin and Confession on the Eve of the Reformation* (Princeton, NJ: Princeton University Press, 1977).

Chapter 16: Laypeople

Eamon Duffy, *The Stripping of the Altars* (New Haven, CT: Yale University Press, 1992).

Anne Hudson, *The Premature Reformation* (Oxford: Oxford University Press, 1987).

Julian of Norwich, *Showings*, tr. Edmund Colledge and James Walsh, *Classics of Western Spirituality* (New York: Paulist Press, 1978).

Chapter 17: Politics and the Church

Brian Tierney, *The Crisis of Church and State, 1050–1300* (New York: Spectrum, 1964).

Brian Tierney, *The Origins of Papal Infallibility, 1150–1350* (Leiden: Brill, 1972).

Walter Ullman, *The Origins of the Great Schism* (Connecticut, CT: Hamden, 1972).

Michael Wilks, *The Problem of Sovereignty in the Later Middle Ages* (Cambridge: Cambridge University Press, 1963).

Chapter 18: The Rebels

R. Cross, *Duns Scotus* (Oxford: Oxford University Press, 1999).

Master Eckhardt, *Selected Writings*, tr. Oliver Davies (Harmondsworth: Penguin, 1994).

Anne Hudson, *The Premature Reformation* (Oxford: Oxford University Press, 1988).

Bernard McGinn (tr.), *Apocalyptic Spirituality, Classics of Western Spirituality* (London: SPCK, 1980).

Bernard McGinn, *Visions of the End: Apocalyptic Traditions in the Middle Ages* (New York: Columbia, 2000).

Michael Wilks, *Wyclif, Political Ideas and Practice* (Oxford: Oxbow, 2000).

Chapter 19: Monks, Saints and Christian Examples

Mark Atherton (tr.), *Hildegard of Bingen: Selected Writings*, Penguin Classics (Harmondsworth: Penguin, 2001).

Peter Brown, *The Cult of the Saints* (Chicago, IL: University of Chicago Press, 1981).

C.H. Lawrence, *Medieval Monasticism* (third edition) (London: Pearson Education, 2001).

Fiona Maddocks, *Hildegard of Bingen: A Woman of Her Age* (London: Hodder Headline, 2001).

P. Matarasso (tr.), *The Cistercian World – Monastic Writings of the Twelfth Century* (Harmondsworth: Penguin, 1993).

Gregory Palamas, *Triads*, tr. J. Meyendorff and Nicholas Gendle, *Classics of Western Spirituality* (London: SPCK, 1983).

Chapter 20: Holy War

W.B. Bartlett, *God Wills It* (Stroud: Alan Sutton, 1999).

Guibert de Nogent, *Gesta dei per Francos*, tr. R. Levine (Woodbridge: Boydell and Brewer, 1997).

J. Riley-Smith, *The First Crusade* (Cambridge: Cambridge University Press, 1997).

Chapter 21: Tradition and Continuity: The Road to Reformation

Gerald Brady (ed.), *Documents of the English Reformation* (Cambridge: James Clarke, 1994).

E. Cameron, *The European Reformation* (Oxford: Oxford University Press, 1991).

Owen Chadwick, *The Reformation* (Harmondsworth: Penguin, 1964).

Alister E. McGrath, *Reformation Thought: An Introduction* (third edition) (Oxford: Blackwell, 2000).

INDEX

excommunication 36–37, 56, 77
exorcism 117–18, 122

F
faith 121
fall of Constantinople *see* Constantinople
fasts 10, 36, 64, 66, 80, 93, 96
feast days (festivals) 10, 21, 83, 89, 94, 131
filioque 32, 37, 110–11
Franks 32, 42, 109
fresco *see* wall painting
funerals 97, 118

G
Gabriel, archangel 131
Galilee 79
Genesis, book of 113, 115
Gennadios, ecumenical patriarch 137
Georgia 135
Germanos I, ecumenical patriarch 45, 46, 98, 130
Germans 33–34
Gibbon, Edward 9
Giotto 132
Glabas, Michael 132
Gnostics 51
God the Father 99–112, 116
  immanence of 89
  transcendence of 76–77, 113, 114
  'uncreated energies' of 76, 111–12
  unknowability of 76–77, 99–100, 111

Goths 22, 33
Great Church *see* Hagia Sophia
Greece 74, 125, 136, 137
Gregory of Nyssa 68, 100, 103

H
Hagia Sophia 20, 24, 27, 30, 35, 37, 43, 48, 91, 92, 130, 136
hagiography 70
healing 79, 96, 97, 106, 121–22
heavenly kingdom 55, 78–79, 88, 98, 114–17, 123
hegumenos see abbot
Helena 78–79
Herakleios 11, 22, 25, 83, 107
heresy, heretics 9, 21, 44, 46, 56, 77, 101, 103, 107, 109–12, 113, 124
Hesychasm 76
hesychia see solitude
hierarchy 38, 50, 85, 116, 130
Hijra 26
Hodegetria icon 86
Hodegon Monastery 86, 87
Holy Apostles, Church of the 134
holy fools 81
Holy Land 30, 37, 78, 79
holy mountains 74
Holy Sepulchre 78
holy sites 78–79
Holy Spirit 21, 32, 39, 50, 76, 88, 99, 101, 103, 110, 111

homilies *see* sermons
homoousios 103
Hosios Loukas, monastery church of 133
hospices 60
hospitals 52, 59–61, 121
hostels 59–61
Humbert, Cardinal 36
humility 81
Huns 22
hymns 24, 30, 75, 83, 92, 118, 124

I
Iconoclasm 25–28, 29, 31, 45–47, 57, 70, 85–87, 94, 108–109, 124, 127
iconography 129, 132, 134, 134
iconophiles 27, 31, 87, 108–109
iconostasis 94
icons 8, 10, 25–28, 29, 31, 43, 46–47, 70, 76, 78, 83–87, 88, 94, 98, 108–10, 121, 123, 128, 129, 131, 132, 136
  as channels of communication 87
  identity 10, 113, 122–24, 136
idolatry 45, 108, 125
Ignatios 30
illiteracy 57
illness 61, 98, 121–22
incubation 121
India 10, 115
Indikopleustes, Kosmas 11, 115
intercession 64, 86, 119

Faith in the Medieval World

B

baptism 165, 166, 187–88, 211, 247
Barlaam 220
Barnabas 175, 185
barons 201, 202
Benedict of Nursia 222
Benedictines 187, 222, 224, 225, 226, 228
Berengar of Tours 170
Bernard of Clairvaux 174, 182, 191, 196, 204, 225, 228, 230, 233, 236
Bible 149, 153, 156, 158, 160, 162, 173–83, 184, 193, 206, 210, 214, 219, 244–47
bishops 167, 187, 188, 189, 190, 191, 194–95, 201–202, 204, 206, 207, 246, 247
Boethius 154, 155, 161, 162, 168, 169
Bogomils 207, 215
Byzantine church, Byzantines 144, 196, 235, 242

C

canon of the Bible 174–75, 178
canonization 229
canons 171, 178, 226, 229, 230
catechumens 165
Cathars 207, 215
cathedrals 145, 171, 181, 226
Celtic Christians 150, 223

charismatics 150, 184, 186, 208, 213, 220, 227, 247
Chaucer 187, 224
cherubim 157
Christ 160, 163–64, 170, 171, 173, 175, 178, 179, 184, 186, 187, 188, 191, 194, 197, 198, 203, 205–206, 207, 208, 213, 215–17, 231, 232, 240, 246, 247
divinity of 150, 206
human nature of 205
see also Jesus
Church 144, 146, 157, 160, 163–64, 165, 166, 167, 168, 171, 173, 175, 179, 180, 184–91, 192, 193, 197, 198–204, 205–210, 211, 212–15, 217–18, 220, 227, 233, 234, 235, 242, 243, 245–49
and state 190, 191, 203–204, 209
Cicero 161, 219, 243
City of God 156, 199
classics 162, 243
clergy 190, 191, 192, 193, 208, 210, 227
Clermont 234, 235
Columba of Iona, St 150
community of faith 144, 145, 164, 165, 173, 174, 184–86, 188, 191, 198, 205, 216, 245
Concordat of Worms 191, 204
confession 187–90, 195
Congregationalists 246

consensus fidelium 186, 213–14
Consolation of Philosophy 154, 162
Constantine, Emperor 147, 175, 190, 198
Constantinople 166–67, 175, 176, 207, 220, 236, 241
Patriarch of 167
Synod of (1368) 220
contemplation 154, 156
conversion 147–150, 151, 152, 154, 198, 214
cosmos 152–53, 157, 248
Council of Bari (1098) 167, 235
Council of Constance (1415) 209
Council of Florence (1438–45) 167–68
Council of London (1382) 210
Council of Verona (1184) 208
creation 153, 156, 158–59, 162, 171, 172, 195, 212, 240, 248
creeds 164–65, 166, 207, 214–15
cross, crucifixion 153, 173, 173, 188, 204, 234
Crusades, the 234–41

D

Dante 157, 204
deacons 186
Dionysius the Areopagite 156
disciples of Jesus 164, 170, 174, 186, 204, 213, 226, 231

Lightning Source UK Ltd.
Milton Keynes UK
UKHW021427020719
345426UK00005B/165/P

9 781912 552269